THE
BLACKSTONE BOOK
OF MAGIC & ILLUSION

THE
BLACKSTONE
OF MAGIC

BOOK
& ILLUSION

HARRY
BLACKSTONE, JR.

with CHARLES AND REGINA REYNOLDS

FOREWORD BY RAY BRADBURY

MAGIC EFFECTS ILLUSTRATED BY ERIC MASON

Newmarket Press
New York

To my wife, Gay,
my daughters, Cynthia, Adrienne, Tracey, and Bellamie,
and to the memory of my son,
Harry Blackstone III

◆

First Edition
1 2 3 4 5 6 7 8 9 0

Library of Congress Cataloging in Publication Data
Blackstone, Harry
   The Blackstone book of magic & illusion.

   Bibliography: p.
   Includes index.
   1. Conjuring—History. 2. Conjuring. I. Reynolds,
Charles R. II. Reynolds, Regina. III. Title.
GV1543.B57 1985   793.8   84-29486
ISBN 0-937858-45-5

Quantity Purchases
Companies, professional groups, clubs, and other organizations may qualify for
special terms when ordering quantities of this title. For information, contact the
Special Sales Department, Newmarket Press, 3 East 48th Street, New York, New
York 10017. Phone (212) 832-3575.

Designed by Deborah Daly

Title page: "Ten Pails and a Tub," the Blackstone duck illusion, c. 1925; Harry
Blackstone, Sr., c. 1943; Harry Blackstone, Jr., 1983 (photo by Harry Blackstone
III).

Manufactured in the United States of America

Acknowledgments

This book could not have been accomplished without the cooperation of many people who were connected with the Blackstone show as employees, friends, or devoted fans. They were free with information and visual material and our thanks go to them all. Of particular aid throughout the writing of the book was Dan Waldron, the preeminent Blackstone scholar who, it is hoped, will one day write his detailed history of the elder Blackstone; Bob Lund, curator of the American Museum of Magic in Marshall, Michigan; Walter Gibson, friend, confidant, and ghostwriter for Blackstone, Houdini, and Thurston; George Johnstone, today a top professional magician, who was an assistant on the Blackstone show in his early days in show business; and our publisher, Esther Margolis, and editor, Katherine Heintzelman, who have helped in more ways than we would care to count.

Others who also helped in different ways are: Robert Albo, Harry Amdur, David Belenzon, Pete Biro, Ina Blevins, Greg Bordner, Floyd Brown, Eliott Caplan, Jack Cunniff, Professor Edwin A. Dawes, Irving Desfor, David Eisendrath, Jim Feldman, Cliff Flora, Neil Foster, Arnold Furst, Carl Fyhrie, John Gaughan, Billie Gillick, John Henry Grossman, Jane Hayes, Doug Henning, the George Hensel Family, Al Hirschfeld, Lewis Horwitz, Ken Howard, Dr. Joseph Inzima, Ricky Jay, Ken Klosterman, Robert Koch, Bill Larsen, Hank Lee, Rick Levin, Charles McDonald, Jay and Frances Marshall, Caroline Merrill, Merrillyn Merrill, Ken Murray, Robert A. Olson, Stanley Palm, Robert Parrish, Jack Rennert, Fred and Peggy Ruckels, Bill Schmeelk, Chan Shedelbower, Siegfried and Roy, Les and Gertrude Smith, Betty Stolle, Phil Temple, Dr. Morris Young, and all of those grownups who, many years ago, held the birdcage or got a rabbit, and in more recent times have come backstage to tell us about it. Final thanks to that very special person who asked not to be mentioned.

Contents

Foreword

As my four daughters were growing up, every night was Blackstone Time. Seven nights a week for years I imagined tales about myself as a boy of seven or eight, walking on air or lost in Egyptian tombs with the Great Magician.

Blackstone was such a part of my daughters' lives that they didn't believe me when, walking down Hollywood Boulevard one noon twenty years ago, I suddenly cried:

"Good Grief, girls, there's *Blackstone*!"

I pointed into a magic shop where stood a gentleman with a great shock of flaming white hair.

"Is Blackstone *real*?" my daughters gasped.

"Real? Oh, *yes*!" I cried. "Wait here!"

I rushed into the shop to shake Harry Blackstone's hand, breathless.

"Mr. Blackstone," I said, "the last time we met was when I stumbled up onstage of the Orpheum Theatre, 1937, to help you with your canary-cage. My daughters think I know you better than I really do, because I've told them stories about you for the last two thousand nights. Can I bring them in?"

"Run 'em in!" said Blackstone. "What did you say your name was?"

I ran the daughters in.

"Ray!" shouted Blackstone. "It's been so *long*! Great to see you again!"

The next half hour was filled with gabble and laughter as the Great One vanished cards, danced handkerchiefs, signed posters and books, and waved us back out into the noonday sun, stunned and happy.

"Blackstone!" my daughters kept repeating.

And Blackstone say I to you.

And again: Blackstone, his son.

What a history is theirs.

And I am a micro-dot part of it.

For, traveling across country in the thirties with my mom, dad, and brother Skip, when we stopped in small towns in Kansas, Oklahoma, or Texas, I hit the dust running for the nearest library hoping to find and devour:

Books on Magic by Blackstone.

At age twelve I suffered a concussion of delight when I found a huge posterbill advertising The Great Magician in an alley in Waukegan, Illinois. Hypnotized by the sight of so many haunts, skeletons, floating light bulbs, and fired Arabian cannons, I backed up, dazed, and crashed down. My head went through the window of a basement barber shop, six feet below. The customers leaped to their feet. The barber almost slit the throat of his prime customer.

I survived the shattered glass to rush onstage later that week and be gifted with a live rabbit from the Great Magician.

Moaning with happiness, I carried the dear beast home, named it Tillie, and watched it, in the months ahead, illusion forth more rabbits.

I promptly became a boy magician and performed minor miracles at Oddfellows banquets and American Legion picnics, sporting a false mustache that fell to the floor as I finished each trick.

After that I began to write stories every day of my life. And thanks to Blackstone, and another carnival sorcerer named Mr. Electrico, I grew up to become not a science fiction writer, as everyone falsely dubs me, but—

A magician.

I lived to make men vanish at Cape Canaveral.

And reappear on Mars.

If *that* isn't magic, what is?

It is only proper and right, then, that I stand up here to acknowledge the wondrous fact that Harry Blackstone pulled me out of a hat when I was a boy, and I have never stopped growing amidst mysteries, miracles, and dreams.

This book, as you will soon see, doesn't need an introduction at all. But the rabbit-child that was me in 1927 would throw a conniption-fit in my subconscious if I didn't dare try these few words.

What this book is, then, encompassed in a bright theatre world and passed on from distinguished father to equally distinguished son, is a history, no less, of mankind.

From the cave to Mars, over some few million years, we have longed to tame fire, lick gravity, control seasons, enchant animals to behavior, cause sabre-tooth smiles to vanish from our ledges, and order mammoths to lie down on huge hamburger buns for immoveable feasts. This we did at first with sorceries, incantations, dust symbols, wall paintings, rain dances. To which, needless to say, gravity and matter paid small attention.

Late in time we sensed that willpower, minus gray matter that could conjure reality into axes or plows or Spanish galleons or Apollo missions, was useless. So we sea-changed magic into science, where the two still lie uneasily abed today, twin desires to shape imagination and rebuild matter for sweet survival's sake.

Blackstone and Son performed in cavern mouths for brute

tribes one hundred thousand years ago. Their scientific twins command electric computer ghosts to bounce images off the Red Eye of Jupiter and skirt Saturn's carousel.

We share history with the Blackstones. Their dreams, their illusions, are ours. But what started as necromancy is now the romancing of atoms to warm bungalows and light school rooms, with fire collectors one day soon adrift beyond Earth.

They are us. We are them. But now we take the final big steps from illusion, or science fiction dreaming, if you wish, to pure blueprint, machined data, and ramshackle immortality, somewhere between here and the Horsehead Nebula.

All this from the Great Blackstone and the Great Great Blackstone, his son? Yes, and all the magicians before them, who started us on the long road from Eden to Moon Port to Pluto. The magic had to come first before we could build mechanical illusions that worked unfailingly and for all time.

Enough. To finish up, this book proves that, to rephrase the old saying, you can teach a *new* dog *old* tricks. Where Harry Senior left off, Harry Junior began. They are a magical ribbon with no seam.

Other magicians will come and go in our age, but our love for the combined history of these two who are one should echo well into the twenty-first century.

And perhaps brighten the stage of the Oriental Theatre on the Red Planet?

No life on Mars, you say?

Hold on!

Where did I stash those rabbits!?

Ray Bradbury
Los Angeles, California
February 1985

INTRODUCTION: THE WORLD OF MAGIC

This book is intended to be a new kind of magic book. It is a person-to-person talk to you, based on a lifetime of experience in a family devoted to magic, about the art of entertaining deception. I was literally born into a life of magic. My father was The Great Blackstone, America's foremost magician in his day, and my mother was an assistant in his big traveling magic show. From my earliest days, I traveled with the show troupe, and, when I became old enough to perform, I started learning from my father. For all of my adult life I have been a professional magician, carrying on the tradition of the Blackstone show and performing many of my father's illusions, and many new ones of my own, all over the world. The year 1985 marks the one-hundredth anniversary of my father's birth (he died in 1965), and the fiftieth anniversary of mine. Both of us spent our lifetimes in magic and, certainly, neither of us regretted it.

The Blackstone Book of Magic and Illusion is an informal introduction to the history, principles, and effects of one of the oldest, if not *the* oldest, entertainment arts. It is not, however, going to tell you *everything* there is to know about magic. Many people, myself included, have devoted a major part of their lives to the study of magic and they are far from understanding it completely. That is one of the major fascinations of magic, whether approached as a hobby or a profession: the more you study it, the more there is to learn.

(Opposite) **Performing the Floating Light Bulb, 1984.**

In teaching you how to do a variety of first-rate magic effects, of all sizes—from making a coin or a salt shaker disappear to cutting a woman in half using ropes instead of a saw—I will tell you not only the methods, but also the *psychology* behind them. I'm not going to show you how a magician makes an elephant disappear or a woman float in the air, because these effects are far out of the range of the amateur magician, and finding out how tricks work just to know the method is one of the best ways to spoil the fun and end the wonder of the magician's art. Every effect I teach you will be one that you, as a beginning magician, can actually do. Even more important, I will try to give you the thinking behind the effect that will allow you to present it in the most baffling and entertaining manner.

Every year there are literally hundreds of books and monographs published on magic. Most of these are specialized works, intended for advanced magicians. There are also hundreds of magic effects put onto the market each year, mostly sold through outlets that supply material to performing magicians. To the beginner, all this can be very bewildering. It can also be a great waste of time and money. What books should you read? What tricks should you buy?

The right answers to these questions can go a long way toward easing the task of the beginner who wants to get started in magic. This book is designed to help get you started, and to point you in the direction of further rewarding adventures in magic. You may find, as I have, that the more you know about the art of illusion, the more fascinating it becomes, and what began as a mild interest may become a lifetime obsession. Dai Vernon, known to magicians the world over as "the Professor" and the dean of American sleight-of-hand experts, has, at this writing, just turned ninety. He started the study of magic when he was six years old. "I wasted the first six years of my life," he is fond of telling people. No matter what age you are, an introduction to the world of magic may lead you to feel the same way.

What Magic Really Is

If a number of people were asked the question "What does a magician do?", the majority would probably answer, "He does magic tricks," and that would be that. If we were to press the inquiry further and ask "What kind of magic tricks?", we would probably be told, "He pulls rabbits out of hats, saws ladies in two, and things like that." If asked whether they enjoy watching magic, most would probably say they do, provided the magician is a good one.

Even in this supposedly enlightened age, there are undoubtedly some people who believe in the existence of "real" magic, but most accept the role of the magician as a professional entertainer who pretends to do the impossible for the amusement of his audience.

Jean-Eugène Robert-Houdin, the greatest magician of the nineteenth century and generally considered to be "the father of modern magic," defined a conjuror (the term by which a magician is often known in England and Europe) as "an actor playing the part of a magician." It is doubtful that this definition will be improved upon. The late John Mulholland, a distinguished American magician, editor, writer, and magic historian of our generation, defined magic as "the art of creating illusion agreeably," an excellent statement of what that "actor playing the part of a magician" should do. That a magician should be an *actor*, that he should *create illusion* and do it *agreeably*, are the key elements of any successful magic performance.

In the late 1930s, an enterprising advertising man whose name has been lost to history came up with the idea of a campaign involving magic to sell his client's cigarettes. The idea was that each ad in the series would expose the workings of a famous magic effect, and the memorable tag line of each was, "It's fun to be fooled, but it's more fun to know." This ad campaign, which suggested that you should not be fooled into buying a cigarette of inferior quality, was soon relegated to Madison Avenue oblivion, perhaps in part because its creators failed to understand some basic facts about the magician's art. First, it is very difficult to "expose" the *real* secrets of magic, and in fact the very effect that has been explained to a supposedly curious public will, presented expertly, continue to astonish. Realizing this, my father had large blowups of some of the cigarette ads placed in front of the theatres where he was playing, with an invitation to the public to buy tickets and see him perform the same tricks they had been reading about. When they saw him perform, they could not believe that the mysteries they were seeing could have such simple explanations, and they were fooled anyway.

Deep in their hearts, people want to believe in magic, and that is why they respond to it when it is entertainingly presented in theatrical form. They do not want to be told that the wonderful illusions a magician performs are in reality just tricks, even though they know intellectually that this is the case. It is this "willing suspension of disbelief" (to borrow a phrase from Coleridge) that makes magic work in its ideal form. There are also, of course, those members of a magician's audience who are there not for the theatrical experience of wonder, but to figure out how the tricks are done. It's part of the job of every good magician to try to win these people over and to turn them from antagonistic puzzle-solvers to participants in an imaginative experience akin to every other work of art, be it painting, film, novel, play, or fairy tale.

Another miscalculation of the advertising executive who conceived the cigarette campaign lay in his choice of slogan for the advertisements. It is *not*, at least under many circumstances, fun to be fooled, and, assuming that the magician has been successful in making his performance enjoyable for his audience, it is certainly *not* more fun to know how.

As we have seen, there are two ways to experience a magic performance. The first is the puzzle experience. The second is the magical experience. The reason audiences can become antagonistic to magic that fools them, but is not entertainingly presented, is that the magician has not succeeded in transcending the puzzle experience. Let us look at a simple card trick to see how this can happen.

The magician has a card selected from the deck and not shown to him. The card is replaced in the deck and the cards are shuffled. The magician looks through the deck and finds the chosen card. The spectator is baffled because he does not know how the magician accomplished this, but it does not necessarily follow that he has been entertained or that the magician, to return to John Mulholland's definition, has demonstrated "the art of creating illusion agreeably." In fact, the act of being fooled may well lead to frustration, which, in turn, leads to annoyance. By knowing how to find the card when the spectator does not know how he did it, the magician has implicitly proven himself smarter that the spectator, or at least in possession of some arcane secret which he is not about to reveal. Such a performer-audience relationship does not lead to agreeable entertainment.

Any successful magician must first and foremost make his audience like him and what he does. Once he helps his audience to transcend the puzzle experience, he can get on to the *real* business of magic. This is a theatrical experience like any other, where the spectator suspends his disbelief in order to become caught up for a few moments or a few hours in a new, artificially created reality that will appeal to his sense of fantasy and wonder.

How does the magician do this? By being an actor and by convincing his audience, as any good actor must, that they should at least temporarily accept the new reality that he is creating for them.

What should the magician not do? He should not be a smart aleck who, through his superior attitude (he knows a secret they do not), alienates his audience.

These observations about the magician-spectator relationship should be painfully obvious, perhaps so much so that they do not warrant the strong emphasis I have given them, but for many beginning magicians they lie at the root of why they are not successful entertainers. Many beginners, particularly young people, are powerfully drawn to magic because, on a subconscious level at least, it gives them a sense of power over the world. Although he is usually not aware of it, the beginning magician often performs his tricks in a way that suggests he is having a wonderful time because of the power he has over his audience. What the audience is supposed to get out of this never occurs to him.

Making an audience like the magician and willingly enter into the world of wonder which he creates is the biggest and most important task for any performer. It is far more difficult than merely fooling an audience, which, as we shall see, is relatively easy. To make magic not only baffling but *interesting* is the name of the game.

Your Place in Magic

Magic is a varied field and there are many ways you can fit into it. They are determined by your personality and interests, as well as your ability (talent does count in magic, as in any artistic endeavor), and the amount of time, energy, and money you have to invest. You will save yourself a lot of confusion and frustration, and certainly have more fun, if before beginning you ask yourself one important question: "What do I want out of magic?" Your answer could be one of many and, of course, it may change over the years if you continue your pursuit of the magical muse.

Perhaps you want a relaxing and intellectually stimulating hobby. This is why most people, at least initially, go into magic. Most of the tens of thousands of magic enthusiasts in the world today are hobbyists. I should emphasize that just because one pursues magic as an amateur (the real meaning of which is "lover," not "inept bungler"), it does not mean that his or her magic should not be skillful and entertaining. Many of the most

Performing the Vanishing Birdcage illusion in my Broadway show
Blackstone!, **1980.**

skillful magicians in the world are, strictly speaking, amateurs, and probably more new magic effects (or variations on older effects) are created by amateurs than by professional performers. This is easy to understand. The amateur is in magic for the love of it. He can afford, given the requisite time, to perfect a sleight-of-hand move or an effect until it pleases him. The professional must attend first and foremost to the business of making money. His effects must be created not to please himself, but to please a paying audience. This is not to say that he does not love magic as much as the amateur. If he did not, he would probably pick some easier and more lucrative way to make a living. I do not believe that I have ever met a good professional magician who did not truly love magic.

When you decide to become involved in magic, you automatically join a fraternity that is worldwide, and which transcends the barriers of language, race, religion, or politics. If you are a magician, you are automatically accepted as a friend by other magicians,

INTRODUCTION: THE WORLD OF MAGIC

and many people have had endless satisfaction out of their hobby of magic by belonging to this special fraternity. There are also many magic organizations that hold meetings and conventions, elect officers, and publish their own books and magazines (for a listing of some of the major magic societies, see the Appendix).

Another area of magic that has given many amateurs great satisfaction is the collecting of apparatus, books, posters, programs, photographs, and numerous kinds of magic ephemera. The collectors have their own society, publish their own journal, and have annual meetings both in the United States and in Great Britain. While most collectors (in common with nearly all magic hobbyists) can perform some tricks, it is their collection of a particular magic-related item, from coins to comic books, that is of primary importance. Some private magic collections are staggering in their scope. Two of the largest collections of antique magic apparatus in the United States belong to Dr. Robert Albo, a physician in Oakland, California, and to Ken Klosterman, who owns a chain of bakeries in Cincinnati, Ohio. H. Adrian Smith (now Dean of the Society of American Magicians), a retired engineer in North Attleboro, Massachusetts, has one of the major private collections of magic books.

Closely related to the collector is the magic scholar, who studies the history of the art, often specializing in some particular area such as card magic or mentalism. Most magic enthusiasts who have progressed beyond the stage of simply wanting to show people tricks (alas, many go no further) are interested in the study of a specialized area of the art.

Finally, there are those who make their living, or a part of their living, out of magic. There cannot be more. than a few hundred full-time, professional magicians, whose magic is their entire source of livelihood, in the entire world. However, there are tens of thousands who make part of their living from magic. Many young magicians learn their craft and supplement their incomes by doing shows at birthday parties, church and school events, and other local bookings (this is, in fact, how my father started before the turn of the century). Many adult magicians, who hold full-time jobs in other areas, earn handsome second incomes as semi-professional magicians.

There are also those who make a living in areas related to the performance of magic but not as performers themselves. There are hundreds of magic dealers, both large operations and small, all over the world (see the Appendix), as well as publishers of magic books. There are builders of special magic apparatus who often create the custom-built illusions used by top professionals. There are also a few magic consultants who help create and sometimes direct effects used by performing magicians, and who devise magic and special effects for theatrical productions, films, television commercials, and other media. It should be pointed out that to be successful in these magic-related areas, it is necessary to have not only a thorough knowledge of the magician's craft but of other areas connected with the particular specialty as well. For example, the proprietor of a magic shop or magic publishing operation must also have a business background if he or she is to succeed. The custom builder must have a thorough knowledge of design, wood- and metal-working, new materials, and technology. The consultant must be grounded in theatre and media as well as in magic.

Finally, there are those who simply enjoy watching magic. While most magic enthusiasts eventually find themselves performing (some well, some not so well), there are some who are simply fans of magic. For example, the movie star Cary Grant has for many years served on the board of the Academy of Magical Arts, which has its headquarters at Hollywood's Magic Castle. Grant has seldom been seen to perform magic, except a few times for his friends (as the Great Carini). Why is he on the board? He simply likes to watch magic. There's nothing wrong with that!

I hope that this book, which is not a book of tricks but a book about magic—its art, its science, its history—will "hook" you on magic as a performer or as a collector or as an enthusiast, by showing you the basic psychological and mechanical principles and why they are fun to perform and witness.

(Opposite) **A montage of images from my father's show.**

FROM CAVEMAN
TO MODERN CONJUROR:

A SHORT HISTORY OF THE ART OF ILLUSION

 here was always magic. Itinerant street magicians, gypsy fortune tellers, and even the soothsayers of ancient Egypt and Babylonia were relative late-comers to the world of power and mystery. In man's earliest beginnings, magic was everywhere, in the winds, in fire and water, in the changing seasons. Every element of his daily existence was ruled by powers far beyond his comprehension. The wiser among his kind reasoned that if they too were to be powerful, whether to appease the irrational gods or to have power over their fellow men, they must take on the semblance of gods themselves—and thus magic and deception found their start on the altars of the early religions.

Was a man not godlike if he could calm a wild animal, cause a bird to fall asleep and awake at his will, make three stones appear where there had been only one? Should he not be superior to all others if he could change a staff into a serpent or raise the dead to life again?

When and how some early shaman discovered that a bird could be put to sleep by tucking its head under its wing, or who first found that certain snakes would become rigid when pressure was applied to them, is information lost to us. But the secrets of Indian fakirs, who buried themselves alive only to rise again, have been observed by men of our time; and the Cups and Balls, one of the oldest recorded tricks of magic, is very likely a variation of Stone Age man's original marvel, in which he caused stones to appear and disappear in some crude form of sleight of hand.

(Opposite) **At the beginning of his career, my father included escapology in his repertoire. In this 1906 studio photograph (when he was appearing under the name LeRoy Boughton), he is shown trussed with rope and encased in wire in preparation for the illusion.**

Mysticism and Ritual: The Art of Magic Begins

Our first historical accounts of magic appear in the writings of an Egyptian chronicler whose work, known today as the Westcar Papyrus, has been dated at about 1700 B.C. In it he relates stories handed down over the previous centuries of the miracles performed by men of magic. One of the characters in these fables is Dedi of Dedsnefru, who allegedly performed before Cheops, builder of the Great Pyramid. He reportedly cut off and then restored the heads of both a goose and a pelican without any noticeable harm being done to either. Though Dedi apparently also set himself up as a seer and soothsayer, there is nothing in the tale to indicate he presented himself as anything other than an entertainer; he claimed no special powers nor intimate contact with the gods, unlike the biblical figures of later times.

Magic history would have it that the Cups and Balls trick was first portrayed in the burial chamber of one Beni Hassan (circa 2500 B.C., perhaps earlier; see left). Though one could question whether the two kneeling figures are actually performing this trick (some have suggested they are simply baking bread or perhaps playing a game), there were many reports of the trick being performed in Greece and Rome, as well as Egypt, by public entertainers who also swallowed swords, juggled, and did ventriloquism and fire-eating as part of their repertoires.

Greece apparently supported many strolling players. *The Iliad* refers to tumblers and conjurors, puppeteers were popular, and there were even schools where conjuring was taught as both an art and a trade. There were even reports of stage illusions, although these seem to have been tied into religious rites. Hero of Alexander, in his *Pneumatics* (written in about the first century A.D.), describes altar doors opening when temple fires were lit and other mechanical wonders, such as productions of thunder and lightning, self-refilling jugs, and trumpets that played without human assistance. The Greek people admired their magicians and flocked to their performances at festivals and games. They even erected statues to some of their favorites—Euclides, Zenaphon, and Theodorus, among them.

Although most of what has been recorded about early magic comes from Egypt, Greece, and Rome, one must assume that other early cultures had their exponents of the art. Persia, China, and India, for example, sustained civilizations at least as sophisti-

Many magicians believe this illustration, from the burial chamber of Beni Hassan, depicts the ancient Cups and Balls trick.

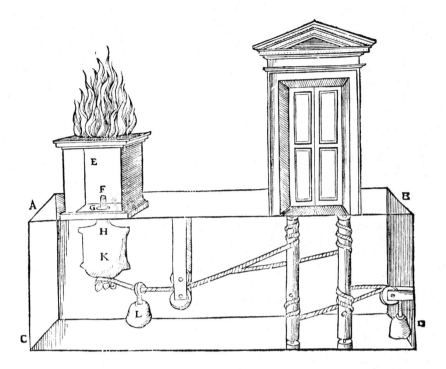

Illusionary effects were in use at an early time, though primarily as part of religious rites, such as this example described in Hero of Alexander's *Pneumatics*. The lighting of the fire caused the temple doors to open.

cated as those already mentioned. Marco Polo relates in his late-thirteenth-century account of his travels to the East that the conjurors of Tibet could cause thunder and lightning and "produce many other miraculous effects," that Chinese magicians could prevent rain, and that magicians in Kashmir could obscure the light of day. As most of these Eastern civilizations had long studied astronomy, the tides, and the change of seasons, these miracles were probably the daily work of these wise men. However, Marco Polo also reported conjuring wonders that were undoubtedly considered just plain entertainment. In the court of Kublai Khan, he reports self-moving pitchers pouring beverages for the Khan and his guests. A few years later, in 1320, Friar Odoric, a wandering priest visiting courts of China, tells us he saw golden cups flying through the air to men's mouths, and statues walking.

In 1355, Abu-Abdullah Mohmed, an Arab from Tangier who called himself Ibn Batuta (the traveler), wrote an account of his extended journey throughout Asia, begun in 1325. In his diary, we hear for the first time of what is undoubtedly the most legendary illusion in magic—the Rope Trick.

Ibn Batuta tells us that, in the center of a palace garden, one of the Khan's jugglers threw into the air a wooden sphere, to which long straps were attached. The sphere disappeared from sight but the end of the strap remained in the juggler's hand. He then commanded a boy to climb the strap, and the boy too

8516-C

disappeared. His master climbed after him, knife in hand, and in moments parts of the boy's body began to fall to the ground. The master then returned to earth and reassembled the boy, who stood up, apparently none the worse for wear!

Tales of this fabled illusion have continued through the ages. It was reported in Venice in the fifteenth century and in Germany in 1550. In the latter report it was a horse, his master, the master's wife, and a maid who disappeared climbing a rope. One hundred years later, the author Pu Sing Ling found the illusion in Chinese folklore: a woman, a man, and a boy were the characters this time, and they climbed a ladder and were never seen again. A dog, a hog, a panther, a lion, and a tiger disappeared up a chain in an account of the Emperor Jahangir of Delhi in the late 1600s.

It is interesting that the legend of the Rope Trick has persisted over the centuries and is also closely aligned with such folk tales as Jack in the Beanstalk. Religious connotations—levitation into Heaven—can of course be seen in it. Large sums of money have been offered through the centuries to anyone who could perform the trick as described in the legendary accounts, but the offers remain unclaimed. Many a modern magician has performed his own version of the trick, however. My father's version of the fabled illusion was a regular feature of his show for many years.

Every illusion that later became part of magic as an entertainment had its roots in shamanism, which seems to have originated in Asia, then moved on to Europe and, by way of Alaska, to the Americas. The rituals of shamanism primarily had to do with curing the sick and calling forth the spirits, and the methods used to obtain these miracles were not unlike those of the modern magician.

One of the tricks often employed was the "removal" of some "diseased" organ from a patient's body. This was usually a stone or piece of bone, hidden on the shaman's person, which he produced at the appropriate moment. Today's "psychic surgeons," relying on the patient's belief in magic, produce the same effect using animal innards.

The Algonquin shamans in North America used ventriloquism to call forth the voices of spirits, and produced carved figures from cloth bags previously shown to be empty. They magically suspended bears' claws from mirrors held upside-down. The Crees and the Ojibwas performed escapes from within trussed animal skins. Both Alaskan and South American Indians reappeared in good health after being locked in boxes that were consumed by flames; another popular effect was the restoration of a piece of twine after cutting it into many pieces.

(Opposite) **The legendary Rope Trick was first reported by Ibn Batuta in 1355 and has appeared in the folk tales of many cultures. A version of it was performed by my father in his full evening show during the 1940s.**

Il Giocatore di Bussolotti, in Roma.

Itinerant magicians were a common sight in medieval Europe, along with other street performers.

Church Suppression and Magic's First Literature

Magician-entertainers were first referred to as jugglers, and were part of the medieval itinerant players' groups which did indeed perform juggling, tumbling, fire-eating, and sword-swallowing, and which told stories, played musical instruments, and did animal acts and other entertainments. Europe was full of these street performers, who appeared in village squares and at special festivals and holiday fairs. All were referred to as jugglers, or *juculatores*, or *jangleurs* (the latter meaning "babbler"!), and also as minstrels in early times, although singers and musicians were considered classier acts, and eventually were classified as a separate and special talent, who had their own guilds and were usually in the service of kings and noblemen. The other performers were also well thought of, however, as witness the naming of streets where they performed: Paris had its Rue des Jouglers (later the Rue de St. Julien des Menetriers, referring to the church and hospital established in 1330 by two performers for the benefit of performers), and Liverpool's Juggler Street dates from the fourteenth century.

All this followed on the heels of church suppression in earlier centuries, when the theatrical arts had been banned as evils. Performing talents were quietly handed down from generation to generation during those bleak times, and the Church's suppression undoubtedly helped foster the "secrets" of the conjuring art. Indeed, it was the Church's condemnation of presumed witchcraft and sorcery that led to the first book exposing the magicians' tricks. The *Discoverie of Witchcraft*, written by Reginald Scot in 1584, set out to dispel the myth of supernatural powers ascribed to victims of the Church's zealots, and to expose them as simple feats of the conjuror's trade.

Wherin the lewde dealing of witches and witchmongers is notablie detected, the knauerie of conjurers, the impietie of inchantors, the follie of soothsaiers, the impudent falshood of cousenors, the infidelitie of atheists, the pestilent practices of Pythonists, the curiositie of figure castors, the vanitie of dreamers, the beggarlie art of Alcumystrie, the abhomination of idolatrie, the horrible art of poisoning, the vertue and power of naturall magike, and all the conueiances of Legierdemaine and iuggling are deciphered: and many other things opened, which haue long lien hidden, howbeit verie necessarie to be knowne. Heereunto is added a treatise upon the nature and substance of spirits and diuels, etc.

King James I, in his *Daemonologie* of 1597, took issue with the *Discoverie of Witchcraft*, railing "against the damnable opinions of two principally in an age, whereof the one called Scot an Englishman, is not ashamed in publike print to deny that ther can be such a thing as Witchcraft" (the other he referred to was a German physician). King James was hardly the first to speak out. In 1150, St. Bernard had railed against jugglers, and another clergyman had said, "the tricks of jugglers never please God"; in 1106, jugglers were banned as residents in some cities of France; and over one hundred years later the King of France, Louis IX, tried to drive "tumblers and players of sleight of hand" from the country altogether.

But the trade of the juggler persisted. To the wandering troupes of conjurors, acrobats, and minstrels was added the mountebank, who sold healing potions and elixirs and often attracted attention by his performance of sleight of hand. He carried with him mysterious bottles and mechanisms purportedly of scientific origin, and indeed many of these charlatans may have had at least limited knowledge of optics and acoustics, and thus produced crude versions of today's stage illusions. Chaucer relates in "The Frankelynes' Tale" of the "tragetours" producing such delights as "a castel al of lym and stoon," "a vyne and grapes whyte and rede," lions, flowers, and even "water and a barge, and in the halle rowen up and down."

These mountebanks also performed many of the less appealing but nevertheless amazing feats of Eastern magicians, such as passing needles through their arms, hands, and tongues, lying on beds of nails, and fondling snakes of various kinds—all performed without harm to themselves, and certainly as advertisements for the wondrous curative powers of their wares.

By the end of the fourteenth century, playing cards had been introduced in Europe, possibly by the Moors when they came to Spain, and possibly by the gypsies who had been wandering the continent since about 1300. The gypsies told fortunes and sold charms, but, although early Tarot cards depicted *Le Bataleur* (the juggler), often shown doing the Cups and Balls, it is doubtful that they performed any of the card sleights done by later magicians, because the cards were so large and thick that they could hardly have been put to that purpose.

Cards were definitely in use for sleight of hand by 1600, and are referred to in *The Art of Juggling or Legerdemaine* (1614), the second book of magic tricks by S. R. (probably Samuel Rid). S. R. simply took most of the tricks listed in Scot's *Discoverie of Witchcraft* and added a few new ones, including "a strange and excellent trick to hold fower Kings in the hand, and by word to transforme them into fower Aces, and after to make them all blank cards, one after another."

In 1622, the *Hocus Pocus* book was published, various editions of which appeared over the next two hundred years. The first edition no longer seems to exist, but the second, *Hocus Pocus, Junior*, can still be found. Although the 1635 edition tells of new tricks, once again most of the text has been stolen from Reginald Scot. Even then, the habits of magicians were well established! The origin of the words Hocus Pocus, and their application to magic, is a mystery in itself. An acceptable theory, advanced as early as 1694, is that they are a variation on the Latin words spoken at the altar in the rite of consecration, a rite in which bread and wine are mystically changed to the body and blood of Christ. During the Reformation, when the Church and its practices were ridiculed, Hocus Pocus could well have served as a name for performers who could mystify by changing one thing to another. Whatever its roots, Hocus Pocus became a name for individual performers and synonymous with conjurors in general.

From Streetcorners to the Courts of Kings: Magic as Entertainment

The street performer began emerging as a respected entertainer during the seventeenth century. Until that time, the juggler had often appeared more as a beggar than a man of talent. His clothes, though usually distinguished by their color and flair, or by their hex symbols and wizard-style cloaks, were more often than not on the well-worn side. But as the oppressive suspicions of the Dark Ages fell away, and all of Europe experienced what then must have seemed great social freedom, so too did the lot of the entertainer improve. Traveling performers devised wagons that opened to form stages, and local inns and taverns not only allowed, but occasionally invited, magicians and their like inside to attract paying customers. The first theatre in all of "modern" Europe, which opened in 1576 (The Theatre, in Shoreditch, London), included performances by magicians and plays with magicians as characters from its very beginnings. At the great fairs, magicians began to set up booths for their shows where they performed at specific times and charged admission, instead of performing whenever they could attract a crowd and then passing a hat for whatever coins the public might offer. The fairs, which had originally been organized to celebrate saints' days and usually benefited the Church, had started in the twelfth century and had evolved into marketplaces for everyone's wares, with diversions to please the crowds.

St. Bartholomew's Fair, started in 1133, was undoubtedly the most famous, but there were many others, such as Southwark Fair, Greenwich Fair, Stourbridge Fair, and the May Fair—all in England—and the St. Germaine Fair in Paris. A great variety of jugglers appeared at the fairs year in and year out, and their group included fire-eaters, water-spouters, sleight-of-hand artists, makers of clocks and automata, and dispensers of every type of "medicine." A number of these performers became well-known

Isaac Fawkes appeared at Bartholomew and Southwark fairs in the early 1700s and later at his own theatre. He is seen here with two "posture-makers" (contortionists), with whom he toured about 1720.

and quite prestigious, among them Isaac Fawkes (or Faux), who gave private performances at both Bartholomew and Southwark in the early 1700s (he later established his own theatre at the Cock and Half-Moon Tavern). It was during Fawkes's day that newspapers of a sort began to appear, and the advertisements they carried give us, for the first time, some specific information about the performers of the period.

Fawkes, already popular and appearing before royalty, advertised in 1720 that he had a booth at Bartholomew Fair where he performed from two to eight daily, and presented "surprising and incomparable dexterity of hand." In addition to his own performance of magic, Fawkes toured with two "posture-makers," or contortionists, and by 1726 was performing along with a puppet show and displaying a musical clock that played various melodies and produced the sound of birds singing. This clock was made by Christopher Pinchbeck, inventor of a copper-zinc alloy that was often used to make gold-colored jewelry (thus the use of the word *pinchbeck* to mean gaudy or cheap). Pinchbeck had been exhibiting his own automata, but by 1727 he and Fawkes were in partnership, showing such wonders as "a prospect of Algiers" and an apple tree that, in one minute, would bear fruit. Fawkes presented the fruit to the audience for eating. When Fawkes died in 1731, he reportedly left £10,000, certainly a goodly sum for a magician! Two of Hogarth's prints feature Fawkes, "Masquerades and Operas" (1724) and "Southwark Fair" (1733).

During all of this period, magic shows were awash with bizarre and rather unseemly acts like that of one Mr. Love, who hammered 12-penny nails into spectators' breeches (while they

A SHORT HISTORY OF THE ART OF ILLUSION

were wearing them), then removed them without pain. Chabert put his head into a fire, swallowed prussic acid, and, for a finale, had fireworks burn the shirt off his back. Signora Josẹphine Giradelli put boiling melted lead into her mouth and had red-hot irons passed over her body. And then there was the pathetic but brilliant Matthew Buchinger, born without legs or arms, who, using his fin-like appendages, performed sleight of hand, played musical instruments, and did calligraphy. Blaise Manfre swallowed water, then regurgitated it as rose water, brandy, beer, and a choice of red or white wine. Something for everyone!

Mechanical figures of every kind were often another prominent part of a conjuror's trade. During the seventeenth and eighteenth centuries one saw exhibitions of a pipe-smoking skeleton; a druggist who dispensed coffee, tea, cinnamon, and other spices; magical clocks; the Sagacious Swan, who guessed chosen cards and read thoughts; talking heads; mechanical peacocks; the Clockwork Duck; the Flute Player; the Writing and Drawing Master; mechanical orchestras that played music; and, of course, the famous Chess Player, invented by Baron von Kempelen in 1769 and later toured by Maelzel. Although many of these were indeed mechanical wonders, the larger and seemingly more complicated of them usually hid a person who operated the mechanism from within, often a child or a midget, sometimes a full-grown man who tucked his legs into the bottom of the cabinet.

Matthew Buchinger was one of many bizarre performers of the 1700s.

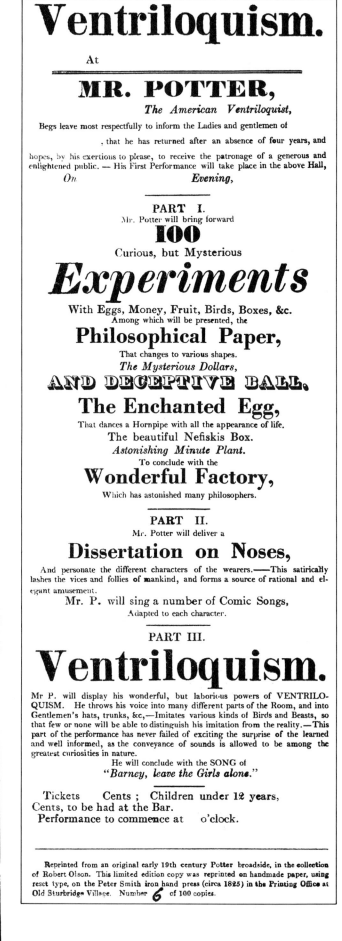

Ventriloquism.

At

MR. POTTER,

The American Ventriloquist,

Begs leave most respectfully to inform the Ladies and gentlemen of

, that he has returned after an absence of four years, and hopes, by his exertions to please, to receive the patronage of a generous and enlightened public. — His First Performance will take place in the above Hall,

On   *Evening,*

PART I.

Mr. Potter will bring forward

100

Curious, but Mysterious

Experiments

With Eggs, Money, Fruit, Birds, Boxes, &c.
Among which will be presented, the

Philosophical Paper,

That changes to various shapes.

The Mysterious Dollars,

AND DECEPTIVE BALL.

The Enchanted Egg,

That dances a Hornpipe with all the appearance of life.

The beautiful Nefiskis Box.

Astonishing Minute Plant.

To conclude with the

Wonderful Factory,

Which has astonished many philosophers.

PART II.

Mr. Potter will deliver a

Dissertation on Noses,

And personate the different characters of the wearers.——This satirically lashes the vices and follies of mankind, and forms a source of rational and elegant amusement.

Mr. P. will sing a number of Comic Songs,
Adapted to each character.

PART III.

Ventriloquism.

Mr P. will display his wonderful, but laborious powers of VENTRILO-QUISM. He throws his voice into many different parts of the Room, and into Gentlemen's hats, trunks, &c,—Imitates various kinds of Birds and Beasts, so that few or none will be able to distinguish his imitation from the reality.—This part of the performance has never failed of exciting the surprise of the learned and well informed, as the conveyance of sounds is allowed to be among the greatest curiosities in nature.

He will conclude with the SONG of
"Barney, leave the Girls alone."

Tickets   Cents ;   Children under 12 years,
Cents, to be had at the Bar.

Performance to commence at   o'clock.

Reprinted from an original early 19th century Potter broadside, in the collection of Robert Olson. This limited edition copy was reprinted on handmade paper, using reset type, on the Peter Smith iron hand press (circa 1825) in the Printing Office at Old Sturbridge Village. Number **6** of 100 copies.

During the eighteenth century performing animals were very popular, among them the Learned Pig, who could recognize selected cards, do addition, and tell time.

(Right) Richard Potter toured the American colonies performing sleight of hand and ventriloquism. He was the son of Sir Charles Frankland and his negro servant, Dinah, and, along with Jacob Philadelphia, was one of the first American-born magicians.

Pinetti presented an extensive repertoire of illusions and mechanical devices, performed escapes, and stole a shirt from the back of a spectator — a trick that is part of the Blackstone show today.

There were also animal marvels such as Morocco, the counting horse; the Learned Goose, who could read numbers; the Learned Pig, who could pick cards by both suit and value, tell time, and add; and dozens of others.

There were magicians everywhere by the 1700s. In the American colonies, Jacob Meyer, the first magician known to be born in what would become the United States, took the name of his birthplace and, advertising himself as the mystic Jacob Philadelphia, toured throughout England, Europe, and Russia. He even did royal command performances for Catherine the Great, Frederick the Great, and Sultan Mustapha III of Constantinople. Massachusetts-born Richard Potter, the son of Sir Charles Frankland and his Negro servant, Dinah, toured the colonies displaying his ventriloquism and sleight of hand. Potter's Place, New Hampshire, where he lived and is buried, bears his name. There was the audacious Cagliostro, who hoodwinked half of Paris until accused, perhaps falsely, of collusion in a scandal involving a diamond necklace intended for Marie Antoinette. Exonerated of that charge, he was soon to be condemned to life imprisonment by the Holy Inquisition for his attempts to establish Freemasonry, a capital offense to the Church. He died in the dungeons of San Leone in Urbino.

And, finally, to round off the century, we have Pinetti, who was a skilled performer and a publicist of the highest order. Probably born in Tuscany of simple parentage, about 1750, he traveled throughout the German provinces and then to Paris, where he entertained for the public and at court. In spite of his penchant for boasting and exaggeration (he claimed to be a professor of mathematics and natural philosophy, a Knight of the Order of St. Philip, financial counselor to the prince of Limburg-Halstein, and a dozen other titles pertaining to science, art, and royal connections), his audiences were very taken with him. His magic repertoire was extensive, and he added to his performances exhibitions of mechanical devices, which enthralled the always novelty-starved French. His Grand Sultan answered questions by striking a bell with a hammer. A talking head in a glass did the same. The Clever Swan, placed in a plate of water, changed course according to request and spelled out cards chosen by spectators.

Pinetti long preceded Houdini by escaping from various types of bonds. He did an early version of the Thumb-Tie trick in which spectators tied his thumbs with cord, covered them with a hat, and, seconds later, he would stretch out one hand to grab a glass of wine with which he toasted the spectators, then threw it

THE BAMBERGS

There have been numerous families in magic, and the Bamberg line is certainly outstanding in its longevity. The first of the Bambergs may have been one Jasper, an alchemist and necromancer of the early eighteenth century, and there are records of Eliaser Bamberg (1760–1833), a magician of Leiden, Holland, who was known as *Le Diable Boitieux* (The Crippled Devil) because he wore a wooden leg (in which he hid many of his magic props). He was famous in his day as a sleight-of-hand performer and a collector of automata.

David Leendert Bamberg (1786–1869), the son of Eliaser, was made court magician in 1834, and his son, Tobias, a scholar and linguist (1812–1870), also became court magician. Tobias's son, David Tobias (1843–1913), was appointed Royal Conjuror and on his touring performances he was assisted by *his* son, Theo.

Theo Bamberg (1875–1963), who was performing before the Dutch king by his eleventh birthday, became severely deaf as a young man and, as a result, he devised Okito, a Japanese character who spoke only his native tongue, giving Bamberg an excuse for doing a silent act. Okito's first vaudeville performance in Berlin was a great success, and, except for a few years working with Thurston under his own name, he performed as the Oriental magician throughout his life (the character became Chinese during the war years). Okito was known for his beautifully crafted magic equipment.

David Tobias Bamberg II (1904–1974) was the son of Theo and the last of the Bamberg dynasty. He chose to perform as the Oriental magician Fu Manchu, and spent most of his years appearing in South America, where he was a great favorite. He made several films in Mexico in which his character performed magic and, in 1947, his *Crazimagicana* was a successful show in Buenos Aires. He retired in 1966, ending the family's long and illustrious magic history.

in the air where it changed into a ball of paper. Dropping the hat from his hands, he revealed his thumbs still tightly bound. Another trick for which Pinetti was famous was that of stealing a shirt off the back of a spectator—a trick that is still a part of the Blackstone show today.

Pinetti left Paris as the unrest that led to revolution began, and tried his luck in London, then Germany and Naples, where he drew large crowds. Finally, he headed for Russia where, unfortunately, he was not to achieve the same success. His money ebbed away, as did his health, and he died there in his fifties. However, even during those bad years he managed to make his mark—he somehow got the emperor to become godfather to his two children!

Magic Enters the Theatres

As the nineteenth century dawned, a certain social maturity began to show itself in both Europe and America, and with it the beginnings of a middle class. Merchants were becoming respected citizens, and men of science, though still a bit suspect, were among the new idols. Businessmen and their families took their place among nobility and came to expect the comforts and graces of their new social standing. Entertaining guests in their new homes, and their own entertainment in theatres and restaurants, called for more talented and prestigious performers, and "stars" began to emerge. Theatres sprang up in every city—not the backrooms of taverns and inns, the village barns, or the makeshift booths of the great fairs, but halls built especially for performances, with upholstered seats, decorated walls and ceilings, orchestra pits, and pleasant lighting.

Magicians were among the first to take advantage of the trend and many, such as André Noé Talon, who performed under the name of Philippe, established their own theatres—his was the Bonne-Nouvelle in Paris—and presented their magic amid extraordinary sets and fanciful costumes. Philippe dressed in a conical hat and robes decorated with cabalistic signs. Bosco, the first of many magicians by that name, dressed in black satin breeches trimmed with lace, a short-sleeved top, and a large ruffled collar, and carried a large wand tipped with a gold ball. Comte, a prominent French conjuror, opened Le Théâtre Comte in Paris

M? PHILIPPE

André Noé Talon, dressed in colorful robes, performed as Philippe in his own Paris theatre.

in 1814, and another Frenchman, Henri Robin, opened the Théâtre Robin, presenting shows that combined magic and science, with a stage full of scientific impedimenta and elaborate magic props.

The preeminent among the new elite of conjurors was Jean-Eugène Robert-Houdin, often referred to as the father of modern magic. Jean-Eugène Robert was a clockmaker, a trade he'd learned under his father's tutelage. As he relates in his memoirs, a bookseller mistakenly gave him a book on scientific amusements instead of horology, and his fascination with the art of illusion began. As he continued his career as an expert clockmaker, he continued practicing as an amateur conjuror. At twenty-five, he married the daughter of a Parisian clockmaker, moved to Paris, and added his father-in-law's name—Houdin—to his own.

Robert-Houdin's expertise as a clockmaker and his interest in magic began to merge, and, at an industrial exposition, he exhibited an automaton figure that performed the Cups and Balls as well as a clock that operated without any visible mechanism. He began to make other curious clocks, mechanical singing birds, and automata for wealthy collectors. At the Universal Exposition of 1844 he won a silver medal and attracted the attention of P. T. Barnum for an automated "writing" man who answered questions, which Barnum bought and exhibited in London.

Robert-Houdin's inventions began to interest many people and he soon had a sponsor who supported him in his desire for a theatre of magic. He opened a salon in the Palais Royal, once the residence of Cardinal Richelieu. Elegantly appointed, it was the perfect setting for his mechanical masterpieces: a blooming orange tree; a magic bottle that poured various drinks; his famous "Ethereal Suspension" (which played upon the new use of ether as an anesthetic), in which he suspended his son horizontally from a single pole—this trick is now usually referred to as the "Broom Suspension"; and his "Pastry Cook of the Palais Royal," which featured a figure going in and out of a doorway bringing various sweets and liqueurs. Considered a mechanical wonder, it was actually controlled by Robert-Houdin's small son, who was hidden inside. Robert-Houdin also performed mentalism, with his blindfolded son identifying objects held by members of the audience. Called "Second Sight," this act proved a sensation (though the basic premise had been demonstrated by numerous other performers), and the French flocked to see it.

Robert-Houdin toured England when the 1848 Revolution closed all the theatres of Paris, and the English, including Queen Victoria, were as impressed with him as were the Parisians. He continued to tour throughout England and the continent for the next few years, but returned often to France, where he established a protégé, Hamilton, who successfully took over Robert-Houdin's "Soirées Fantastiques." Robert-Houdin also opened a new theatre on the Boulevard des Italiens and bought an estate in the country where he continued his scientific research, inventing many practical electrical and mechanical devices that he displayed at various industrial expositions.

Robert-Houdin's mechanical inventions were very much a part of the Western world's interest in what would become the Industrial Revolution, and yet one of the most curious incidents in his life reflects the underpinnings of mysticism that have remained with all civilizations from time immemorial. In 1856, when the marabouts (religious leaders) of Algeria were advocating dissolution of that country's ties with France, Robert-Houdin was sent as a special envoy of Napoleon III to dazzle those shamans into submission. In spite of the fact that he was putting on public performances at a theatre in Algiers, simply as entertainment, Robert-Houdin totally convinced the tribal leaders of his (and France's) supernatural powers. Hard to believe, but apparently true: After a display of well-done but hardly outstanding tricks—productions of flowers and cannonballs, and the transportation of coins from his hands to a closed crystal box—he challenged a strong man to lift a wooden box from the floor. The man lifted it easily, then replaced it. Asked to lift it again, he found it impossible, then suddenly cried out and ran. This and another illusion, in which a young boy disappeared from under a cone, convinced the marabouts that they shouldn't fool around with France and her wonderworkers!

The unliftable box was held to the floor by an electromagnet, and an electric shock was the cause of the man's pain and fear. The boy under the cone simply dropped through a trap door for his disappearance. Even in our time, among the most sophisticated of us, there are those who would believe in such "miracles"!

Robert-Houdin died at the age of sixty-five in 1871. He left behind a literary legacy in magic. Until Robert-Houdin, relatively little had been written for or by professional magicians. In addition to his memoirs, he wrote books on card manipulation, sleight of hand, stage illusions, and the psychology of deception, which have been translated into many languages. He also raised the conjuror's image from charlatan and itinerant performer to artist and man of science, respected and admired. It is interesting to note that the Théâtre Robert-Houdin lasted for over sixty years, finally closing at the onset of World War I. It was sold by Robert-Houdin's daughter-in-law in 1888, to Georges Méliès, who refurbished it and a few years later excited audiences with a new kind of magic—moving pictures.

The Théâtre Robert-Houdin opened on the Boulevard des Italiens in 1852 after Robert-Houdin's lease on the Palais Royale came to a close. It lasted over sixty years and, after 1888, was for some time managed by Georges Méliès, who presented early motion pictures there.

Jean-Eugène Robert-Houdin.

The First Great Stars: Magic Takes On an Image

The Herrmanns were certainly among the first families of magic in the nineteenth century, from Carl (or Compars), born in 1816, to Adelaide, wife of Alexander Herrmann, who gave her last performance in 1928 at the age of seventy-five. Carl and Alexander (who was twenty-seven years Carl's junior) were the sons of a doctor and undistinguished conjuror, Samuel Herrmann, who wrongly tried to dissuade them from considering magic as a profession. By the age of thirty, Carl was touring England and

CHUNG LING SOO

In a scenario that could put mystery writers to shame, Chung Ling Soo, the famous Chinese conjuror, was shot to death on the stage of the Wood Green Empire Theatre in London on March 23, 1918, as he performed the "Defying the Bullets" act before a full house of spectators. Born William Ellsworth Robinson in New York in 1861, Soo had toured in his twenties as Achmed Ben Ali, presenting one of the early "Black Art" shows in America. He worked as an assistant and illusion builder to the Herrmanns and to Thurston. He first appeared in Oriental garb as Hop Ling Soo at the Folies Bergère, but changed to Chung Ling Soo when he went to London. He carried the characterization so far that he insisted on translators when he dealt with the press, and, when challenged by a real Oriental magician, Ching Ling Foo, Soo claimed it was he who was being imitated.

At the time of his death, he was appearing with his wife of many years, who was billed as Suee Seen. She however was not the mother of his three children, and what their relationship was at that time it is hard to say. Soo was also heavily in debt and had been trying to put his finances in order.

Scotland Yard decreed Soo's demise as "death by misadventure." but no one will ever know the real story.

Europe (presenting as his own many of the inventions of Robert-Houdin). It was Carl who established the image of a magician that has come down to us through the years. He wore a large black mustache and goatee, making him appear slightly satanic, and he often wore a cape. He was sophisticated in his performing style, and even produced a rabbit out of a hat (though he was not the first to do so). His brother, Alexander, was very much the same in appearance, as was their nephew, Leon, who toured as Herrmann the Great after Alexander died in 1896. Although he was born in Paris, Alexander became one of the first great American magicians, and his wife, Adelaide, was certainly one of the great women performers of magic. After years of performing with her husband, she took over his show when he died, and became very successful in her own right.

It was during these times that advertising started taking on the importance that it has to this day. Magicians from early times had printed broadsides and called out their talents as they arrived in each town, but with the emergence of star performers, who could promote themselves to a substantial theatre-going public, the advertising began to outdo the entertainment.

John Henry Anderson, who billed himself as the Great Wizard of the North, had carriages covered with his posters driven through the streets of London while men marched carrying letters spelling out his name. He and others printed their programs on silk and satin, and magnificently colored lithographs began to appear. Adjectives were a dime a dozen, and one reads of the wonderful Talking Machine, the Smallest Man Alive, Incompara-

Alexander Herrmann, though a European, became the leading American magician in the late nineteenth century. He toured with his wife, Adelaide, who later became a star magician with her own large show.

John Henry Anderson, the Wizard of the North, was one of magic's great publicists. He gave away premiums, distributed posters and handbills, and paraded his announcements through the streets of London.

ble Entertainments, the Most Daring Illusion of the Age, Colossal Combined Shows, and the Eclipsing Sensation. Every other performer was the King or Queen of something. Magic posters implied illusions far surpassing anything the audience would ever see on stage—spirits, decapitations, conflagrations, floating pianos and girls, escapes from water, fire, and shackles. There were red devils, white-winged fairies, and golden butterflies. There were ducks and horses and birds, elephants and rabbits. By the time an audience arrived at the theatre, the anticipation was at a fever pitch. There were also magnificent portraits of the artists done in poster form. The Herrmanns, both Alexander and Adelaide, used them, as did Kellar, Carter, Thurston, Chung Ling Soo, and Houdini. As late as 1934, one of my father's posters advertised him as "Blackstone, King of Magicians" (see Color Plate 6).

SERVAIS LEROY (THE TRIPLE ALLIANCE/ LEROY, TALMA, & BOSCO)

Jean Henri Servais LeRoy (1865–1953) was born in Belgium, but ran away as a boy to England, where he toured with a heavy-drinking magician named Captain Henry Hill, and, after several misfortunes, with the good captain's brother. The tour did, however, lead to other bookings in England and the United States. In 1898, a theatrical promoter created the "Triple Alliance," combining the talents of three magicians, Imro Fox, Frederick Eugene Powell, and Servais LeRoy, who toured together for two years. Fox, a German who had originally been a chef, performed as a burlesque magician, using only mechanical props; Powell, an academic and businessman from Philadelphia, was known for his cremation illusion, called "She," and his "Second Sight" act. One of the novelties of the show was that one magician performed on stage while the other two performed in the audience. They were advertised as the "Three Crowned Kings of Magic."

Servais LeRoy was married to an attractive young lady, Mercedes Talma, who worked as his assistant on stage. When she became an excellent sleight-of-hand performer and was

Throughout the 1800s, a bizarre phenomenon was taking place: starting in the United States, spiritualism soon took hold in England and Europe. Although its disciples would not have it so, it was (and is!) very much a part of magic, both as a mystery and as an entertainment. Communion with the dead was believed possible long before recorded history, and was practiced by many a shaman and charlatan, but in the "modern" world of 1848, it seems incredible that two little girls in upstate New York, the Fox sisters, were able to convince the multitude that mysterious rappings were messages from departed loved ones.

Katherine and Margaretta Fox discovered they could startle their parents and the neighbors by making odd noises by cracking their toe joints against various surfaces that would carry sound. It was a wonderful game and they pretended to be as

LeRoy, Talma, & Bosco, and successfully toured Europe, North and South America, Australia, England, and South Africa. Talma performed her coin manipulations, and Leon Bosco was the comic relief. He fumbled the tricks and caused general mayhem on stage, to the audience's delight. So successful was the character that when Leon Bosco left the act, LeRoy replaced him with a series of others who always performed as "Bosco."

LeRoy was the creator and presenter of many of the now-classic illusions of magic, among them the "Asrah," in which a hypnotized lady floats in the air and then vanishes. He also performed "The Three Graces," an illusion involving a transposition of bodies and one that was also performed by Blackstone in the 1920s, by Jansen (later Dante), and by Doug Henning and others.

baffled as anyone else, but their mother, unnerved by the proceedings, called in others to witness the "miracle." Exploitation was just around the corner in the form of their older sister, Leah, and so spiritualism began.

While Leah was out promoting the ability of her sisters to carry messages back and forth across the border of death, dozens of others, both innocents and mountebanks, were hopping on the psychic bandwagon. There was Daniel Dunglas Home, who floated in the air, levitated tables, and claimed second sight. Florence Cook and Rosina Showers produced ghosts (Florence's ghost was called "Katie King," and Miss Showers produced "Florence Maple"). Eusapia Paladino caused objects to leave the room (and

THE GREAT LAFAYETTE

I n a small crypt at Piershill Cemetery in Edinburgh, Scotland, lie the remains of two devoted friends, constant companions in death as they were in life. Buried here are Sigmund Neuberger (1872–1911), known as The Great Lafayette, and his beloved dog, Beauty.

Beauty had been given to Lafayette by Harry Houdini when the two magicians were struggling young performers, and the dog became a stepping stone to success for Lafayette; he put her into his act, where she proved herself a good performer and a great audience pleaser. He moved on up to the major vaudeville circuits and became a top performer in both the United States and Great Britain. Lafayette doted on the dog, putting up signs in his house that read, "The More I See of People, the More I Love My Dog," and "You May Eat My Food, You May Command My Servants, But You *Must* Respect My Dog!"

Lafayette constantly told tales of Beauty's great abilities and intelligence, such as the time the lion got loose in his famous illusion "The Lion's Bride" and attacked him. According to Lafayette, had Beauty not distracted the lion by barking, he would not have survived (the performer was afterward prosecuted by the Royal Humane Society for having electrified the floor of the cage to shock the lion, causing him to roar ferociously on cue).

not return!), and produced a third arm from under her dress. And so it went.

In 1865 the Davenport Brothers, Ira Erastus and William Henry, traveled throughout England presenting themselves as spirit mediums. They asked spectators to tie them up and were then enclosed in their "spirit" cabinet. Seconds later, the "spirits" were playing musical instruments, tossing things in the air, and ringing bells. When the cabinet doors were reopened, there sat the brothers, still securely tied.

At one of their exhibitions, a young man went up on stage as part of a committee called upon to ensure there was nothing fraudulent about the spirit manifestations. The young man was

To what extent Lafayette's stories of Beauty's wondrous deeds were true, and how much he promoted his devotion to her to enhance the public's image of himself as an eccentric, is hard to discover, but there is no doubt that he truly loved Beauty and that he supplied her with unusual comforts. In his London house, she reportedly had her own room and bath, and she wore a leather collar studded with silver tags engraved with the names of the fashionable hotels that had been willing to accept her as a guest. As an alternate, she had a gold collar studded with diamonds.

Beauty grew old and feeble and died on May 4, 1911, while Lafayette was appearing at the Empire Palace in Edinburgh. In his sorrow, he had the dog's body embalmed and insisted she be buried in a cemetery for humans, not for pets. Outraged officials finally agreed it could be done if Lafayette bought a crypt in which he would one day also be buried.

The waiting period was short. Five days later, in a back-stage fire that took ten lives, The Great Lafayette perished, and his ashes were placed between the paws of his beloved Beauty (who had been buried sitting sphinx-like, "in the attitude of one of the Trafalgar Square lions," in an oak coffin with silver handles). In the funeral cortege, the hearse was followed by Lafayette's motor car, draped in black and occupied solely by another of his dogs, Mabel. Houdini sent a floral wreath in the shape of a dog's head with the words, "To the memory of my friend Lafayette,

THE DAVENPORT BROTHERS'
PUBLIC CABINET SÉANCE.

NOW BEING HELD AT
THE QUEEN'S CONCERT ROOMS,
HANOVER SQUARE.

This Drawing is the Copyright of Messrs. Robert Cocks and Co., London.

Ira and William Davenport purported to be spirit mediums and continued to attract large audiences even after John Nevil Maskelyne and George Cooke exposed their trickery.

John Nevil Maskelyne, a descendent of Nevil Maskelyne, Astronomer Royal (for whom the moon crater was named). John Maskelyne was skeptical of the increasingly popular performances of spirit influence, and when an accidental shaft of light fell upon the cabinet during the Davenports' seance, revealing to him the manner in which the spirits were manifested, he decided to expose the fraud to the public. He and his friend George Cooke put together an act imitating that of the Davenports and, a few months later, they presented it to great acclaim. It led Maskelyne to a career in magic lasting well into this century.

After two years of playing the provinces, Maskelyne and Cooke brought their act to London's Crystal Palace in 1869, and appeared there again in 1873. Their second appearance there was an enormous success and they remained in London, moving first to the St. James Hall, and finally to Egyptian Hall, where they played until 1904. Egyptian Hall, in Piccadilly, had been presenting theatrical attractions since 1811—menageries, circus performers, art shows, and illusions. Various magicians had appeared there, including Alexander Herrmann, Dr. Lynn, and Charles Morritt, but it was John Nevil Maskelyne who established it as England's first "Home of Mystery."

Maskelyne was an ingenious inventor, and, during his years at Egyptian Hall, he presented numerous mechanical devices. Many of them—including winking moons, talking parrots, animated tables, and dancing canes—appeared in the magic skits he was fond of. His automatons, Psycho (which played whist) and Zoe (which drew pictures of celebrities), were popular attractions for years. Maskelyne also presented one of the first levitations in which a hoop was passed over the floating subject. He is credited with inventing the coin lock (which led to the pay toilet), a ticket-dispensing machine, a keyboard typewriter, and a cash register, and with being one of the first to present the theatrical matinée.

John Nevil Maskelyne and George Cooke established Egyptian Hall as England's "Home of Mystery" in 1873. They performed there until 1904, when Maskelyne built a new theatre at St. George's Hall.

In 1904, George Cooke died and the owners of Egyptian Hall wanted to replace it with offices and shops. Maskelyne bought St. George's Hall, built a new theatre there, and went into partnership with David Devant, a young magician who had been appearing throughout Britain for some time and who shared with Maskelyne an interest in developing new illusions (he had already presented the new "animated pictures" at Egyptian Hall and on tour). "Maskelyne and Devant Mysteries" became a household word in Britain, and audiences flocked to see their shows. Ten years later, Devant went touring on his own again, and, sadly, was soon after stricken with a debilitating disease that caused his retirement. John Nevil Maskelyne continued managing his theatre and even performing until May of 1917, when he died at seventy-

Maskelyne went into partnership with David Devant in 1904; "Maskelyne and Devant Mysteries" became a household word in Britain.

DAVID
DEVANT
BY ARRANGEMENT WITH
MASKELYNE & DEVANT,
ST. GEORGE'S HALL, LONDON, W.

T. NELSON DOWNS

Billing himself as the "King of Koins" was a young man from Iowa who'd been a railroad telegrapher. T. Nelson Downs (1867–1938) was extremely skilled as a coin manipulator and became a successful variety performer at a young age, playing such big houses as the Palace in London and the Wintergarten in Berlin. He made a considerable fortune, enabling him to buy real estate and give up touring. He wrote two important books, *Modern Coin Manipulation* and *The Art of Magic* (with John Northern Hilliard), and invented the "Continuous Back and Front Palm" with coins, and "The Miser's Dream," "catching" coins in the air and dropping them into a top hat (today usually a bucket is used).

seven. His son, Nevil, continued "Maskelyne's Mysteries" until his death in 1924, when Nevil's son, Clive, took over. Clive died four years later at thirty-three on his way to Tibet to produce a film, and his brother Jasper became managing director of St. George's Hall; but a few years later two other brothers, John and Noel, outvoted him and took over. In 1933, St. George's Hall became a radio studio, and the last performance of the longest-running magic show was presented the following Christmas at London's Little Theatre.

Jasper Maskelyne continued touring performances of many of the famous illusions presented by his father and David Devant. When World War II broke out, he entered military service, performing for the troops and working as a camouflage artist, an experience he described in a book, *Magic—Top Secret.* He retired to a farm in Kenya and died there in 1973. Another generation of Maskelynes lives on, none of its members involved in magic, and England's great Home of Mystery has been relegated to glorious memory. It represented the finest of craftsmanship and creativity in a subculture often riddled with a lack of both.

The Great Blackstone: Vaudeville and the Rise of the Big Magic Shows

When my father was born, on September 27, 1885, in Chicago, the world was a very different place than it is today. Chicago was one of the new, great centers—America's second city—a hubbub of commercialism and aggressiveness, attracting thousands to the opportunities it offered. But where did these hordes come from? From the farms and rural outposts of a still-frontier country, filled with wide-eyed innocence and only the beginnings of sophistication. The medicine shows, the tents and circuses, the showboats had all passed this way, but when vaudeville and the stars it made famous began arriving, it seemed the world was at the front door and every prairie boy dreamed of distant adventure.

My father's family name was Boughton, and his father had opened a flower shop in Chicago in 1881. My grandfather had died when my father, the third of seven children, was only fifteen, and my dad started early to make his own way. As a boy, he'd thought of being a cabinetmaker (and that interest stood him in good stead throughout the years), but his natural career was firmly established long before he'd really had time to consider alternatives.

At McVicker's Theatre in 1897, he sat entranced as the great Harry Kellar performed sleight of hand and levitations, and presented his automata and spirit cabinet. Kellar by then was the major rival of Alexander Herrmann for the title of America's leading magician, and when Herrmann died in 1896 Kellar had few competitors.

Kellar had been born in Erie, Pennsylvania, in 1849, but had been performing all over the world before he made a success in his own country. He had toured small American towns as a boy assistant with the Fakir of Ava, a magician from England. By eighteen he was performing on his own, but without much success. In 1869, he took an assistant's job with the Davenport Brothers and Fay, the famed spirit-mediums who were soundly denounced by other conjurors but who, nevertheless, continued to convince gullible audiences of their psychic abilities. They had added William Melville Fay to their show to lecture on spiritualism and to substitute for one or another of the brothers when necessary. Kellar soon became the company's business manager,

HORACE GOLDIN

Born Hyman Goldstein in Poland, Horace Goldin (1873–1939) came to the United States at age sixteen and was still speaking only broken English by the time he became a performer. Embarrassed by criticism of his accent, he began doing a silent act, and, to make up for not speaking, Goldin presented as many tricks as possible in the allotted time. Audiences were fascinated as he performed "45 Tricks in 17 Minutes." Starting out in side shows and dime museums, Goldin soon was playing the Keith vaudeville circuit; and before he was thirty, he was appearing all over the world. He had a great flair for publicity and often devised illusions that represented current news stories. When he presented his version of "Sawing a Lady in Two," in which the girl's head and feet hung out of either end of the box, many magicians imitated him, so he changed it, presenting the first version using a buzz saw. He publicized the large insurance policy he carried on the girl and stationed ambulances and nurses outside the theatre to dramatize the danger. Another popular illusion was "The Tiger God," in which a girl, thrown into a cage with a Bengal tiger, is rescued when the magician causes the tiger to disappear.

After receiving gifts of jeweled stickpins from King Edward, King George, the King of Siam, and the Queen of Saxony, Goldin billed himself as "The Royal Illusionist." The stickpins survive today in a private magic collection.

watching the daily performances, and in no time he had perfected the act himself. When he had had enough of the Davenports' difficult personalities, he quit, taking William Fay with him. Presenting the same seances as the Davenports and adding magic, they hit the road. Their first performances were in Canada, then on to Cuba and Mexico. Their adventures were many and were the beginnings of Kellar's foreign travels, continued throughout his career.

The great magician Harry Kellar inspired my father when my father was quite young.

Kellar, who became a truly great performer, often adapted the ideas of others. One can forgive his adoption of the Davenports' act in the days of his youth, but throughout his long career he seldom hesitated to usurp other's inventions and put them into his own performances. When he saw Buatier de Kolta do his Vanishing Bird and Cage at Egyptian Hall, he bought it from him and then traded the secret with a magic builder in New York for something he wanted more. On tour, he advertised his company as The Royal Illusionists—the name used by Maskelyne and Cooke. He later exhibited his copy of Maskelyne's automaton Psycho. A couple of years after, he managed to get hold of the plans for three more Maskelyne automata. Still later, through Paul Valadon, a young German magician who had appeared at Egyptian Hall and whom Kellar seemed to be grooming as his successor, he got the plans for a levitation of Maskelyne's. In 1884, he leased the Masonic Hall in Philadelphia and opened it as Egyptian Hall!

A SHORT HISTORY OF THE ART OF ILLUSION

NICOLA AND VON ARX

C harles H. Nicol (1872–1958), who performed as Von Arx, and his brother, William Mozart Nicol (1880–1946), the Great Nicola, were the sons of one John Nicol, who performed as Nicoli, and grandsons of another magician, a Scot whose name was McNicol. As children they appeared in their father's act and each later used the name Nicoli. Von Arx, for a short time, did an act with Blackstone called Bouton & Kelso, with Von Arx as Bouton—a variant of Blackstone's real name—and Blackstone playing Dr. Kelso. Von Arx also appeared for a time as Chalbert. He spent most of his performing years touring Africa and the Far East, and, during World War II, entertained American troops in Europe.

Nicola was also one of the great touring magicians, performing in Europe, India, and the Orient as well as in the United States. He appeared often before royalty and heads of state, and received gifts of jewels from many of them. He was known as a gentleman who never stole ideas and illusions from other magicians and who always showed great respect for all the members of his company.

Even with all of this, Kellar was a great and charming performer, and my father's exposure to his show convinced him magic was the life for him. He went back to see the show again and again and began reading books on magic. One of the first tricks he learned was in Professor Hoffmann's *Modern Magic,* and it was a trick he used throughout his performing life. It was called "How to Tie a Knot in a Handkerchief and Make It Disappear" (it is also a part of my show today). Another trick he always presented he claimed he first saw done by the spirit-medium Anna Eva Fay. One of her "spirit manifestations" was a dancing handkerchief. It charmed him then and his version of it charmed audiences for years.

My father's interest in magic was entertaining him, but it wasn't feeding him and he had to find jobs to support his interests. At seventeen, he got a position with a woodworking shop as a pattern maker. One of his jobs was to manufacture magic props for Roterberg, a prominent Chicago magic dealer. Whenever he made one of these props, he made a duplicate for himself.

In the ensuing years, my father played dates at lodge halls, churches, schools, and small theatres in the Chicago area. By 1906 he had ventured as far afield as St. Paul, Minnesota, where he played his first out-of-town date on a bill with the movie *The Great Train Robbery,* early evidence of a burgeoning form of entertainment that was to profoundly change show business in the years that followed. But many years were to pass before movies killed vaudeville, and there were plenty of places for a young magician to play and perfect his act.

For a while in 1908, my father was part of an acrobatic act, "The Famous Byrnes Brothers in the New 8 Bells," doing gymnastic stunts and filling in with magic. During 1909, he joined an act called "Martini and Maximillian," playing the part of Martini, who did serious magic, while Maximillian (whose real name was Bobby Landis) did comedy burlesque of the straight magic. This combination of serious magic and comedy was to form the basis of an act that, shortly afterward, he was to do with his younger brother, Pete. My father, as the "straight" magician, was dressed in formal evening clothes, while my Uncle Pete, attired as a clown in bald wig, whiteface makeup, and baggy pants, performed a "crooked magic" burlesque of my father's feats.

In the season of 1910–1911, my father and uncle successfully toured their act on the Sullivan-Considine Circuit, and my father dropped the "gh" from his name, calling the act "Harry Bouton and Company in 'Straight and Crooked Magic.'" Another act on the bill that season was the Karno Troupe in "A Night in an

A SHORT HISTORY OF THE ART OF ILLUSION

My father and his brother, Pete Bouton, toured in "Straight and Crooked Magic" in 1910–1911.

Pete Bouton played the clown in "Straight and Crooked Magic."

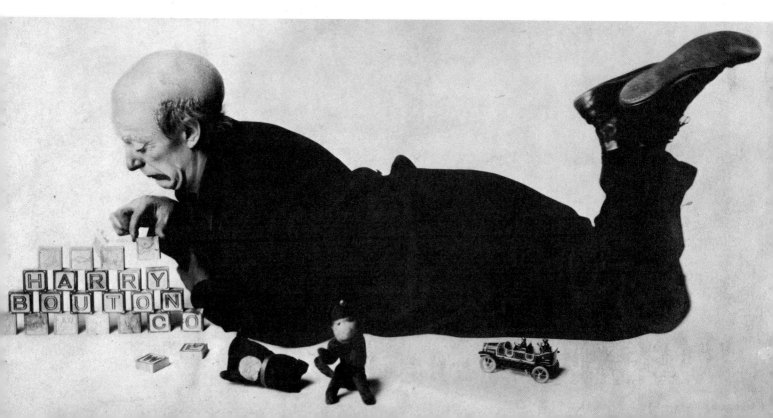

A very young Harry Bouton posed with his magic props in 1905.

Harry Bouton *(right)* did magic in a serious vein and brother Pete burlesqued his performance.

My father shows a card trick to old friend Stan Laurel at Hal Roach Studios, Hollywood, 1933. Oliver Hardy looks on.

English Music Hall." Among the then-obscure actors in that group with whom my father became good friends were two young Englishmen, Charles Chaplin, who shortly was to move to Hollywood and worldwide fame, and Stan Laurel, who was later to team up with Oliver Hardy and become another screen immortal. Also in the Karno Troupe was a young man named Ted Banks, who later became my father's stage manager until his death from a heart attack the night after the Decatur, Illinois, theatre fire (the story of which is told on pages 62–63).

In 1913, my father acquired several large illusions from the estate of a magician named Albini, including the spectacular "Bridal Chamber," in which an entire bedroom, complete with the bride and her maid, were produced from nowhere. It was to remain a feature of his act for the ensuing four decades.

For the next three years, my father and Uncle Pete played every conceivable kind of date including small-time vaudeville, burlesque, carnivals (sometimes reading palms and telling fortunes), and even (in 1916) a showboat out of St. Louis called the "Goldenrod." During a Los Angeles engagement, the great magician Harry Kellar attended their show. Kellar, who had been living in Los Angeles in comfortable retirement, came backstage to tell my father that he was the best all-around magician he had ever seen. Many years later, after Kellar's death, my father obtained his wonderful levitation illusion, thought by many to be the greatest stage illusion of all time, and added it as a regular feature to his full evening show.

The Boughton brothers were on their way as performers, and little by little they built their reputation. My father had a chance to buy some posters from a printer at a very low price— posters intended for a magician who had quit the business, called

My father appeared under many names during his early performing days. The transition from "Fredrik the Great" to "Blackstone the Great" took place in a three-day period in January 1918. These two similar posters show him in 1917 as Fredrik the Great, and in 1920 as Blackstone.

Fredrik the Great—and saw no reason to let such an opportunity pass by, so he called himself Fredrik the Great and began to advertise. Their act took on a more professional cast and things started looking up. Fredrik the Great was only one of several names he used in those early years. The Great Stanley, Francisco, Harry Careejo, Mr. Quick, C. Porter Norton, LeRoy Boughton, and Beaumont the Great were among the others.

A SHORT HISTORY OF THE ART OF ILLUSION

P. T. SELBIT

ne of the major inventors of stage illusions was an Englishman, P. T. Selbit (Percy Thomas Tibbles, 1879–1939). He had been a journalist before going into magic and although not an overnight sensation he became a very successful performer, playing at Maskelyne and Devant's St. George's Hall at various times for over thirty years, and in music halls throughout Britain. He invented the original version of "Sawing Through a Woman," and numerous other magic illusions that put young ladies through various tortures such as stretching and crushing. He created an audience-participation illusion in which strong men did battle with "The Mighty Cheese" (inside which a gyroscope was hidden). His illusions were copied by almost every stage magician of his time and many of them are widely performed by present-day magic performers.

Numerous sources have been given for the name Blackstone, but my father's first wife related that during World War I, when anti-German sentiment was high, business took a nose dive because people thought Fredrik the Great was German. Taking a walk one night in Wappokineta, Ohio, talking over the show's misfortune, she and my father spotted an advertisement for Blackstone cigars, and decided to give the name a try. On January 4, 1918, in Celine, Ohio, "Fredrik" gave his final performance. On January 7, at the Grand Theatre in Tiffin, Ohio, "Blackstone" gave his first. Whatever the source, it was to become a name synonymous with spectacular magic for the next forty years.

My father married Inez Nourse in Ingallston, Michigan, on November 3, 1919. Inez was a young musician who played the banjo and, after touring with the Reed St. John Trio and Crossman's Banjophiends, had gone on her own as "Inez Nourse, the Little Banjo Fiend." She was pretty, lively, and talented, and came to the show in 1916 when she heard it needed a music director. Inez brought good music to the show, and as its fortunes increased, added costumes and production qualities. The Blackstone show

flourished during the next ten years. The marriage did not; they were divorced in 1929. Inez died in October 1983, at the age of ninety-four.

During the early years of Blackstone's career, he had two major competitors: Harry Houdini and, perhaps more important, Howard Thurston. It was not Paul Valadon who became Kellar's successor but rather Thurston, who, in 1908, purchased the Kellar show.

Both Thurston and Houdini started out in American side-shows and carnivals, and went on to make their reputations in Europe before becoming real successes at home. They were both proficient at card magic (and indeed each, at one time, advertised himself as the King of Cards), but Houdini went on to become known for his escapes and his exposure of fraudulent spirit mediums, while Thurston became one of the great magicians of the theatre.

Howard Thurston returned from tours in Australia and the Orient at the age of thirty-nine, just as Kellar was ready to retire. The two toured together for a year as "The World's Greatest Magicians." Throughout the tour, Kellar introduced Thurston as his successor and, when Thurston took out his show the next season, it opened with a giant book on stage displaying pictures of Robert-Houdin, Philippe, Herrmann, and Kellar. Finally Thurston himself stepped from the pages of the book.

The Thurston show grew every season, filled with great illusions and Thurston's traditional act of card manipulations. Girls appeared in nests of boxes and in glass-lined trunks; sometimes they were levitated and sometimes caused to vanish, along with an automobile, and at other times with a piano. He was so successful that he put out road companies, one headed by Dante (Harry Jansen), and another by Tampa (Raymond Sugden). A third company, headed by Thurston's brother, Harry, did not make a go of it.

Thurston also tried his hand at writing. He wrote his autobiography, *My Life of Magic*, with Walter Gibson (who also wrote for Blackstone), and a mystery play, *The Demon*, which culled good but not great reviews. He kept himself fit and face-lifts kept him looking youthful. At sixty-five he married his fourth wife, a young lady of twenty-seven; but within the year he'd suffered a stroke, and he died in 1936.

It's a toss-up as to whether Harry Houdini is remembered more for his escapes from various restraints or for his failure to return from the bondage of death. Houdini's sincere interest in an afterlife and those who claimed direct communication with the dead had probably begun at the time his beloved mother

(Opposite) Inez Nourse, "the little Banjo Fiend," became music director for the Blackstone show in 1916. She and my father were married in 1919.

Harry Kellar passed on the "Mantle of Magic" to Howard Thurston in 1908.

died. Many writers have suggested his devotion to his mother was extreme, but, in his generation, to hallow one's mother was a basic concept. And for the millions of sons of struggling immigrant parents, as Houdini was, it was especially justified.

Houdini found no mediums he didn't recognize as fraudulent and, no matter how sincere his investigations, he saw no reason not to incorporate his findings into his performances and his publicity. On stage, he presented seances in full light, showing audiences how easily they could be taken in by the spiritualists. He testified on fraudulent mediums before a congressional committee, and he rode herd on the likes of Margery, the Boston medium. He told his wife, Bess, that if there were any way to return from the dead, he would find it and achieve the greatest

DANTE/THE GREAT JANSEN

When Howard Thurston was sending out touring companies of his very successful show, he hired Harry Jansen to head up one company and advertised him as "Dante," and it was as Dante that Jansen performed for the rest of his life.

Jansen (1882–1955) had come to the United States from Copenhagen at age six. He became interested in magic at an early age, and was touring with a small act by the time he was twenty. For a while he had his own Chicago-based illusion-building company, but he found performing more lucrative. He toured the Far East and in vaudeville until going on the road as Dante. After four years with the Thurston show, he went out on his own, playing successfully in South America, Europe, India, Australia, China, and Japan. He titled his show *Sim Sala Bim*, magic words from an old Danish nursery song, and, in 1940, opened it at the Morosco Theatre on Broadway to excellent reviews. After another five years touring the United States, Canada, and Mexico, Dante retired to his ranch ("Rancho Dante") in southern California. In his last years he appeared in films and acted as a magic consultant for a television show.

escape of all. For ten years after his tragic death from peritonitis at age fifty-two (he had suffered a ruptured appendix after a blow to the stomach by a student who thought Houdini's strong muscles could withstand it), Bess held a seance each year on the anniversary of his death, hoping for his message.

As a young man, Harry Houdini (born Ehrich Weiss in Budapest in 1874) read *The Memoirs of Robert-Houdin* and, adding an "i" at the end, adopted the author's name. He first performed with a friend, then with his brother, Theo, and eventually with his young wife, Beatrice, known as Bess. They did small magic and he became very adept at card manipulation, but his one large stage illusion was, in a sense, the forerunner of his career as an escape artist. This was an illusion called "Metamorphosis," in which he was placed in a knotted bag with wrists tied and put into a locked trunk, from which he not only escaped but managed to exchange places with his partner, all in a matter of seconds. (My father performed this same illusion as a feature

A SHORT HISTORY OF THE ART OF ILLUSION

of his act in 1906, when he was playing small-time vaudeville under the name of LeRoy Boughton.)

As time went on and his reputation grew, Houdini accepted challenges to escape from anything and everything. He was trussed up, handcuffed, locked in jails, safes, and milk cans, and, of course, in his famous Chinese Water Torture Cell, in which he was suspended upside-down in a locked tank of water. He emerged before a terrified audience two minutes later.

Houdini also performed many underwater escapes in icy rivers and streams as a means of advertising himself, but he was only one of many who did such stunts. My father did it numerous times and suffered many bruises and close calls just trying to get his name in the papers.

Harry Houdini and Harry Blackstone were "friendly enemies."

BLACKSTONE AND HOUDINI

My father once described his relationship with the great escape artist Houdini as that of "friendly enemies." Houdini, who was ten years older than my father and who had achieved stardom when the younger magician was still struggling in small-time vaudeville, did not take kindly to competition. My father was definitely competition, particularly in the area of escapes, which Houdini considered his special province. Houdini was a great showman and second to none in his ability to present sensational escapes, although as a magician he was much inferior to Blackstone, Thurston, and other of his contemporaries. Once, when asked about Houdini's abilities as a magician, my father commented sardonically that "Houdini could not put his hand in Central Park without rattling the leaves." In another interview, he explained that he and Thurston, a friend but his major

(Left) In 1914, Houdini posed before attempting one of his famous underwater box escapes.

(Right) There is reason to believe that my father preceded Houdini in performing the underwater box escape.

Photo by
FRED HESS + SON.
ucf. Cy

13

competitor, had divided up the United States, with Thurston playing the theatres east of the Mississippi and my father playing those to the west. When the interviewer asked, "What about Houdini?", my father replied, "We've given him the Mississippi to do his underwater box escapes."

It was, in fact, the underwater box escapes that my father periodically performed that most rankled Houdini. While Houdini had been performing underwater escapes, trussed in chains and handcuffs, since the early years of the century, there is good reason to believe that the idea of escaping from a chained and sealed box underwater originated with my father, who was performing such a feat several years before Houdini started doing it in 1912. The main feature of this escape was showing the box still tightly sealed after the magician had escaped and reappeared above the surface of the water.

Like Houdini, my father used underwater escapes to promote public interest in his stage performances and to keep his name in the papers.

My father being trussed up in preparation for an underwater escape.

My father reportedly got the idea for the feat from a highly impractical escape from a barrel, published in an early issue of *Popular Mechanics*. The method for the underwater barrel escape, which was possibly inspired by Houdini's highly publicized underwater escapes from chains and handcuffs, involved breaking apart the barrel, which was never recovered after the magician appeared free. My father realized that it would be a much stronger effect if the container could be raised from the water still securely sealed. He also designed the effect to be performed in a heavy metal box instead of a barrel. The secret of the box, which contained a hidden sliding panel that could be unlocked from within, was given by my father to his friend Walter Gibson for publication in one of Gibson's books.

When Houdini returned from theatrical triumphs in Europe, he heard of my father's feat and added it to his

A SHORT HISTORY OF THE ART OF ILLUSION

own repertoire, but with one important improvement. Instead of using a special box, which could easily be tricked up, Houdini had the box constructed by local carpenters in a lumberyard in each city where he played. This not only made the escape more baffling but also eliminated the necessity of carrying a heavy, specially constructed box from city to city. My father immediately recognized the wisdom of Houdini's idea, and, putting his specially constructed box into storage in New York, began doing underwater escapes from locally constructed packing boxes in each city where he played.

Houdini was furious. Not only was Blackstone doing escapes, an area of show business that Houdini considered exclusively his (actually, there had been escape artists before Houdini), but he had appropriated the idea of an underwater escape and had also had the temerity to

Giving a cheerful smile just before the final plank is nailed to the escape box.

The still-tied box is raised from the water.

come up with the good idea of doing it from a sealed box. Now, to make matters worse, he was using Houdini's improvement on the feat.

Houdini immediately brought my father up on charges in front of the National Variety Artists association, tried to have him kicked out of the Society of American Magicians, and threatened him with a lawsuit. My father was not terribly troubled by all of this, but did defend himself to the NVA by saying that he could produce the special box that he had been using for several years before Houdini did the escape. When they went to the warehouse where it was stored, the trunk, along with some other magic props, was not there, perhaps because the storage charges had not been paid. Nevertheless the NVA cleared my father of the charges against him since he apparently was able to establish that he had done the box escape at an early date. The threatened lawsuit never materialized, and the files of the Society of American Magicians indicate that he was never banished from that organization.

The story of Blackstone, Houdini, and the box escape has a strange ending. Many years later, after Houdini's

A SHORT HISTORY OF THE ART OF ILLUSION

death in 1926, the great mind reader Joseph Dunninger, a close friend of Houdini's, was visiting the Houdini house on 113th Street in New York City to buy some of the great escape artist's props from his wife, Bess. When Dunninger asked for a trunk to pack them in, Bess told him that the basement was full of trunks and boxes and to take any of them. Dunninger, sensing that it was some kind of escape prop, picked an interesting-looking metal trunk. When he got it home, he examined it to see how it worked, and, knowing that Walter Gibson was a close friend of Houdini's and the editor of his papers, asked Gibson if he knew anything about the box. Gibson immediately recognized it as the original Blackstone underwater box, and told Dunninger how the secret panel could be opened. How the box disappeared from the warehouse and ended up in Houdini's possession remains one of magic's many historical mysteries.

Finally, my father appears, safe and released from his bondage.

The Blackstone style was very different from that of his major competitors. Thurston was a gentleman of the old school, and Houdini, though he certainly had a sense of humor, always took himself very seriously. My dad performed each show as if he'd just thought up a new game in which he and the audience must participate. He teased and cajoled, used dreadful puns, and always made himself a part of each illusion he presented. It's hard to see clearly the public image of one's own father, but over the years hundreds—by now, perhaps, thousands—of those who saw him have spoken and written of his particular charm on stage. He dressed in white tie and tails, but often wore a huge cowboy hat (while cutting a lady in two with a revolving lumber saw). He kidded his own illusions, vanishing a horse but leaving himself with a saddle between his legs. When he presented the Buzz Saw illusion, audiences were astounded, but their terror was assuaged when his strong but soothing voice rolled out, "It is said that in the Himalaya Mountains they use hypnotism to stop the flow of blood during surgical operations," or, "I shall cut a little lady in two—so help me!" And thousands of grown men and women still tell with pride of being the child chosen to go on stage and receive a rabbit from him.

He loved illusions with animals, and believed audiences did too. Besides the rabbits he used ducks, donkeys, doves, canaries, and geese, and he tried vanishing a camel as well as a horse (it didn't work too well; the camel was determined to do its own version of the illusion and was demoted to stage decoration). He also loved spectacle and lots of assistants and toured the largest illusion show to hit the road— traveling with up to thirty assistants and two ninety-foot railway baggage cars full of equipment.

My favorite description of my father's performance was written by Daniel Waldron, the major Blackstone historian, for a series on "Famous Michiganians" for the Michigan Department of State.

When Harry Blackstone stepped onto the stage you knew you were in the presence of "A Magician." Striding in, shoulders thrown back, arms thrust slightly outward from his sides, elbows bent, his sturdy hands poised as though ready to grapple with unseen forces, he seized the imagination instantly. And when he stood center stage, erect as a pillar, his great white head of hair glowing in the spotlight, a sudden smile of pleasure passing over his face as the gloves which he briskly tossed into the air turned into a fluttering dove before your very eyes—at that moment there was no doubt in your mind that you would relax and be assured of enchantment. Nor was there any fear, as the sonorous, good-humored voice rose without electronic amplification to the last

(Opposite) My father often wore a large cowboy hat while "sawing a lady in two."

A SHORT HISTORY OF THE ART OF ILLUSION

THE THEATRE FIRE

Perhaps the greatest feat my father performed was not one of his standard tricks at all. It happened on September 2, 1942, when the show was playing the Lincoln Theatre .in Decatur, Illinois, and I was along as an eight-year-old assistant. It was a matinee and the house was packed with 3,200 enthusiastic spectators. Just as my father was introducing the next illusion, Ted Banks, the company's stage manager, walked out on stage and spoke quietly to him. The building next to the theatre was on fire and there was danger that the flames would spread. My father, completely unruffled, walked to the footlights and announced to the audience that they were in for a special surprise. He had created an illusion so spectacular and vast that it could not be performed on a theatre stage,

My father surveys the Lincoln Theatre in Decatur, Illinois, from which he had just evacuated the audience in the fire of September 2, 1942. Behind him stands Ted Banks, whose death from a heart attack the following day was attributed to his efforts in saving the Blackstone show.

he announced. He invited the audience to join him in front of the theatre and to look up, where he would perform the biggest trick they had ever seen. From the stage he supervised the orderly evacuation of the theatre, one row at a time. The stage crew and assistants helped usher the audience out; I remember one very fat lady who got stuck in her seat, and my father and a stagehand had to unscrew the seat from the floor. I walked her out of the theatre, still stuck in the seat.

There is little doubt that my father's ruse avoided panic and almost certain loss of life. After the audience was outside, we returned to the theatre and carried the apparatus out into the alley behind. Supervising all of this was my father's stage manager and dear friend, Ted Banks, whom he had first met so many years before when he and my Uncle Pete were on the bill with the Karno Troupe. When the theatre was evacuated and all the props safely stacked in the alley outside, Banks returned exhausted to his hotel room to rest. The strain had been too much for his heart, and, when he lay down on his bed to take a short nap, he never awoke. The fire in the building next door was brought under control and the Lincoln Theatre did not burn.

Smoke rises from the Lincoln Theatre, where the Blackstone show had been playing, September 2, 1942.

BLACKSTONE PLAYING TO
5000 PEOPLE TWICE DAILY I[N]
WORLD'S ONLY CORN PALA[CE]
MITCHELL, SOUTH DAKOTA

The Blackstone name drew crowds at the Corn Palace in Mitchell, South Dakota, in 1924.

row of the uppermost balcony, that you would have to strain to help lift the dusty cares of life away. You could give yourself over to the astonishment, laughter, awe, and delight which lay ahead as horses vanished, princesses floated, handkerchiefs danced, gorgeous girls were buzz-sawed in half, birdcages disappeared from your own fingertips, and people, rabbits, flowers, ducks, burros, bottles, and silken shawls appeared from nowhere, behaved in incredible ways, underwent breathtaking transformations, or vanished completely from human sight in the twinkling of an eye. You were in good hands. You would leave the theater refreshed, full of wonder, and wholly satisfied.

During the 1920s, Thurston, Houdini, and Blackstone, along with many other performers, began to feel the pinch brought on by the demise of vaudeville. Along with his involvement with spiritualism, Houdini tried making adventure movies starring himself. Thurston and Blackstone tightened up their programs and headlined on bills featuring motion pictures. Fortunately, this period is the one that brought the greatest fame to my father.

Thurston's death in 1936 left my father the preeminent illusionist in America, and although the country was in the midst of the Great Depression, movies and their accompanying stage shows were pulling in the crowds. The theatre has always done well during bad times, the escape it offers obviously a welcome

A SHORT HISTORY OF THE ART OF ILLUSION

relief to the dreariness of everyday existence. Even the theatres themselves were built for fantasy, decorated with pagodas, sailing ships, Egyptian temples, medieval fortresses, Dutch villages, country gardens, and Spanish haciendas. Lions, tigers, cupids, gods, and goddesses decorated grand staircases and Moorish arches. Magic fit right in!

My father played many of these picture palaces year after year, among them the Oriental Theatre in Chicago, where the walls were so overdecorated with plaster creatures that the architects themselves were embarrassed; the Fox in St. Louis, where sworded Turkish warriors mixed with Persian throne chairs while elephants gazed down from under a circus-tent ceiling; and the Fabulous Fox in Atlanta, a Moorish marvel where sunrise and sunset take turn in a desert sky behind the fortifications that still adorn the balcony, and even the fire escape, made of stripes of cream-and-tan brick to match the rest of the exterior, is decorated with arched windows and doors. I played there with my show in 1979, and can only thank the preservationists for keeping this wonder of an age gone by.

My father headlined in vaudeville theatres and presented his "Rabbit Giveaway" at children's matinees, c. 1920.

c. 1920.

c. 1920.

(Opposite) Devil Shadow portrait, 1920s.

1950s.

(Left) c. 1946.

(Right) c. 1946.

Onstage with my father on my seventh birthday, Colon, Michigan.

BACKSTAGE: GROWING UP WITH THE COMPANY

Starting in the 1920s the Blackstone show headquartered in Michigan, first at Sand Lake and later in the small town of Colon. The company would spend most of the summer months there (all touring shows cut back in the summer because of the lack of

A SHORT HISTORY OF THE ART OF ILLUSION

air-conditioned theatres), refurbishing the props and enjoying a respite from the grueling road trips of the winter, and over a period of years my father, the company, and magic itself took over the town.

My father bought a strip of land on one of Colon's small lakes, and it became known as Blackstone Island. There he constructed a house and barn where he built the illusions for his *Show of 1001 Wonders*. The company members lived nearby in various cottages and many bought houses in Colon, where they remain residents to this day.

I was born in nearby Three Rivers in the summer of 1934. My mother, Billie Matthews, had auditioned for the show at age sixteen, toured with it for a short time, then returned home to Buffalo; a few years later, she joined the company again. She was tall, with a lovely figure, and became a prominent performer in the show. She and my father married in 1933. It was a short union, and when the marriage dissolved it was to Colon and my father that I turned. I spent happy childhood summers there and even a winter or two in the care of Sally Banks, wife of Ted Banks, the company's stage manager, when it was not possible for my father to take me with him on the road.

Lifelong friendships were made in Colon. One of my childhood playmates, Merrillyn Merrill (whose father, Fred Merrill, was my father's advance man), has in recent years been governess and aunt-by-adoption to my youngest daughter. Her mother, Caroline, lives in Colon still. The little graveyard on the outskirts of town keeps the company together. My father is buried there, and near him my Uncle Pete, and my Aunt Millie, who was the show's wardrobe mistress, Fred Merrill, and Ted and Sally Banks.

Over the years Colon became known as the "Magic Capital of the World," and every year magicians came from afar for a week of shows, lectures, and special events known as the Abbott Get-Together. Percy Abbott and my father were briefly in business together, and Percy continued making magic equipment under the name of the Abbott Magic Novelty Company, which is still in business today. Each year for one week in August, the schools, the library, every restaurant and bar, and many households in Colon are abuzz with talk of invisible decks, disappearing rabbits, multiplying coins, and stage illusions old and new. Then its strange and magical visitors depart and, like Brigadoon, the town reverts to the quiet little mid-western village my father found so long ago.

It seems odd in retrospect, but as a child I didn't realize there were magicians other than Blackstone. I started attending magic conventions with my dad in the 1940s, and the first

A BLACKSTONE SCRAPBOOK

Alfred Boughton (c. 1895) and Barbara Deegan Boughton (c. 1905), parents of Harry Blackstone, Sr.

Harry Blackstone, Sr. and his first Studebaker, 1918.

Blackstone, Sr. wrestles a cow; postcard sent to his mother, 1911.

The company on the Million Dollar Pier, Atlantic City, New Jersey, 1922.

The gang in the barn, Colon, Michigan, 1920s.

Blackstone, Sr. and members of the company with the camel Sand Lake, Michigan, 1923.

Blackstone at a magicians' gathering in the early 1920s. To his left are Harry and Bess Houdini.

Truckload of magic props leaving Colon for the railroad in Three Rivers, Michigan, mid-1930s. Kneeling in front: Bud Doremus, then stage manager for the Blackstone show.

The Blackstone and Billie Matthews wedding, Colon, Michigan, July 1933.

Blackstone, Sr. on dock, Colon, Michigan, c. 1933.

The Blackstone, Sr. troupe visit the Hal Roach Studios, Hollywood, California, 1933.

Blackstone, Sr. does a handstand on the dock in Bermuda, holding a fan of cards in his toes, 1928.

Harry and Billie Blackstone, Greenfield Village, Michigan, c. 1935.

Relaxing in the alley behind the theatre between shows, 1936.

Skiing in Denver, Colorado, c. 1935.

Harry and Billie Blackstone with Harry, Jr., Detroit, Michigan, 1934.

Merrillyn Merrill and Harry Blackstone, Jr., 1935.

Colorful magic props by the barn, Colon, Michigan, 1940s.

Movie great Harold Lloyd, Bess Houdini, and Blackstone, Hollywood, California, 1933.

Father, son, and rabbit, c. 1939.

Crowned King of Magicians, Detroit, Michigan, 1934.

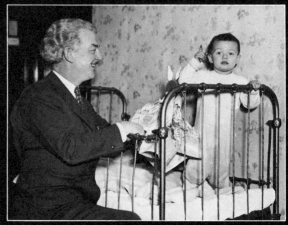

Father and son, New York, 1935.

Shirley Temple's birthday party at her Hollywood home, 1939, with rabbits produced as a gift for her by Blackstone, Sr.

Father and son; Christmas card, 1941.

The famous Vanishing Horse, 1940s.

Blackstone does Rope Trick with cactus at Triple H Ranch, Tucson, Arizona, 1949.

Blackstone and some of the 153,000 rabbits he gave away during his career; late 1930s.

Harry and Harry, Jr. at the piano, c. 1944.

The great magician Al Flosso has a card selected by another great magician, New York, 1952.

A young Blackstone, Jr. meets Georgie Jessel, Albuquerque, New Mexico, 1961.

Harry and Gay Blackstone on stage with (from left) daughters Cynthia, Adrienne, and Tracey, Colon, Michigan, 1979.

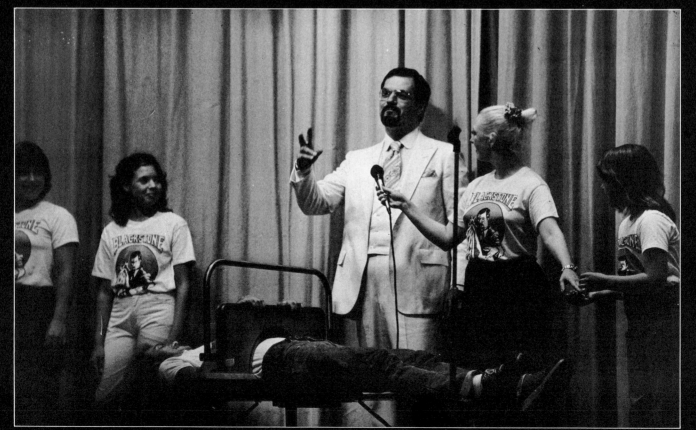

Harry Blackstone, Jr. and Gay Blackstone receive 1979 Magician of the Year award from Bill Larsen, president of the Academy of Magical Arts, Hollywood, California.

Harry Blackstone III and Bellamie Blackstone.

Bellamie Blackstone, age three, on Misty, the Blackstone vanishing elephant.

magician I saw perform was Virgil. Once when my dad was touring with the USO and couldn't take me with him, Virgil and his wife and assistant, Julie, took care of me for a couple of weeks. They let me appear on stage to help them perform a trick in which they baked a cake in a hat! I'd often been in the Blackstone show—at six months of age, I had been produced, along with my mother, in the "Artist's Dream" illusion; starting at about age six, I carried on props, went on stage with the kids from the audience for the "Vanishing Birdcage" trick (as my children have often done when I'm performing it), and appeared in production numbers (in costumes made by Aunt Millie to match those of the adults). When I was in military school, I would arrive for visits in my cadet uniform and my father would introduce me as a "midget Turkish general," other times as commander of a battalion of Lilliputians.

I once had occasion to introduce my father from the stage. When I was a student at the University of Texas, I wrote my thesis on levitations and performed a show of which levitation was a part. Unbeknownst to me, my father had come from California to be in the audience. When I received my applause, I heard a special whistle he had always used with me. I introduced him to the audience, and he performed for thirty minutes! My professor gave Dad an A; I got a B, with the added comment that it "had been difficult to judge Harry Blackstone, Jr., with the other act on the bill."

During the early 1940s, Blackstone toured extensively with the USO doing shows with such popular performers of the day as Alan Jones, Edgar Kennedy, Frances Langford, and George Burns and Gracie Allen. When the war ended, he started doing full evening shows and continued with them until his retirement in 1960.

In those days, for thirty rail tickets you could have the use of a ninety-foot baggage car, so he found it cheaper than shipping to buy forty-five tickets, which allowed one and a half baggage cars for Blackstone equipment. As a result, there were many traveling companions. A frequent favorite was Walter B. Gibson, who wrote many articles for and about Blackstone and who, under the pseudonym of Maxwell Grant, was the author of over two hundred and fifty full-length novels of *The Shadow*. In the early 1930s, there was also a mysterious young British magic enthusiast who briefly rode along with the show when it was going through Canada. It seems he was truant from a Canadian State visit! (My father had originally met the future Edward VIII at a private party in Canada.)

(Opposite) **USO poster, c. 1943.**

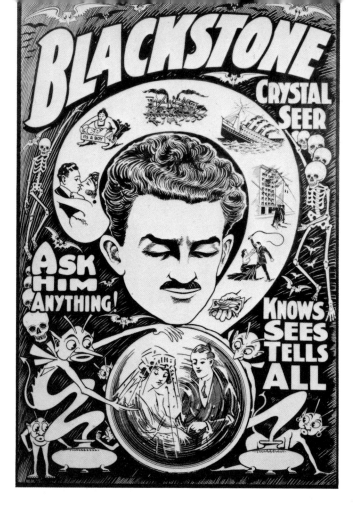

BLACKSTONE AND THE SPIRIT WORLD

From the earliest days, magicians' advertising strongly suggested that the wonder workers were in league with the spirits (if not actually in partnership with the devil!). As audiences became more sophisticated, this linkage of stage magic and supernatural forces became less believable, but magicians continued to "read minds" and to present pseudo spirit phenomena. My father was one of the first (perhaps *the* first) to add a special "spook night" to his performances, to pull in those more interested in spooks than in magic (see color plate 3). In earlier (and leaner) times, my father worked a crystal-gazing act in carnivals and small towns, but said he decided to give it up when he discovered that people were taking it seriously. He maintained his friendship with Joseph Dunninger, "the master mentalist" of radio fame *(opposite)*, and once they collaborated on a seance, held on Halloween, the anniversary of the death of their famous contempor-

ary Houdini. Among the spirit phenomena hoped for(?) was that the spirit of the great escape artist would open a pair of handcuffs that had once belonged to him. Perhaps Houdini, from beyond the grave, was reluctant to give free publicity to his arch-rival Blackstone. The cuffs did *not* open, but the story made the wire services anyway.

My father also emulated Houdini by publicly challenging "mediums, fortune tellers, and those who claim to possess psychic powers and to hold communication with departed spirits," and offering to duplicate their effects on stage. Each performance of my father's show and of mine still features some spirit phenomena "just for fun," in the classic dancing handkerchief trick.

THE BIG SELL: ADVERTISING AND PROMOTING MAGIC

Blackstone was one of the magicians who truly used the media of his day. In city after city the newspapers carried personal stories about him, and local stores and products were endorsed by him. On a national scale, there was *Blackstone, the Magician Detective*, a syndicated fifteen-minute radio program featuring a Blackstone adventure plus a simple trick that could be done by listeners, and *Super Magician Comics*, starring Blackstone, could be bought at the newsstand. Houdini and Thurston, of course, had done the same. Houdini used the infant art of film, starting with a serial, *The Master Mystery*, in 1918. Playing the part of an undercover agent, he escaped from one entrapment after another for fifteen

BLACKSTONE IN THE COMICS

In 1941, pulp writer Walter B. Gibson, my father's longtime friend and creator of "The Shadow" (under the pen name of Maxwell Grant), approached him with the idea of a Blackstone comic book that would feature him as "the world's only living comic book character." Gibson went to Street and Smith Publications with the idea of *Super Magic Comics*, which would relate largely fictitious adventures of Blackstone based on illusions in his show at exotic locations all over the world (actually, my father never played outside of the United States and Canada, except for one engagement in 1931 in Bermuda). Gibson, who was at that time writing "The Shadow" comic book for Street and Smith, suggested that they try the idea as a one-shot and, if it was successful, turn it into a regular monthly comic book. Since the average run of a comic book was 200,000 copies in those days, Gibson made the proposition particularly attractive to the publishers by offering to have my father buy 50,000 of the press run at five cents per copy (the newsstand price for a comic book in the 1940s was ten cents). My father, in turn, would offer these comics as a premium to children at his matinees, and the theatre managers would pay half the newsstand price of the comics distributed for this promotion. For an additional nickel a ticket, the theatres' business was increased and the books thus cost my father nothing.

A SHORT HISTORY OF THE ART OF ILLUSION

Gibson wrote the first issue on the train from Boston to New York, and the Street and Smith editors were delighted with the adventures he had concocted. It was immediately turned over to their comic book artists to illustrate and soon the first issue of *Super Magic Comics* was on the newsstands. When my father went to get his 50,000 copies, he was astonished to find that none were available. The first issue was such a hit that it was completely sold out. Already they were pressing Gibson to write Volume 1, Number 2 (its title changed slightly to *Super Magician Comics* to put more emphasis on Blackstone), to fill the demand. Thus Blackstone joined Superman, Batman, and Flash Gordon as a genuine comic book hero for hundreds of thousands of American youngsters.

After a successful run of some five years for Street and Smith, Blackstone continued as the feature character in *Master Magician Comics*, and later as *Blackstone, the Magician Detective*. Blackstone was so popular with his young followers that, in 1944, the *Blackstone, the Magician Detective* radio show (also created by Walter B. Gibson) ran for seventy-eight episodes. In 1949 a comic character named "Whackstone," obviously based on my father, appeared in Al Capp's immensely popular *Li'l Abner* comic strip. In the strip, he was seen performing the pickpocket act that was an important part of his show and is still a feature of the Blackstone show today.

© 1984 Capp Enterprises, Inc.

episodes. He followed the serial with feature films—*The Grim Game, Terror Island, The Man from Beyond,* and *Haldane of the Secret Service.* None received any critical acclaim, but they kept his name before the public.

Thurston took to the airwaves when recovering from the plastic surgery he thought would keep him looking young. He also used adventure as his theme. Probably the most curious success in radio was Dunninger, the mentalist. It is fascinating that radio audiences were completely accepting of "mind reading," something to which they could not be privy. Dunninger was a rough-and-tumble boy from the Lower East Side of New York who, early on, realized the importance of promotion. He dressed with a flair, wearing spats and diamond stickpins, and publicized his abilities by driving blindfolded through the streets in search of hidden objects. He gave "demonstrations" of the "science" of mind reading for civic groups and journalists' clubs, assuring that there would be mention of his talents in the press.

And he was, indeed, impressive. Calling himself a researcher rather than an entertainer or a psychic, he "read" with his mind the secret thoughts of audience members. He "assisted" local police departments in finding missing automobiles (usually his own!), and, in a strange switch, took on exposing frauds à la Houdini.

Dunninger had tried a series on radio (unsuccessfully) as early as 1929, but by 1943 he felt his mind reading could be sold over the air if he performed in front of a live audience which would serve as witness. This time he had indeed read the collective mind of his listeners: the show was a great hit. It usually featured a celebrity guest and a "Brain Buster," in which he guessed the serial number of a dollar bill that lay in a block of cement at the bottom of the East River, or described a sketch drawn by someone in a plane flying over New York, or some equally fantastic feat; but his greatest effect was telling audience members what was on their minds. In 1948, Dunninger's show moved to television. He continued to perform for several years, but he was already suffering the early signs of Parkinson's disease and his career soon came to an end. He died in 1975.

The Blackstone show continued to delight audiences until his retirement in 1960. Tens of thousands of rabbits had been given to as many happy children, and the Dancing Handkerchief, the Buzz Saw illusion, and the pickpocket routine called the Committee had made Blackstone, in the minds of millions, "the greatest magician I ever saw." He was seemingly the last of an age of charismatic magic personalities, and indeed it was several years before the emergence of any new magic superstars.

PLATE 1. Blackstone — The World's Master Magician. c. 1920.
Erie Lithographic & Printing Co., Erie, Pennsylvania. Collection of Posters Please, Inc., New York City.

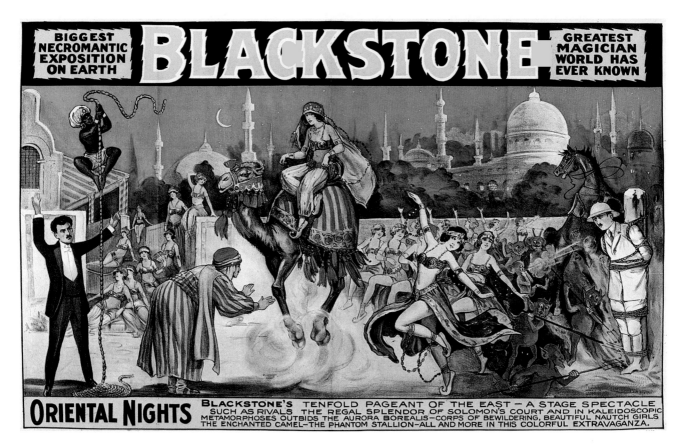

PLATE 2. **Blackstone — Oriental Nights. c. 1920.**
Erie Lithographic & Printing Co., Erie, Pennsylvania. Collection of Posters Please, Inc., New York City.

PLATE 3. **Blackstone — Congress of Spooks. c. 1920.**
National Printing & Engraving Co., Chicago, Illinois. Collection of Posters Please, Inc., New York City.

PLATE 4. **Blackstone and His Show of 1001 Wonders. 1945.** Globe Poster Corp., St. Louis and Chicago. Blackstone Collection.

PLATE 5. **Blackstone and His Mighty Wonder Show. 1929.** Artwork for a poster never printed. Courtesy American Museum of Magic, Marshall, Michigan.

PLATE 6. Blackstone — King of Magicians. 1934.
Erie Lithographic & Printing Co., Erie, Pennsylvania. Blackstone Collection.

PLATE 7. Blackstone Concert Tour. 1984–1985.
Artist: Robert Watts. Blackstone Collection.

Scenes from *Blackstone!*, on tour and on Broadway, 1979–1980.
Photography by Ken Howard.

PLATE 8. The Enchanted Garden.

PLATE 9. Merlin.

PLATE 10. Oriental Magic.

PLATE 11. Americana.

PLATE 12. Moorish Fantasy.

PLATE 13.   Circus of Mystery.

PLATE 14.   Circus of Mystery.

PLATE 15. Blackstone! 1979–1980.
Artist: Miller. Blackstone Collection.

CARTER THE GREAT

Charles Joseph Carter (1874–1936) was another Blackstone contemporary, but did most of his performing outside the United States. Carter had started performing magic as a young boy, billing himself as "Master Charles Carter, America's Youngest Prestidigitator," and had made enough to put himself through college, where he earned a degree in law. He toured a full evening vaudeville show throughout his twenties, then commenced touring the world, mostly the Orient. He preferred performing for weeks at a time in each city, rather than the short-term bookings he'd done in the United States. He always traveled in great style—often in a custom-built automobile that boasted a refrigerator and a decorative horn shaped like an asp.

Carter was a tremendous success in Japan, and greatly admired. During his stay there he presented a silver-encrusted saddle to the emperor, but when he attempted to leave the country, the Japanese confiscated all his earnings. Carter took his case before the court, serving as his own legal counsel, and won, but the Japanese told him never to return. Infuriated, he demanded the return of the saddle. He never forgave the Japanese and during the years he spent at Carter Castle, his home overlooking San Francisco Bay, he prophetically insisted to everyone that they were mining the harbor in preparation for attacking the United States. Ironically, after World War II, Carter Castle served for some time as the Japanese consulate.

Carter had two unsuccessful theatrical ventures in the United States—a permanent magic theatre in New York and a "Temple of Mystery" at the 1933 Chicago World's Fair, neither of which was self-supporting—and he then returned to his world tours. He died in Bombay, India, of a heart attack, but his long-time assistant, Evelyn Maxwell, claimed he had never fully recovered from being crushed against a wall by an elephant several months before.

Ralph Edwards, host of the television show *This Is Your Life,* poses with my father and me after the program devoted to my father's life story.

My father had always suffered from asthma, and it was in a sanitarium where he had gone for treatment in 1950 that he met the woman who became his third wife, Elizabeth Ross. In 1960, they gave up the apartment in New York that my father had maintained since 1926 and moved to Los Angeles. He was interviewed by Edward R. Murrow on his *Person to Person* television show, and *This Is Your Life* devoted a program to him, giving him an opportunity to be reunited with various members of the old company. He spent his last years doing special shows and performing for fans at the world-famous Magic Castle in Hollywood. There, younger magicians who had admired him for a lifetime listened with rapt attention to his stories and watched him perform. For him, it wasn't the same as being on the road with the big show, but it was very gratifying.

When he died on November 16, 1965, at the age of eighty, an important era of magic came to a close. The great personalities who had toured from large city to small town, across America and to distant corners of the world, were gone. My father had carried into this century a tradition of style and flamboyance that lasted more than one hundred years. The color and spectacle of those shows had brought magic to millions in spirit as much as in fact, and magic had come of age as an art form.

Decline and Rebirth: Nightclubs and Early Television

In the late 1940s, Blackstone was billed as "The Last of the Great Magicians," and indeed it did seem for a time that the great days of magic were over. They weren't, of course. During these years, magic clubs and societies flourished as they had always done, magic books were read by enthusiasts old and young, and "Mysto Magic" sets were given to thousands of delighted children every year. But audiences seemed disinterested. Just as World War I had drastically changed America from a mostly rural society to an urban one, and from an isolationist country into an international power, World War II had disrupted and changed our lives as well. The war had brought women into the work force and they wanted to continue earning. Service in the military made people eligible for the G. I. Bill, which offered money for further education and for mortgages. All across the country, people were involved in bettering their personal lives, buying homes and automobiles, having babies, and going to college. And they traveled—not just the wealthy, who even during the Depression had made luxurious crossings on the great ocean liners, but all of Middle America. They crisscrossed the United States by car, bus, and train, and they went to Europe—at first on such ships as the "United States" and the "Ile de France," and then, as the schedules expanded and the prices shrunk, by plane. There was no longer much need for a traveling show to visit the towns and small cities. Audiences were doing the traveling, and the need to escape from the stress of the Depression and the war years was gone.

Roy Benson, the comedy magician, c. 1945.

Jay Marshall and "Lefty."

Nightclubs and a handful of early television programs seemed to be the only workplaces for magicians, and this changed the nature of their performances. Clubs were intimate rooms with small audiences and no place for large illusions. Sleight of hand, card and coin manipulation, and sophisticated comedy magic became popular in such places as the Blue Angel, Billy Rose's Diamond Horse Shoe, the Empire Room at the Waldorf, and the Rainbow Room in New York, and the Chez Paris in Chicago.

Magicians had to learn to "work the room." They had to deal with the distractions of clinking glasses and clattering dishes, with drunks and with showoffs who wanted to join them on stage, and they had to devise magic that could be performed in arena-type settings. Because much of small magic depends on angles of vision, sleight-of-hand performers had to develop new ways of presentation. Among those who not only adapted but became experts as cabaret performers were Cardini, Frakson, Channing Pollock, Russell Swann, Dell O'Dell, Roy Benson, and Jay Marshall.

Cardini (born Richard Pitchford) was a Welshman who mimicked a British gentleman and did outstanding manipulations of cards and cigarettes. Attired in top hat, white tie, and tails, and wearing a monocle and white gloves, he pretended astonishment as fans of cards kept materializing in his hands. Then billiard balls appeared and multiplied, and when these were subdued, cigarettes appeared. Through it all, he remained elegant and acted somewhat tipsy. He was a great success and appeared with his wife, Swan (who dressed as a bellhop in the act), not only at clubs but at the Palladium in London and at Radio City Music Hall and the Palace Theatre in New York.

Frakson appeared on the scene at about the same time as Cardini. He also wore gloves and manipulated cards and cigarettes, but he presented himself very differently. A Spaniard from a family of magicians, he displayed a very warm stage personality and his performance was filled with humorous asides. He also played the Palace.

Channing Pollock was not the first to present dove productions, but he is the magician with whom the act is associated. As handsome as any screen star (and, indeed, he did appear in several films), Pollock, dressed in white tie and tails and using red silks and white doves, did one of the most beautiful acts ever to be seen. Many have presented similar acts since, but Pollock's personality and style have not been matched.

Russell Swann, Dell O'Dell, Roy Benson, and Jay Marshall all did comedy, but they were expert magicians as well. Russell Swann was the true Rotarian, never forgetting a name, always

WOMEN MAGICIANS

I t has usually been the lot of women in magic to be mutilated and restored in some bizarre fashion by a magician who took all the applause while she stayed backstage packing the props. As any male illusionist will attest, however, it is not the illusion but the lovely assistant who is the real secret of the magic. My wife, Gay, is invaluable in the Blackstone show, just as Bess Houdini, Marion Nicola, and Moi Yo Miller of the Dante show were in theirs. There have also been a few women in magic who had the talent and the nerve to forge careers for themselves that netted both fame and fortune.

Adelaide Herrmann (1853–1932) was one of the most outstanding performers to appear on the stage. Born Adelaide Scarcez in London of Belgian parents, she married magician Alexander Herrmann in 1875 when he was already a star in both London and the United States. With Alexander, she toured their big show and they lived a life of comfort with a large house on Long Island, New York, a yacht, and their own private railroad car.

When Alexander died of a heart attack in 1896, Adelaide kept the show on the road, bringing in Leon Herrmann, her husband's nephew, as the new "Herrmann, the Great." The company lasted three seasons, but she and Leon did not work well together and when they parted, she performed successfully at such large variety houses as the Folies Bergère in Paris, the Wintergarten in Berlin, and the Hippodrome in London. She returned to the United States and opened the "Temple of Magic" at Luna Park, Coney Island, and continued to play the Keith Circuit. She was already well into her sixties and as beautiful as ever. At seventy-five, the "Queen of Magic" appeared at the Keith Orpheum in Brooklyn. This was her last performance, however, and she died four years later at seventy-nine, having performed on her own for over thirty-one years.

Mercedes Talma (1868–1944), born Mary Ann Ford, was hired as an assistant by Servais LeRoy when he was appearing at the Royal Aquarium, Westminster. She was vivacious and beautiful and audiences adored her. So did LeRoy. They married and, under the name of Mercedes Talma, she began taking a prominent role in LeRoy's show. Amazingly proficient at coin manipulation, Talma performed as the Queen of Coins, part of "LeRoy, Talma, and Bosco—the Monarchs of Magic."

At various times, Talma appeared without her husband, performing magic with silks and other small items as well as her coin specialties. She and Servais LeRoy eventually retired to New Jersey where she died at seventy-six.

Adelaide Herrmann.

Mercedes Talma.

Ionia (Elsie DeVere) was the daughter of a Parisian magic performer and manufacturer, C. V. DeVere. As "Ionia, The Goddess of Mystery," Miss DeVere toured Europe and England in the early 1900s and was scheduled to be in Florenz Ziegfeld's Follies in 1903 but, for some long-forgotten reason, never appeared. Her illusions were lavish and her settings and costumes were in an Egyptian-Oriental vein (although she seems to have produced such out-of-place items as a bear and a girl in a large "Merry Widow" hat). She apparently lost most of her show and was restricted to her hotel for three months in Moscow in the early days of the Russian Revolution; she never put the show together again, but married and retired from the stage in 1919.

Anna Eva Fay and *Eva Fay*. Anna Eva Fay was a late-nineteenth-century spiritualist whose audiences of believers never minded that she mingled magic tricks with her psychic programs. A tiny woman with a great presence, she answered questions about the future and beyond and performed such classic magic of the day as the "Dancing Handkerchief," a levitation, and a spirit cabinet. She held private seances and appeared as a vaudeville headliner until 1924. Her daughter-in-law, Ann Norman, performed as Eva Fay. Married to Anna Eva's son, John, Eva Fay worked with him in an act called "The Fays" until his suicide in 1908, then went on to a career as successful as that of her mother-in-law, touring England and the United States as "The High Priestess of Mystery."

Susy Wandas (1896–   ). Susy Van Dyke was from a Belgian theatrical family, the child of a magician whose wife, Elizabeth, performed in the show with him. Susy appeared on stage with them as early as age eight and, when her father died young, formed a new act with her mother and brother called "The Wandas." This act became "The Wanda Sisters, Queens of Magic" (mother and daughter) when her brother left for service in World War I. They toured Europe for many years. Elizabeth was proclaimed Dean of Belgian Magicians in 1954, but died soon after. Susy toured alone as "Susy Wandas, the Lady with the Fairy Fingers, the Paganini of the Cards and the Virtuoso of the Cigarettes." In 1959, she married Dr. Zina Bennett, and moved to the United States where for a short time she continued to perform. For the past few years, she has often attended magic conventions and she continues to maintain friendships in the magic community.

Dell O'Dell started out giving lectures on health and the benefits of physical culture for women, promoting exercise items and demonstrating them with humor. She was a great success on the vaudeville circuit before becoming interested in magic

When she did, she started a new career as the "Queen of Magic" and became a star in nightclubs, at industrial shows, and at private dinners. She could play it with elegance or be rough enough for a workingmen's club, but she was always a lady. Dressed in sophisticated gowns, she produced rabbits, doves, and goldfish, and worked through the audience bringing smiles to café society matrons and union members alike.

She married Charles Carrer, the "King of Jugglers." When the nightclub era began its demise, they moved to California, where she did a children's television show and ran her own magic shop for a time. Although she was stricken with cancer, she continued performing until her strength ebbed. She died in 1963.

◆

There have been many other women through the centuries whose talent and charm made them outstanding magic performers. I've mentioned some of those who performed as single acts, but there have been many who always remained part of their husbands' shows who were, nevertheless, expert individual performers within that framework. Among these were the beautiful Litzka Raymond (now Mrs. Walter Gibson), who performed with The Great Raymond; Jane Thurston, who did her own act as part of her father's show; and Gerrie Larsen, who, as The Magic Lady, delighted many California children, taking time out only to be mother to Bill and Milt Larsen, the founders of Hollywood's Magic Castle.

Today there are women magicians working in many areas. Shari Lewis has been a star puppeteer and magician with her own television shows and tours since girlhood; Debbie (Mrs. Doug) Henning performs her own magic in her husband's touring shows and has appeared with him on his television specials and in his Broadway show *Merlin*; Dorothy Dietrich performs escapes and magic for stage, television, and industrial shows and is a partner with her husband (Richard Brooks) in the Magic Townhouse in New York; June Horowitz, an excellent close-up magician, performs mostly for other magicians at seminars and conventions; Diana Zimmerman performs in clubs, trade shows, and theatres and presides over and encourages budding junior magicians at the Magic Castle in Hollywood; Shelly Carol (real name: Carol Shelly) performs in clubs and trade shows; and Frances Willard performs (with her husband, Glenn Falkenstein) a marvelous Spirit Cabinet act once done by her mother in her father's (and grandfather's) show, billed as Willard the Wizard. And Frances Marshall (wife of Jay Marshall) not only runs Magic, Inc., Chicago's great magic shop, but for years has been an outstanding children's magic performer.

Dell O'Dell.

remembering a birthday. He used audience participation, as did Dell O'Dell, a rowdy, good-humored extrovert who had been a circus strong woman (she balanced a sofa on her chin). Roy Benson brilliantly manipulated billiard balls and did a routine with cigarettes, and his comedy was sharp and very much of his time. Jay Marshall, in addition to doing skillful magic, invented Lefty, a charming puppet made from only a white glove worn on his hand. Lefty was and still is a strong personality, perhaps the most likeable presented by a ventriloquist since Edgar Bergen's Charlie McCarthy.

Early television variety programs such as the *Ed Sullivan Show* and the *Milton Berle Show* used magicians, and many small stations had regular magic shows headed by local personalities. There were special magic shows from time to time, including *It's Magic*, on which my father made one of his rare television appearances. Each of the major networks carried a program highlighting magic: CBS had *Masters of Magic*; ABC had *Super Circus*, which presented magician Jack Gwynne for a long run and others for numerous appearances; and ABC stations also presented a weekly half-hour show starring Dell O'Dell, the Queen of Magic. In 1957, NBC presented the first television magic special on *Producer's Showcase*, a prestigious ninety-minute program. The man who put the show together was Milbourne Christopher, author of some of magic history's most astute articles and books. Titled *Festival of Magic*, the show featured Chinese magic with Li King Si, and Indian magic performed by Socar. Robert Harbin did illusions and a straitjacket escape; Cardini did his classic sleight-of-hand act; René Septembre produced bowls of water and goldfish, and ducks and doves; and Christopher did the famed "Bullet Catch."

Another magician to put the new medium of television to use was Mark Wilson. Wilson grew up in Dallas with an interest in magic and a flair for business. As a teenager he worked in a magic shop, and by the time he entered college as an advertising major, he realized magic should be used as a promotion tool for commercial products. He convinced local business of his expertise and was soon presenting a television show sponsored by major companies. It drew high ratings, and Wilson began developing and promoting television magic. *The Magic Land of Alakazam* was a long-running series of thirty-minute shows presenting many ingenious illusions, starring Wilson and his wife, Nani, and, in the 1970s, Wilson did a series of one-hour specials called *The Magic Circus*. Wilson now creates magic for industrial shows, amusement parks, and world's fairs.

Finding My Own Place in Magic: A Second Blackstone Builds a Show

During these years in which magic started reaching new audiences, I had grown to adulthood, and, though my interest in magic remained, I had not considered it my life's calling. Perhaps this was because the Blackstone show itself had been my home, the "place" to which I returned from school. Whether the show was in Chicago or Milwaukee or St. Louis, or headquartered in Colon for the summer, it was my unofficial residence.

I attended various schools over the years, mostly military academies, but I did spend a year going to school in Colon after the Georgia Military Academy (where my dad had transferred me from a California school during World War II, because he was afraid the Japanese might land there) suggested they could do without such a difficult child! My father's company manager picked me up and I toured with the show until I could be put in school in Colon. During these years I studied piano, was in the school choir, a barbershop quartet, and a madrigal group, and played polo. My favorite school was Southern Arizona School in Tucson, from which I graduated on a Friday the 13th in 1951. Surely I should have realized what lay in store for me!

After graduation, I joined the show for the first time as a paid performer, and although I entered Swarthmore College in Philadelphia at mid-term of that year, I came back again to the show during the next summer. The following year I took a job with a paper company while taking some summer courses, and got involved with a repertory company in Valley Forge and other small theatrical efforts.

When I enlisted in the army a year later, I qualified for the Army Language School, and it was there that I learned Mandarin Chinese, in which I am still fluent. I was stationed (after all that training in Chinese!) in Tokyo, where I began doing a few small magic shows at the officers' clubs to get out of doing KP. By the end of my military service, I had done several things with the Tokyo Amateur Dramatic Club and appeared in the Far East company of *The Lark* and in *Teahouse of the August Moon.* And, to the best of my knowledge, I was the first Occidental to perform at Kabuki-za, as a magician who can turn into any form. I broke tradition and actually performed magic in the role, which was accepted, though not condoned, by the Japanese purists.

After my tour of military duty, I returned to the United States, completing my undergraduate work at the University of Southern California, and attending graduate school at the University of Texas, where I began working as a radio announcer. This career was followed by one as manager of the west coast companies of *Hair*, and one working with the Smothers Brothers on both their Las Vegas show and their CBS *Comedy Hour.* I began to realize I would never leave show business, and that performing magic was where I really belonged. I was, indeed, my father's son.

I think that when my father died in 1965, magic began to take on a special meaning for me that I had not experienced through all the years with him. It had been so much a part of my life that perhaps I didn't recognize it as the unique and marvelous

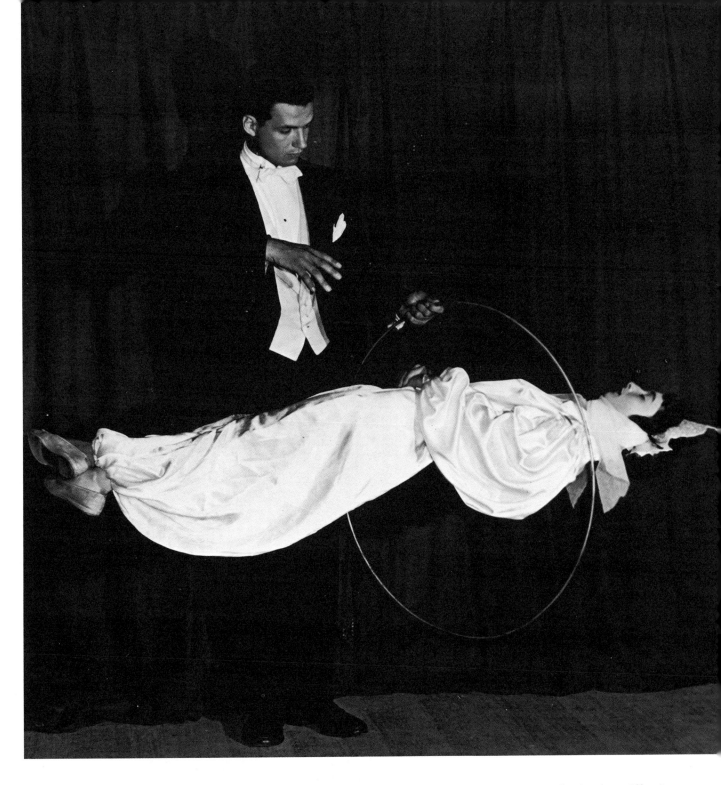

Performing a levitation illusion, 1954.

art that it is. The sights and sounds of it were with me—musty black velvet curtains, the smell of gunpowder for the cannon trick, white satin and ostrich feathers, magic buffets hosted by local enthusiasts in every town after the final show, the boxes, the trains, the crates, the illusions, the gadgets that made them work—and yet, the wonder of the magic itself had perhaps eluded me. I had never really experienced the enchantment magic had created for millions of people.

An early version (1920s) of the "Who Wears the Whiskers?" transposition illusion, always a feature of my father's show and the climactic illusion of my performances today.

My father pictured with his beautiful assistants.

I could perform magic well and had done so many times, but
it took courage to take the first step toward making it my life's
work. I started small, like everyone else. The Blackstone name
may have brought attention, but after that I was on my own.
Incorporating some of my father's tricks and illusions and some
of my own, I put together a nightclub act and got a few bookings.
I toured with an ice show, the 1965 edition of *Holiday on Ice*,
playing such diverse locations as Madison Square Garden in New
York City and the arena in Kalamazoo, Michigan. I appeared on
any television show I could book. Finally, it all began to pull
together. I regularly worked the Playboy clubs, I had bookings in
Las Vegas and at all the large hotels across the United States, and I
was being requested for major television shows. I taped two
Home Box Office specials with Dick Cavett, appeared three times
on the *Tonight Show*, and was a frequent guest on the Mike

The dancers and I are dressed for the "Americana" production in *Blackstone!*, the Broadway show of 1980.

Douglas, Dinah Shore, Phil Donahue, and Merv Griffin shows. I appeared in my own special, *Magic, Magic, Magic.* I was also to be seen as an actor (often playing the part of a magician, as in one episode of *Hart to Hart*), and serving as a technical director for various shows such as the *Mandrake the Magician* series (in which I also appeared) and the television movie based on Harry Houdini's life, *The Great Houdinis.*

I had married Gay Blevins, a dancer who had been performing since childhood, on October 14, 1974. At two, Gay had been on the cover of *Look* magazine. At six, she was on the *Howdy Doody* show. In her teens, she was touring Japan and Thailand with Bob Hope's USO unit, and soon after became one of the Goldiggers on the *Dean Martin Show*. Show business held no terror for her, and when she was asked to be a magician's assistant to Orson Welles, she was game to try it. In 1970, she

"The Magic of Love" (1939), co-authored by my father and Thomas-Ken Byron (Barney Young), was often used as a giveaway. "Oriental Magic" (1980), by Michael Valenti, was part of the original music written for the Broadway show *Blackstone!*, and was featured as part of a concert performed by the Goodman Orchestra in August 1980, at Lincoln Center, New York City.

was asked to be my assistant on the Milt Larsen production of *It's Magic* in Los Angeles. She not only greatly enhanced the act but proved to be the perfect partner on and off stage. We've worked together ever since.

I began to think about the old Blackstone show and what it had really meant to me—and also what it had meant to audiences who had come back to see it year after year. Would they come again, in this day and age, to see a big traveling magic show? Were audiences too sophisticated now to enjoy it? The more I thought of it, the more I believed in the idea. No matter how times change, magic survives, and I determined to take the Blackstone show back on the road.

(Opposite) A publicity shot from the Blackstone show of the 1940s. The bearded figure at the left is my Uncle Pete, and I am inside the cat suit at the right.

What a struggle it was to get the show I wanted! The financing alone was a full-time job and the figures frightened me. What a difference in prices since my dad's day. There was no Aunt Millie to stitch up costumes—they had to be designed and made by specialists. There was no barn in which the props could be built—they had to be constructed by expert illusion builders. And trains didn't seem to be offering those ninety-foot baggage cars any more. There were trucks and buses to be rented, choreographers to be hired, airline tickets to be scheduled, unions to be negotiated with. And there were all those people with titles— Lighting Designer, Set Designer, Lighting Technician, Illusion Engineer, Wardrobe Supervisor, General Manager, Company Manager, Stage Manager, Animal Handler, Magic Consultant, Music Director. (I remembered once when I was a boy, going to Lyon and Healy and Fisher Music in Chicago and whistling the Blackstone show music for the librarian. The music, some of which went back to vaudeville and silent films, had been lost in transit. From sitting so often in the orchestra pit during performances, I was able with the librarian's help to re-create the full orchestrations.) The details were endless.

We tried out several versions of the show, old ideas and new. Finally, it was mostly the classics that won out. The Dancing Handkerchief, the Buzz Saw, the Floating Light Bulb, the Vanishing Birdcage, the Rabbit Giveaway, and the Committee (a pickpocket act), some done just as my father had done them, some my own versions, were the highlights. To this program were added lavish and colorful production numbers such as the Moorish Fantasy, which featured an elephant vanish, the Girl Without a Middle, the Asrah Floating Lady, and a camel which, as in my father's show, did nothing. It just walked from left to right stage, staring at the audience, which always got a tremendous laugh. The Circus of Mystery presented the disappearance of a girl from a trapeze, my wife, Gay, shot from a cannon into a nest of boxes hanging from the proscenium, Gay, changed into a tiger, and a surprise switch, always a feature of my father's show, at the finish. The Americana production number involved Gay's appearance from a drum dressed as the Statue of Liberty and the production of an elephant and a donkey, symbols of the two political parties, from behind flags; and the Oriental number had, in addition to many smaller effects, a girl disappearing from a box (an old one hand-painted by my father for his show), to a swing inside a suspended lantern, then vanishing into the coils of a great fire-snorting dragon, and finally reappearing inside a pagoda. And finally, the show featured a re-creation of the Enchanted Garden production from the Blackstone shows of 1930 to 1935. As the

(Opposite) **A comely assistant of the 1920s reposes in the "radio cabinet" from which she was shortly to vanish. This prop, still bearing my father's artwork, is used in my show today.**

(Overleaf) **"The Bridal Chamber," early 1920s.**

"The Artist's Dream" was the opening production illusion in the Blackstone show of the 1920s. The woman in the center is Inez Nourse, the first Mrs. Blackstone.

number progressed, doves appeared, a bowl of water became a fountain, and great bouquets of flowers came from everywhere. At the end, the stage was filled! It was a bit of nostalgia, a glimpse of what an old-time magic show had really been like.

The show toured across the United States to 156 cities, and opened on Broadway on May 13, 1980, for a limited run of 118 performances, the longest run of any pure magic-and-illusion show in Broadway history. Every review was a rave and had it not been for the phenomenal costs of maintaining a show on Broadway, I think we would have run it longer. For a performer, opening on Broadway remains the greatest theatrical thrill—none of us is ever too jaded to feel its impact. I wish my father could have played there (he did appear in conjunction with movies at nearby picture palaces such as the Loew's State), but I brought so much of him with me that I feel we both played there together.

In 1983, we did a two-hour television special for the Public Broadcasting System. Called *Magic!!! Starring Blackstone*, it is based on the Broadway show which is thus, happily, preserved.

"The Enchanted Garden," *Blackstone!*, 1980.

(Opposite) "The Enchanted Garden" as it appeared in my father's show, late 1940s.

Famed theatrical cartoonist Al Hirschfeld produced this sketch of me during a New York engagement.

Doug Henning and friend.

The New Stars: Today's World of Magic

While straight magic shows have been rare on Broadway, there have been plays and musicals that featured magic as a predominant theme. On May 28, 1974, *The Magic Show* opened at the Cort Theatre in New York. It was a major event in the revival of public interest in magic. The critics thought the show only fair, but they loved the magic.

The show featured a young Canadian magician named Doug Henning who had been appearing at the Royal Alexandra Theatre in Toronto in *Spellbound*, a magic show he had created. Broadway producers saw it, added a book (by Bob Randall), and music and lyrics (by Stephen Schwartz), and brought it to New York as *The Magic Show*. It ran for almost five years and it made Henning a star.

Henning's image was totally unlike the one people had come to expect in a magician. There was no cape, no white tie and tails, not even a tuxedo. He wore no goatee nor satanic expression, nor was his demeanor that of the commanding, all-powerful wizard. Slight of stature, with long hair, he dressed in T-shirt and blue jeans, and seemed as amazed as the audience at the wonders he produced.

After *The Magic Show*, Henning starred in a television special for NBC-TV. He insisted that the show be done "live" in front of an audience, and that the camera shots present what the television viewers would see had they been watching in the studio. No camera trickery was allowed, no part of the show was taped out of context. It was a difficult job for everyone involved. Television had left live shows behind because of the many problems they presented. It was too easy for something to go wrong on camera.

As Henning was not well-known to television viewers, the producer, David Susskind, backed him with strong personalities—Bill Cosby as co-star and Gene Kelly as host (Orson Welles, originally scheduled as host, was replaced because of illness). Henning did new twists on several classic illusions that hadn't been seen for many years, the de Kolta "Vanishing Lady" (in which singer Lori Lieberman instantly disappeared from a covered straight chair), and Houdini's famous Water Torture Cell. The show was the highest-rated special for that network in the entire year, and became the first of Henning's now-annual "World of Magic" specials.

Other magicians were attracting large, enthusiastic audiences. In Las Vegas, two Germans, Siegfried Fischbacher and Roy Horn, were presenting a razzmatazz display that was making them the hottest item on the Strip. Siegfried and Roy had met while working on a cruise ship, Siegfried as a bartender who also did some magic, and Roy as a steward. Roy had grown up with animals, and suggested that a cheetah be added to the magic act; their phenomenal career was on its way. Today they advertise themselves as "Superstars of Magic" and have their own showroom at the Frontier Hotel in Las Vegas, where they present acts filled with beautiful showgirls, extravagant sets and special effects, and stage

Siegfried and Roy with assistant.

illusions featuring Bengal tigers, a black panther, an elephant, and a lion, and sometimes a Brahma bull, sometimes a white stallion. The animals live with them on their lavish estate, and Siegfried and Roy have become leaders in trying to save and breed rare and endangered species, among them lepjags (from the mating of leopards and jaguars) and more recently, rare white tigers. Siegfried's fair complexion and Roy's dark one are enhanced by flashy but beautiful costumes and jewelry.

David Copperfield (née Kotkin) has become another of magic's top personalities through the medium of television. As a boy, he was as interested in music and dance as he was in magic, and in his shows today those early interests are interwoven. While still in his teens, Copperfield culled fine reviews as "Omar, the Magnificent" in *The Magic Man*, a song-and-dance show produced in a small theatre in a bank in Chicago. It was Copperfield and his magic that drew attention.

Copperfield went on to perform in nightclubs and in Las Vegas, and he worked in industrial shows for major corporations and as spokesperson for Eastman Kodak in their promotions. In 1977, he appeared in the first of his television specials, *The Magic of ABC Starring David Copperfield*. His programs always surround the magic with comedy skits, music, and dance, all done by Copperfield.

On a hill overlooking Hollywood, there stands a curious old mansion that attests to the renewed interest in magic. The building houses the Magic Castle, clubhouse of the Academy of Magical Arts. It is the brainchild of Bill and Milt Larsen, whose father, William Larsen, Sr., a lawyer by profession but a devotee of magic, had often talked of starting such a place. Larsen, Sr., had been editor of the magic magazine *Genii*, and for a time was owner of the Thayer Magic Company. He often did magic shows with his wife and sons, and the Larsen family tended to host members of the local magic community and visiting magicians. When William Larsen died in 1953, the idea of a gathering place for the magic fraternity was put aside but not forgotten by his sons.

Both Bill and Milt went on to careers in television, Bill as a producer, Milt as a comedy writer, but their interest in magic remained. Bill took over the editorship of *Genii* (a role he fills to this day), and Milt created and produced the *It's Magic* revues in Los Angeles, which have been sell-out annual events for almost thirty years.

Milt, who also had a great interest in the restoration of old theatres and was a collector of theatrical music and memorabilia, saw the old house on Franklin Avenue one day, and knew it was the perfect spot for the Academy of Magical Arts. With Milt doing much of the physical work himself and Bill promoting it, the Magic Castle opened in 1963. Its membership started at 150 and now numbers in the thousands. As well as magicians, many members are magic enthusiasts who delight in the atmosphere and enjoy the company of the greats of the profession. In addition to a theatre, the club has smaller rooms where close-up magic can be performed. There is a museum and numerous special effects, including Irma the invisible pianist, who'll play whatever you request. There are three bars and several dining rooms, a library for members, and a room dedicated to my father, where in his last years he would frequently perform. Any night of the week, the Magic Castle is full, and people wait in line to see the performers.

The Academy of Magical Arts holds an annual banquet at which it honors those who have been contributors to the art of magic (I received their Magician of the Year award in 1979). They honor not only outstanding performers, but also those who write about magic, producers, and people who contribute ideas.

The Magic Castle has spawned other places where magic can be enjoyed—among them, Magic Island in Newport Beach, California, and Houston, Texas, private clubs with a magic theme that feature performances by top close-up and stage magicians, and Magic Pizza, a "family entertainment center" that offers shows and illusions for both children and adults. Numerous bars and restaurants across the country feature close-up magic for their customers.

There are many places today where magicians are performing. In addition to the hotels and showrooms of Las Vegas and Atlantic City, the revival of nightclubs has given them new places to be seen, and given an opportunity to young magicians whose names are not yet household words. Street magicians can now be found in all of the major cities, performing their miracles for the passing crowds just as they did centuries ago. In addition to the big network specials, television presents many magicians on general variety shows. *Merlin*, an extravagant musical starring Doug Henning, opened on Broadway in 1983 and, though the show received mixed reviews, the magic was highly praised.

And the road shows? They're still out there, doing fine. Copperfield toured in 1983, Henning in 1984. The Blackstone slow also continues—sometimes the full stage extravaganza, sometimes a smaller concert show, in cities across the United States and in many faraway places—Saudi Arabia, Colombia, Hong Kong— wherever there are people who believe in magic.

Bill *(right)* and Milt Larsen, proprietors of Hollywood's famed Magic Castle.

THE SCIENCE
OF ILLUSION

T hus far in this book, we have talked about the history of magic, about the great magicians, and about some of their amazing performances. From our discussion, you might have come to the conclusion that it is not the magician's tricks that really count, but rather the performer's *personality*, and his or her ability to make the tricks entertaining. However, this is only partially true.

Magic, as we have seen, is about power—a seemingly magical power used and expressed by a skilled actor to create the illusion of miraculous happenings. What is not really of great importance is how these miraculous happenings are accomplished, as long as their accomplishment achieves its purpose of fooling the audience and entertaining them. But there is another kind of power in magic, and it lies in the nature of the magic effects themselves.

The Why and How of Magic

Magic is really a form of storytelling, with each trick a small, self-contained drama. The stories it tells are closely akin to dreams

(Opposite) **A traditional routine in every Blackstone show involves the production of a rabbit, which, just as it is being given to a youngster from the audience, mysteriously changes into a box of candy. Just as the child thinks he or she will never get the rabbit back, the magician makes a rabbit out of newspapers and, tearing it open, finds the real rabbit inside.**

and fairy tales. The things a magician does in his performance fulfill many of the same fundamental human needs. The effective magic trick addresses our subconscious wishes, needs, and concerns in exactly the same way that myths and legends do. Magic at its best expresses, in symbolic form, the concerns of life, death, and rebirth, of the rotation of the seasons, and of dealing with the constraints of natural law that have held man since earliest times. When these concerns, both conscious and subconscious, are dealt with in theatrical terms by a magician who is a good actor and a master of his craft, the result is both entertainment and the emotional cartharsis associated with all good theatre.

What are these magic effects that can be so powerful? On analysis, we discover that there are relatively few of them, less than twenty, and only about half of them make up the major tricks and illusions that most magicians do.

A great deal of what magicians do is making things apparently appear and disappear, and magically move from place to place. The great magic inventor Stewart James describes the magician as "a choreographer of objects," and the three fundamental effects of productions, vanishes, and transpositions constitute much of that choreography. Let us look at each of these effects individually.

PRODUCTION

Magicians generally refer to the magical appearance of objects as *productions*. Most magic performances are full of productions. In my stage show, I produce a stage full of flowers, and then, later in the same number, pigeons out of empty air in a net. Finally, from under a cloth, I produce a fountain spurting water in the center of the flower-filled stage. In another number, I produce banners and a girl from an empty drum, and then from under the banners are produced a burro and a full-grown elephant. Spectacular effects, such as these involving people and large animals, are called *illusions* in magicians' terminology, as opposed to effects using smaller objects, which are usually referred to as *tricks*. All of the basic effects discussed in this section of the book can be, depending on the size of the objects used, either tricks or illusions.

There is no limit in size to what a magician can miraculously produce. The only limit is in his skill and ingenuity in doing it. Bear in mind, however, that the production of a small object such as a coin or a thimble, properly performed under the right circumstances, can be just as amazing as the production of an elephant on the stage of a theatre.

Perhaps the best-known production in magic is an effect that is very rarely seen nowadays: the production of a live rabbit out of an empty hat. In the heyday of this effect, a tall silk opera hat could be easily borrowed from some gentleman in the theatre audience, and the trick was immeasurably more effective because the hat was borrowed. Today the wearing of opera hats (or any kind of hat) to the theatre is almost unheard of, and a great trick, so closely identified with the magician's image, has nearly passed into oblivion. But let us examine the classic rabbit-from-the-hat trick and see how we could perform this effect if we wanted to.

The production of a girl inside a cage was an illusion featured by my father in the early 1920s.

If a rabbit is going to be produced from an apparently empty hat, one of two conditions must prevail. Either the hat is not really empty and the rabbit is already in it, cleverly concealed, or the hat is really empty at the beginning of the effect, and the rabbit must be secretly introduced into it.

In the first scenario, the rabbit could already be in the hat, covered by a black flap, so that if the interior of the hat were casually "flashed" to the audience, it would appear empty. If the rabbit were held securely in place by the black flap that covered the hat opening, then the hat could be turned over, perhaps as the magician brushed off the crown, thus subtly suggesting that if anything was inside it would have fallen out. It would have been a fatal mistake for the magician to say, "Here I have an empty hat," for this would merely have suggested that it was *not* empty. Magicians have been known on occasion to stoop to trickery, and it is very likely that some members of the audience would not have believed him. There is another important point here: most hats, when they are not on people's heads, are empty. Why should this hat not be? The late Al Baker, a famous magician of his day, said, "Don't run when nobody's chasing you." When performing magic, this is a good thing to keep in mind.

A major aspect of making this effect baffling to an audience is the magician's acting ability. He must act as if he were handling an empty hat, not a hat with a rabbit in it. The hat, by the way he handles it, must seem lighter than it really is, and he must in all ways *suggest* that the hat is empty without ever putting himself in the embarrassing position of having to *prove* that it is.

If the hat (with the rabbit already in it) is to be borrowed from a member of the audience, there is one other major problem. The audience member must be a confederate. This fact would be enough to discourage most magicians, for the use of a stooge (except in the most extreme cases) is a kind of cheating that can be very messy. The stooge must be depended on to keep the secret, and even if he does keep his silence, it is a very crude and unsophisticated way to fool an audience. If there is a better way, why not use it, if only for your own self-esteem as a magician.

There *is* a better way, and that is to secretly sneak the rabbit into the previously empty hat. Let's examine just one of many ways to do that. Perhaps the magician could "load" (the magician's term for introducing something secretly into something else) a smaller object into the hat and then, under cover of the "misdirection" (we will talk more about misdirection later) of producing that smaller object, he would introduce (load) the rabbit.

Let's put the rabbit in a black cloth bag and hang it on the

THE SCIENCE OF ILLUSION

back of a solid-backed chair on stage. The bag can hang from a headless nail, ready to be scooped into the hat. Now let's sneak something else into the hat that is easier to conceal than a rabbit, perhaps a tightly rolled string of silk handkerchiefs, tied together at the corners. To make them look like an even longer string, the "silks" (another magician's term) can be cut in half diagonally and tied at the corners. As the hat is borrowed, this tightly rolled ball can be "stolen" from under the coat and "palmed" in the right hand, which conceals it momentarily behind the brim of the hat, while the inside of the hat is clearly shown. Then the right hand, with the concealed ball of silks, reaches inside and begins to unroll the ball. The magician moves near the chair so that the long string of silks, as it is pulled out, can be allowed to pile upon the seat. As the final long length of silk is pulled out by the left hand, it is held high in the air by its end, and the magician looks intently at it, smiles at the audience as if expecting applause (which he should get), and triumphantly lets the last arm's length of silk drop onto the chair. At that very moment, while the audience is applauding and the silks are being dropped (the trick is apparently over), he scoops the rabbit into the hat. It probably would be a good idea to have some larger silks in a (waterproof!) compartment of the rabbit bag so that those can be produced (standing now well away from the chair) before the grand climax, when the rabbit is produced.

This detailed analysis is given only to show one way a magician can produce the classic effect of a production. The thing that is produced can vary from a coin or thimble to a fishbowl full of water to a live Bengal tiger, but, as we shall see as we continue our study of magic, many of the same principles apply.

VANISH

Making something disappear is exactly the opposite of a production. Since the beginning of history, magicians have been vanishing things of all sizes and shapes. There are two types of vanishes, the visible vanish and the covered vanish, where the vanish takes place under a cloth or within a box or other container.

There is no effect in magic more startling than a really good visible vanish. In my stage show, there are three good examples of the different forms a visible vanish can take. An effect that I and my father before me made a specialty is the Vanishing Birdcage. In it, a square cage containing a canary visibly vanishes from my fingertips, and then the startling vanish is repeated with

The Vanishing Birdcage was a feature of my father's shows just as it is today in mine. After the cage vanishes the first time, I repeat the visible vanish with spectators from the audience holding the cage.

members of the audience actually holding the cage. It is one that audiences always remember. This trick, which takes years of practice to do really well, is not one for the beginner.

During the Moorish segment of our show, I make a live six-ton elephant visibly disappear. This original version of the illusion differs from other versions (like Houdini's, in which the elephant vanishes from a closed box) in that the pachyderm is in full view up to the second it vanishes. Another smaller but equally effective vanish takes place in the circus finale, in which a an aerialist visibly vanishes while high in the air, leaving only the empty trapeze and her costume behind.

One astonishing visible vanish feat used by many sleight-of-hand experts involves tossing an object into the air, where it

THE SCIENCE OF ILLUSION

seems to simply fade away. This trick is an excellent example of the use of psychological conditioning to achieve a magic effect. A small object such as a ball is tossed in the air several times, and caught with both hands. As this is done, one side of the performer (say, his right side) predominately faces the audience. The toss and catch are repeated several times. On the final toss, the ball is not thrown at all but is simply palmed in the right hand (the back of which is toward the audience) while the magician *acts* as if the ball has once again been tossed in the air. His actions on the fake toss are *exactly* the same as the previous ones, and his eyes follow the imaginary flight of the ball to a point in the air where it apparently disappears. Spectators, conditioned to seeing the ball as it is tossed and caught, will actually believe that they saw the ball go up in the air and disappear.

TRANSPOSITION

A transposition is simply a combination of a vanish and then a production of the same object. Something vanishes in one place and reappears in another. Big illusion shows are full of effects where a girl vanishes from one box and reappears in another. In the climactic circus number of my stage show, my wife, Gay, is loaded into a large cannon which is fired at a box suspended over the audience. The cannon is seen to be empty and she has

In the 1920s my father featured an illusion in which he was tied to the mouth of a cannon and "blown to oblivion," only to be revealed a few seconds later as one of the men who fired the cannon.

Gay Blackstone is loaded into a giant cannon and fired invisibly into a nest of three trunks hanging high over the stage proscenium, a classic transposition illusion from today's Blackstone show.

gone. When the suspended box is lowered to the stage and opened, a smaller box is found inside. That box is opened, revealing still a third box, and inside that tiny, 17"-square box she reappears.

The oldest and probably the greatest close-up effect in magic (a version of which you will be taught in this book) is simply an elaborate combination of production, vanishes, and transposition of small balls covered by some kind of cup. Nearly every major culture produced its own version of this trick in its early history. Only the shapes of the cups and the balls varied.

THE SCIENCE OF ILLUSION

TRANSFORMATION

Another of the magician's common effects is to change one object into another. Some of the early magicians were referred to in their advertising material as "transformists," and for good reason. One of the most effective tricks in close-up magic is to have one coin change into another, and there have been many deceptive methods devised to accomplish this simple but startling effect. In one good card trick, the magician tries to find a spectator's selected card only to apparently fail and then have the wrong card change magically into the right one. On a considerably larger scale, one of the effects in my stage show is to change a girl into a live 450-pound Bengal tiger.

Things can magically change in many different ways. They can change their identity (as in girl-into-tiger), their shape (a round sponge ball changes into a square one), their color (a red silk handkerchief changes to a green one), or their size (a short man changes into a tall one). Changes can take place when an object is covered or visible; they can also occur slowly or instantaneously.

These first four effects, production, vanish, transposition, and transformation, constitute the most common things that a magician does, but there are others that make up an important part of most magic performances.

In the circus number of my current show, one of the many transformations involves putting Gay into a cage and transforming her into a 450-pound Bengal tiger.

RESTORATION

Beyond the four basic effects, the theme of destruction and restoration has certainly been one of the major ones in magic since its beginnings. The earliest account of a magic performance from ancient Egypt involved the apparent decapitation of an animal and then the restoration of its head; and four centuries ago, in the *Discoverie of Witchcraft*, a decapitation of a man is described, the first explanation in print of what magicians today would call a "stage illusion"—although the explanation does not say that the illusion is concluded by putting the head back on again so perhaps, strictly speaking, it is not a restoration. The same book has the explanation of how to cut a string and restore it, an effect that, in various forms (sometimes with rope or ribbon instead of string), is still done by many magicians today. Doug Henning has made almost a trademark of tearing up a full

A classic restoration illusion that has been a Blackstone tradition is sawing a young woman (in this case Gay Blackstone) in two and then restoring her good as new.

newspaper and visibly restoring it. One of the classic restoration effects is the stage illusion of cutting a girl in two and then restoring her. Originally this illusion was done with the girl in a large box, with her head out one end and her feet out the other. The method there was for the box to contain two girls. The version that is done today uses a very small box that could not possibly contain two girls. In my show, and in my father's, the box has been dispensed with altogether, and Gay lies on a thin table and is cut in half in full view with a large buzz saw. A piece of wood underneath her is also cut to "prove" that the whirling blade goes through her.

There are literally dozens of stage illusions in which assistants (usually pretty young ladies) are apparently mutilated (stretched, burned, crushed, etc.) in some way and are subsequently restored as good as new. All of this sounds rather bloodthirsty and distasteful, but the style nowadays with most magicians is to present these old illusions in a lighthearted way and, while the audience may be amazed and amused, they rarely are asked to believe that they are actually seeing a person killed in front of their eyes. A good example of the lighthearted approach to such a restoration illusion is Robert Harbin's wonderful "Zig-Zag Girl," an effect that has, since its invention about twenty years ago, become a modern magic classic.

In this effect, a girl is put in an upright cabinet (containing holes through which her face, hand, and foot are visible), which is then divided into three parts by metal blades. The center section of the cabinet is then slid over to the side, giving a zig-zag effect to the girl's body that is certainly more humorous than it is gruesome. The Zig-Zag Girl is a classic restoration effect, but with no hint of the Grand Guignol about it.

A favorite effect of an older generation of magicians was to borrow a spectator's ring or pocket watch (in those days men carried pocket watches), apparently destroy it and then reproduce it fully restored in some other place, such as tied around the neck of a dove or a rabbit that has been magically produced.

It is in these illusions of restoration that one of the strongest links between modern magic and the ritual magic of the early priesthood of Egypt, Greece, Rome, and other early civilizations is seen. Today, when a magician restores a cut rope or a lady who has been apparently divided into pieces, we are reminded of those early rituals performed by priests and shamans which celebrated the birth, death, and rebirth of the seasons and the resurrection of the crops, or reminded of the gods that are so much a part of early religions and persist in some form in religious observances of the present day.

ANIMATION

Another effect, done less frequently by today's magicians than many of the other effects we have discussed, but with its roots strongly in the rituals of ancient magic, is the animation of inanimate objects.

Perhaps the most talked-about feature of my father's show was not one of his big stage illusions, but a relatively small effect in which a spectator's handkerchief was borrowed and "brought to life." It danced all over the stage and assumed a definite personality of its own. This effect, which is also a regular feature in my own show, is another example of the importance of acting in magic. The handkerchief must be seen as more than a piece of cloth that mysteriously jumps around. The trick's effectiveness depends on the fact that the handkerchief is seen as a person, with its own reactions to the magician who tries to control it. The effectiveness is far more dependent on the performer's acting ability than on the simple means by which the trick is done.

A classic example of an animation illusion was an effect in the programs of the great illusionists Thurston and Dante, which they called "A Rag, A Bone, and a Hank of Hair" (it was also sometimes called "Creo" or the "Vampire"). Three sticks were shown and set up in a pyramid configuration, and the plaster bust of a woman was fastened to the top of them. A wig was put on the bust and the form was draped with a dress or robe. Finally, the head was given a lifelike look with makeup that the magician applied. The dramatic climax was when the eyes opened and the figure came to life—an apparently real woman created from inanimate sticks and plaster. This effect, seldom seen today, is a feature in the program of Landis Smith, a rising young American magician.

One of the most popular card tricks of days gone by, also not often seen today, is the "Rising Cards," in which several cards are selected from the deck and replaced, only to become animated and rise from the pack at the magician's command. Before the great American illusionist Howard Thurston had his big show, he did a specialty card act in vaudeville. His feature was his own version of the Rising Cards and it made him famous. The Rising Cards remains not only one of the best animation tricks, but one of the best card tricks there is.

A borrowed handkerchief that becomes alive and dances about the stage is a favorite animation effect in the Blackstone show.

The penetration of a pretty woman by twenty-four tubular light bulbs has been a feature of the shows of Blackstone father and son.

PENETRATION

One of the unchangeable laws of nature is that two things cannot occupy the same space at the same time. Naturally, it should be expected that magicians would devise effects that would defy that law. One of the great classic effects of magic, the "Chinese Linking Rings," is a penetration effect where apparently solid metal rings visibly pass through one another, linking and unlinking in various designs and combinations. This trick has been a part of magicians' programs for hundreds of years and will, doubtless, remain so. It is not an easy trick to do well, but performed skillfully it is one of the prettiest and most baffling effects to watch.

There are hundreds of effects in the magician's repertoire in which one object mysteriously penetrates another, leaving no hole or other indication of how the solid through solid was accomplished. Sheets of glass and mirror have been penetrated by everything from knives and blocks of wood to live young ladies. Inflated balloons have been penetrated with long steel needles, and the great Houdini, and magicians that followed him, made a feature out of walking through a solid brick wall.

The brick wall feat is an excellent example of the type of trick that is almost better in the advertising than it is in the doing. The idea of being able to walk through solid walls has a strong element of wish fulfillment, as much good magic does. And although Houdini did the trick only a few times in his career, and the method he supposedly used was widely exposed, he became known as "the man who walked through walls" (that billing was even used as the title of a popular biography of him). The idea of walking through walls still has a strong appeal to the public. Both Doug Henning, in America, and Paul Daniels, in England, have featured their own versions of the feat (each different from the other and each different from Houdini's) on their televison shows.

ANTI-GRAVITY

If one were to imagine an effect universally identified with a magic performance—along with pulling a rabbit from a hat and sawing a lady in two—certainly it would be floating a lady in the air. Here again is a magic effect with its roots strongly in myth and legend. The element of flying or levitating is a common one in most people's dreams. To be able to defy gravity, one of the great constants of the real world, has a strong wish-fulfillment appeal, and most stage magicians find levitation and anti-gravity effects among the most popular in their programs.

There are dozens of different levitation and suspension feats that magicians perform. (Technically, a levitation is an illusion in which the object *rises* into the air. A suspension is one in which the object is placed, and stays, in a position defying gravity.) Probably the greatest levitation, described by many as the most beautiful illusion in the history of magic, was the levitation of the Princess Karnac, invented and performed by John Nevil Maskelyne at St. George's Hall, his permanent theatre of magic in London. A version of it became Harry Kellar's famous illusion in the United States, and, upon Kellar's retirement, was passed on to his successor, Thurston, who presented his version of it for many years. After

The levitation of a glass of milk was a precursor of the Floating Light Bulb, one of the illusions closely identified with both my father and me. Here my father performs both illusions; he is assisted in the light bulb effect by my mother, Billie Matthews.

My father's version of the Levitation of the Princess Karnac came from the estate of Harry Kellar. In its sheer impossibility, it was considered by many to be the greatest of all the levitation illusions.

his retirement, Kellar continued to work on the illusion, and his improved version was passed on to my father, who presented it as a feature of his full evening show for many years. After my father's retirement, and because of the complex technical requirements of presenting it in modern theatres, it has never since been performed in its full form. Why was it such a great illusion? Because the effect it presented was as close to perfect and totally impossible as probably any magician has presented.

In the center of a fully lighted stage, a girl slowly rose from a couch and remained, apparently asleep, in mid-air, where a hoop was passed completely over her. It was as simple as that, but the simplicity and purity of what the audience saw made it almost a mystical experience. The hushed awe with which the audience regarded the floating princess, holding their applause until she returned to the couch and was awakened from her hypnotic sleep, was proof enough of that. They were seeing as close to a miracle as modern magic could provide, and somehow they knew it. Today most stage illusionists, myself included, present a version of the floating lady, but none can approach the awesome beauty of the Karnac levitation. Perhaps if the economics of the contemporary theatre will allow for it, it will someday be revived.

Of course, many other things, from small objects like cards and balls to very big ones like pianos complete with players, have been levitated over the years. A feature in my program, developed and improved from an illusion my father did for many years, is the "Floating Light Bulb," which floats about the stage and through a hoop, finally floating off the stage and over the heads of the audience only to be returned, still lighted, to the lamp from which it was removed.

The effect of defying gravity and floating an object in the air is one of the most beautiful effects in magic, but good things do not always come easily and a really good levitation is one of the most difficult technical challenges there is in the profession.

SYMPATHETIC REACTION

Much early magic, particularly as it was practiced by the high priests and sorcerers of ancient religions, was sympathetic magic. The idea was that by carrying out some symbolic ritual on earth, a similar reaction would be elicited in the heavens. Even today in some primitive religions, such as voodoo as it is still practiced in Haiti, people believe that if a doll in the likeness of a particular person is injured by, say, sticking pins in it, the real person will be similarly injured. The amazing thing about this type of sympathetic magic is that, if the person being acted upon *believes* in spells being cast, even on a subconscious level, they often work!

In magic, there are some very good effects based on the idea of sympathetic reactions. One magic classic is the "Sympathetic Silks," in which three scarves are tied together and three other scarves, previously shown to be separate, also become tied. When one set of scarves is then untied, the other set also unties itself.

There are similar effects with cards, in which one packet of cards is arranged in a particular order and another packet magically arranges itself in the same order. A very good card trick based on the sympathy effect is what magicians refer to as "You Do As I Do." In it, the magician and the spectator select cards, apparently at random, from two decks of cards, only to discover that they have miraculously selected the same card. There have been a myriad of methods devised to accomplish this trick over the years, but the *effect* remains the same. As I have said before (and shall, very probably, say again), it is the effect that counts with an audience, not the method, and the method should be chosen by the magician because it suits his or her particular abilities and approach to performing.

TIME CONTROL

It would be wonderful if a magician could realize the age-old dream of being able to move backward and forward in time, and even to make time move fast or slowly as he willed it. This ability to manipulate time has been the plot of many science fiction and fantasy stories, from H. G. Wells to the present day, but relatively few magicians have used it as a plot for their magic.

One classic effect does use the idea of accelerating time, and that is the rapid germination of plants. It dates back to ancient fertility myths, through the legendary feats of the Indian street magician (or "fakir," as he was known), in which a seed (under cover of a small cloth tent) grows to a shoot, then to a sapling, and, finally, to a full-grown mango tree. A feature of Harry Kellar's show was the magical growth of flowers in pots covered by metal cones, and later magicians, such as Karl Germain, Dante, and Dell O'Dell, featured a rose bush that visibly grew real roses. In all of these effects, time seems to speed up so that a germination that would take days, weeks, or even months in the real world takes place in only a few minutes.

As I noted, the fascinating idea of moving backward and forward in time has been little explored in magic, but a few magicians have performed feats in which a number of actions were accomplished and then, after the clock has been set back, it is shown that all the things that had been done were undone, and everything is as it was before.

◆

The ten effects that I have just described are, in my opinion, the basic ones a magician has to work with in putting together his or her performance. The scale of the effects, the objects used, and, of course, the methods by which they are accomplished can vary widely, but the effects remain the same.

Before we leave our discussion of the basic effects available to the magician, there are several other kinds of magic-related mystery entertainments that we should consider. While they are not, strictly speaking, magic, they are often found in one form or another as part of the repertoire of many magicians. These are escapes, demonstrations of apparent supernatural power (including ESP and spirit effects), and demonstrations of apparent invulnerability and other physical anomalies.

ESCAPES

It is ironic that the best-known magician of all time was not primarily a magician at all, but an escape artist. This was, of course, Houdini. Most reports, by those who knew Houdini and saw him perform, were that he was a compelling stage personality and only an average magician, but a sensational escape artist and a genius at publicity. Theatrical presentations of escapes from restraints of all kinds—ropes, handcuffs, straitjackets, trunks, milk cans, and anything else within which a person could be contained—were tremendously popular with audiences in the early years of this century. Probably one reason why this type of entertainment struck such a popular note is that what the performer was doing on stage was, in symbolic theatrical form, exactly what many members of the audience were involved in, in their day-to-day lives. They too were escaping, from the ghettos of Europe into the promise of the new world, and from the farms into the cities that offered new opportunities. In his ability to escape from all restraints Houdini was, at least on a subconscious level, a message of hope to his audiences. Most magicians realized the appeal of escapes and included them in their programs. They also capitalized on the crowd-pulling potential of outdoor escapes from straitjackets while suspended high above the street or from sealed packing cases thrown into the local river. These kinds of publicity escapes brought the public into the theatres, and many magicians, my father included, capitalized on them.

By the early 1920s, audiences had changed and so had the appeal of the escape artist. While magicians still included escape feats in their programs, Houdini, with his usual sensitivity to what would bring people into a theatre, had moved onto other things, making an elephant disappear on the stage of the New York Hippodrome and exposing fraudulent spirit mediums in each town where his show played. By that time Houdini had added a considerable amount of magic to his show, but this, apparently, was never as strong as the escapes had been in his heyday. His policy then was to feature one sensational escape, the "Chinese Water Torture Cell" (in which he was locked upside-down in a glass tank of water), and devote the rest of his show to magic and spirit exposés.

MENTALISM

Another area closely related to magic is that of mentalism and pretended supernatural powers. Since the heyday of spiritualism as a religion (roughly 1900 to 1920), and the devastating exposés by Houdini who, for all intents and purposes, put the fraudulent mediums out of business, many magicians have, in a light-hearted way, included spirit effects in their programs. These have often consisted of spirit cabinet effects in which various phenomena take place, using such arcane props as talking skulls, rapping hands, spirit clock dials, and spirit bells that answer audience questions. Many of these effects, which were a wonder in their day, have been rendered virtually obsolete as entertainment, since the audiences have become sophisticated about such technological advances as radio and remote control.

Quite another form of mystery entertainment, in terms of audience appeal, is mentalism, or the pretended exhibition of Extrasensory Perception. It is a fact that sizable numbers of the general public believe in ESP as a reality, and an even larger number believe in it as a distinct possibility. My opinion as to what degree this belief seems justified, based on current statistical evidence, is almost beside the point, in the face of the fact that audiences are ready to believe it and even *want* to believe it. Even though most ethical psychic entertainers are quick to insert a disclaimer into their programs, saying that they possess no supernatural powers, it is amazing how many members of their audiences believe that they possess genuine extrasensory abilities. If there is such a thing as genuine ESP, and who can definitely say that there is not, it is certainly not the sort of power that is both infallible and on call at a moment's notice to entertain an audience. The skilled mentalist uses the same psychological principles to manipulate the minds of his audience that a good magician does, but there is one big difference. He does not ask for the "willing suspension of disbelief' as a magician does. For many in that audience, real belief, or the strong susceptibility to it, has taken care of that.

INVULNERABILITY TO PHYSICAL LAWS

Finally, even more tenuously related to magic, but related nevertheless, are the fake freaks who claim to be invulnerable to harm and pain or, through some other contrivance, to be unique in some special way entirely contrary to the known laws of nature. On one hand, there is the fakir who lies on the bed of spikes or enters the red-hot oven, only to emerge unhurt while the steaks he took in with him have been cooked. There is the fire-eater and the man who swallows swords or is buried alive or sealed in a cake of ice. All of these involve the principles of magic or, at the very least, a special learned ability (not supernatural in any way) on the part of the performer.

In more naive times, there were exhibits in dime museums and carnival and circus side shows that displayed, among other amazing things, headless ladies, and living heads on table tops and on the bodies of giant spiders. Audiences were asked to believe that these were real, and, no doubt, some of the most gullible of the onlookers did. It is unlikely that today's audiences would accept them for any more than what they are, clever optical illusions that use many of the same principles employed by stage magicians to accomplish more sophisticated deceptions.

These, then, are the effects that you, as a magician, can accomplish. If you perform these effects in whatever form, much will depend on your knowledge of the magician's art, something that will grow over the time that you study and practice it. The next step for us is to examine the principles by which these seemingly miraculous effects can be accomplished.

Psychological Principles

Before we begin, it's a good idea to dispose of some of the popular clichés about the secrets of magic. The hand is *not* quicker than the eye; the tricks are *not* "all done with mirrors" (actually very few of them are); and there is seldom "something up the magician's sleeve." The fact that these misconceptions and many more are ingrained in the public's idea of the "secrets of magic" actually makes the magician's task easier because it diverts the audience from the real secrets, which are psychological, not mechanical.

All of the magician's effects that defy explanation and are seemingly impossible to accomplish by natural means are theatrical illusions, and modern audiences accept them as such. Because they are fooled by them, the audience assumes that the technology accomplishing them must be very sophisticated. Actually, the technology is very simple; it is the *psychology* that is sophisticated. That is why the audience is fooled. They are looking in the wrong place for the solution to the mystery.

In our rapidly expanding technological society, the relatively naive technology of magic cannot (and should not) compete with the computer, for an important part of its power to deceive lies in its simplicity. Magic can only function *within* the most complex and sophisticated computer of all—the human brain.

All illusions ultimately take place in the mind of the person who perceives them. They are the result of the brain's interpretation (or misinterpretation) of clues that it receives from the usual five senses. These illusions are, at the same time, both positive and negative in nature. They are *positive illusions* in the sense that the audience *sees* something which, in reality, *does not exist*, and they are *negative illusions* in that the audience *does not see* something (by overlooking it, or misinterpreting it) that *does* exist.

SENSORY ILLUSIONS

The brain basically perceives three different types of illusions. The first of these are natural illusions that appear in the real world because of known scientific principles that force us to perceive things in an incorrect way. For example, if we put a pencil into a glass of water so that part of it sticks up above the surface, and then look at the pencil at the point where it enters the water, we see an apparent bend or jog in the pencil. This is because the refraction of light through water is different from that through air, and this produces the natural illusion of the pencil bending. Other natural illusions involve other senses, as when the pitch of a train whistle seems to get lower as the train moves away from us and higher as it moves toward us. This apparent change in frequency (produced by what is called in physics the Doppler effect), is a natural illusion, for the actual pitch of the train whistle, at its source, remains the same.

A second type of illusion occurs because of our mistaken perception of sensory phenomena. We have all had the experience of seeing the full moon rise over the horizon appearing very large, only to see it a few hours later, high in the sky, where it

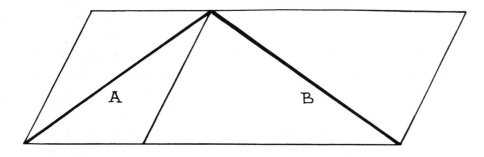

appears quite small. If we were to hold up a stick or piece of string in front of our eyes, and measure against it the size of the moon in both positions, we would see that it remained exactly the same size.

There are also many classic optical illusions (often created by psychologists studying perception) in which straight lines seem to bend and figures seem to reverse themselves, or in which the lengths of lines, really equal, seem to be radically different. For example, in the figure above, the lines A and B seem to be of very different lengths, yet when they are measured, we are amazed to find that they are exactly the same. Another startling example of faulty perception is the famous "Aristotle Illusion" (said to have been discovered by the Greek philosopher), in which your second finger is crossed over your first, and both fingers are used to feel a round object, such as a marble or the tip of your nose, with your eyes closed. The strong impression is that you are feeling two objects. Try it and be amazed!

These natural illusions and illustrations of misinterpreted sensory data do not really fool the eye or ear or other organs of sensory input. These organs merely record and transmit sensory data to the brain, and it is there that the real deception takes place.

While these types of illusions are sometimes used by magicians in creating effects, they occupy a very minor role as tools of the magician's craft. The third type of illusion is of major importance, and this is created by what magicians call *misdirection.*

MISDIRECTION

This is the central principle in the art of magic. It is the means by which the magician casts the psychological spell that makes the deception work and the illusion seem real. Through misdirection, the magician controls what his audience sees or, perhaps more accurately, what they *think* they see.

Misdirection is exactly what it sounds like. It means to direct the attention, or the thought processes of the audience, *away* from that path by which the deception is accomplished. The spectator, under the spell of the misdirection (for modern magicians cast a spell just as surely as those in storybooks and legends), sees both *more* and *less* than is really there, and an illusion is created. The intended result of *misdirection* is thus *misperception.*

Why do we need misdirection? Every magic trick has a secret method by which it is accomplished. If the illusion is to be effective, it's imperative that the audience not discover the method. On its most basic level, the purpose of misdirection is to divert the audience's attention away from the secret of the trick.

It would be wonderful if there were such a thing as a perfect magic trick, in which the method is completely undetectable and invisible. In my almost half-century in magic, I have never found such a trick. There is always *at least one* weak point that must be concealed from the audience. Needless to say, the fewer the weak points, the better the method.

There are two basic types of misdirection: *physical misdirection* and *mental misdirection.* Both are used, sometimes separately but more often in combination, to achieve a magical effect. It is difficult, if not impossible, to attend to more than one thing at a time. The purpose of *misdirection* is to control the spectator's attention so that he is looking at the wrong thing at the right time and away from that vulnerable weak point that can expose the working of the trick. If you are watching the magician's left hand, you will not be aware of what his right hand is doing. If you are intently watching the action on the right side of the stage, you cannot attend to what is happening on the left side. It's as simple as that—but on this simple principle many of the most effective close-up and stage effects are based.

As early as 1635, *Hocus Pocus, Junior*, a book devoted to the art of magic, offered an excellent description of physical misdirection. The unknown author of the book observes that the skillful magician uses "such gestures of body as may lead away the spectator's eyes from a strict and diligent beholding of his manner of conveyance."

The most obvious way to get a spectator to look at a particular thing is to physically point it out to him. Pointing one's finger at something is perhaps a rather unsubtle use of the "gesture of body" referred to in that old magic book, but sometimes, if it is properly done, it works. Considerably more subtle is the use of the eyes to direct the spectator's attention. *If you look in a particular direction, your audience will look in the same direction.* A non-magic example of this is the old prank of standing on a busy street and looking up at the top of a tall building, at which point you will undoubtedly attract a crowd, all looking up to see what you are looking at.

The same principle applies to some of the most basic sleight-of-hand manipulations in magic. Suppose you have a coin in your right hand, and you pretend to place it into your left hand but do not really do so. Eventually, you open your left hand to show that the coin (which the spectators believe to be there, but which is actually secretly retained in your right hand) has vanished. Why are the spectators fooled by such a simple ruse? Why do they believe that the coin was placed in the left hand in the first place? The answer is twofold. First, you have mastered the mechanical motions of appearing to place the coin in the left hand without actually doing it (this is referred to by magicians as a "move" or a "sleight"). Second, and even more important, you have learned to *act* convincingly the action of placing the coin in the hand. An essential part of this acting is the physical misdirection of looking where the coin is supposedly placed. When you pretend to place the coin in your left hand, you must look intently (but not *too* intently, for nothing is more unconvincing than overacting) at the hand. If, even for a moment, your gaze steals back to your right hand (where the coin is really concealed), the audience will immediately suspect that it is there. Good magicians *believe* in the actions they perform, even if those actions serve to cover up the deception, and believing is an important part of good acting.

If you look someone in the eyes, they will look up to meet your gaze. And when they are doing this, they are not looking at your hands. This technique can be very useful, particularly in close-up magic where certain sleight-of-hand maneuvers must be performed unobserved.

There are factors other than the direction of the gaze that will point the spectator's attention in a particular direction.

If something appears on the perceptual scene that is more intense than what was previously there, people will automatically look at it. A loud noise, a sudden movement, a bright color, or an unusual happening will draw attention from the crucial spot where the deception is taking place. One of many examples of this took place in my father's show, in a barnyard number that involved the production, subsequent vanish, and final reappearance of a number of ducks. At one point in the number, the ducks were shooed into a small house named, appropriately, Duck Inn. Shortly after this, a commotion involving a loose duck and an assistant pursuing it happened at another point on the stage (an apparently unplanned event), commanding the audience's attention. Later Duck Inn was dismantled, revealing that the ducks had vanished. Where had they gone? I will reveal to you a well-kept secret. When the audience's attention was on the assistant, the ducks were spirited out of the house and backstage. Anyone looking at the house at that time would have seen them go, but, of course, they were not looking there. They were looking at another point on the stage. I sometimes perform this number in my own magic show. If you should see it, I will fool you anyway, the misdirection is that strong!

Novelty will command attention. This is closely related to the previous rule, but if something strange or unusual appears, it will immediately attract curiosity, and, thus, attention. If a tiger or a gorilla appears, people will look at it; or, to take an example from classic close-up magic, if a lemon appears under a cup (instead of the expected small ball), people will look at it instead of the hand, which can be involved in a deceptive move. Many stage magicians have made use of this principle by using pretty girls in their acts, a very effective kind of misdirection!

Another aspect of physical misdirection involves not drawing our attention away from the spot where the deception is taking place, but instead, occupying us with something else so that we are not attending carefully to what is right before us. For example, let us say that in a particular trick, we must obtain an object from a holder under our coat or from a pocket, and, it is important that the audience does not see us do it. One solution is to use the principles already mentioned to lead the audience to look elsewhere. For example, the left hand could produce an object from the air while the right hand (to which attention is not directed) "steals" another object from the pocket or from under the coat. Another solution is to occupy the audience with some reaction to the magic so that they are not paying close attention. The two best ways to do this are to get them to laugh or to applaud. When a spectator is laughing or applauding he is rarely paying close attention to what the magician is up to. Thus a skilled magician can make use of these moments of relaxed attention to accomplish his deception.

There is another secret of physical misdirection that is the exact opposite of directing the spectator's attention to a particular place, in order to conceal the deception somewhere else. It is to make the crucial part of the trick that must be concealed so natural-looking, and unobtrusive, that it is simply not noticed.

As we go through each day, we are bombarded by literally millions of sensory impressions. To keep from being driven insane by all this confusion, our minds filter out most of them. Try this experiment if you wear a nondigital watch. Without looking at your watch, try to recall whether the numbers on the face are Roman or Arabic. You probably are not sure because, though you look at your watch dozens of times a day, you simply have not noticed; it was not important to you. What *do* we pay attention to? The things that are called to our attention and that interest us. As we have seen, we can use these to control audience attention. But what about the things that audiences do not attend to? They can be used also to accomplish deception.

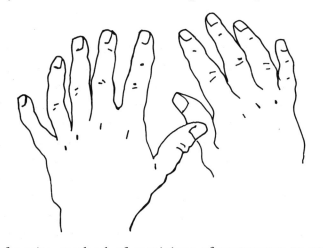

A favorite method of magicians of yesteryear to produce a silk handkerchief from their bare hands was a device known as the "sixth finger." This was simply a hollow, flesh-colored finger made of celluloid that the magician put between the two middle fingers of one hand. When the two hands were shown to be empty, the audience simply did not notice that one hand had six fingers instead of five. When the hands were brought together, the silk handkerchief was pulled out and miraculously produced.

Another very simple but very good trick that will fool audiences today, just as it did a hundred years ago, is the suspension of a table knife or a pencil from the palm of the hand. Here's how to do it. Hold your left hand, palm up, and place the knife across it (any other object such as a ruler or a magic wand will do, as long as it extends beyond both sides of your hand). Explain that you are about to defy the law of gravity through magic, but that absolute steadiness is required for the experiment to work. Hold your left wrist with your right hand, with the right thumb on top, and fingers on the bottom. Explain that the only way the knife could remain on the palm of the hand, if you were to turn it palm down, would be for you to hold it in place with your thumb. Demonstrate this by putting your left thumb on the knife and turning your open left hand palm down. As you do this, your right hand, which is lightly grasping the wrist, stays in exactly the same position. That is, the left wrist turns within your right hand,

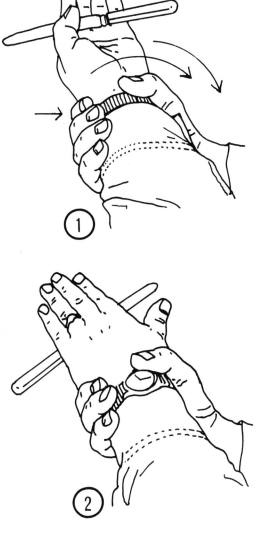

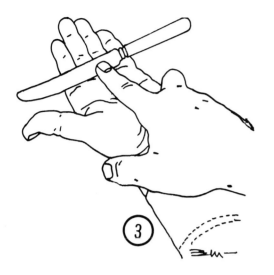

which holds it only loosely, and when the left hand is palm down, it is still being grasped by the right hand in *exactly the same manner*, with thumb on top and fingers underneath. It is at this point that a secret move is done, one that is covered by misdirection. As the hand turns palm down, the right first finger is secretly extended to hold the knife against the palm. This small movement is masked by the wrist, and the left hand is also completely covered by the larger movement of turning the hand over (one of the rules of physical misdirection is that *a large movement will always draw attention away from a smaller movement*). Remove the left thumb (apparently holding the knife in place) and show that the knife is suspended against the palm-down left hand. There is only one discrepency (remember that every trick has *at least* one weak point), and that is that the right hand holding the left wrist only has three fingers and a thumb showing (the invisible forefinger is holding the knife!). This might seem obvious, but it is not, because of strong misdirection. The spectators are amazed by the knife sticking to the palm, and are concentrating on that rather than on the number of fingers holding your wrist. Also you are intently staring at the knife, holding it in place by concentration (or magic), and at no time do you look at the right hand, holding the wrist. Why should you? And if you do not, why should they?

Now for the climax to the trick. Explain that, at their command, the magic will cease. Ask someone to say "Now!", and, as they do, withdraw the forefinger, so the knife drops to the tabletop or floor. As this is done, follow the knife with your eyes, and put your forefinger back in its original position, grasping the left wrist. Under the very strong misdirection of the knife falling, the spectators will never see this.

This is a very simple trick, and a very good one. The misdirection makes it work. When the secret moves are made, the spectator is always looking somewhere else, at something that, to him, seems more important; and, like the false finger that conceals the handkerchief, the missing finger on the hand grasping the wrist is simply not noticed.

This same principle of misdirection—that the natural and the commonplace will pass unnoticed—applies to the handling of all natural-appearing props. Suppose you are doing a trick that requires the use of a drinking glass and suppose that, for this trick to work, the glass has its bottom cut out (this odd prop, which is called, not surprisingly, "a bottomless glass," can be purchased at any magic shop). The general public does not know about bottomless glasses, and would think them a stupid idea even if they did because all the liquid would run out. The magician should

THE SCIENCE OF ILLUSION

therefore not set about proving that the glass has a bottom; he should handle it as if it were an ordinary glass. The audience will assume it is—most glasses *are* ordinary. The magician should never say, "Here I have an ordinary glass," as this will only plant the seed of doubt that it is not ordinary. It is good to remember again (as we did when considering the rabbit-from-the-hat trick) Al Baker's advice not to run when nobody's chasing you, for the magician who "doth protest too much" about the ordinariness of his props will bring suspicion upon them.

It's important to keep this rule of naturalness in mind when practicing all kinds of magic. If the action that we discussed previously, of pretending to place a coin that is in the right hand into the left hand where it will be shown to have vanished, looks *exactly the same* as the real action of placing the coin into the hand, the very naturalness of the action will serve to conceal it. This is why all of the sleights and moves in magic should be examined in terms of their naturalness. Some of these moves, used by magicians for scores of years and beloved by them because of their technical cleverness, look impossibly "tricky" and could not be accepted by any audience as other than what they are, a means to fool them. The best way to practice any "move" in magic is first to practice the particular action *without the move*. If the move is the pretended transfer of an object from one hand to another, first practice actually transfering the object (preferably in front of a mirror), to get a clear idea of what it looks like. Later, after the pretended transfer has been rehearsed, care should be taken to see that it looks exactly the same as the real transfer.

Many beginning magicians (and some who are not beginners) find it very difficult to learn to do moves naturally. A major reason for this is that the performer, at least on a subconscious level, feels guilty about the fact that he is doing something deceptive. This guilt often manifests itself in unconscious mannerisms like closing the eyes, sucking in the breath, or even nervously coughing at the exact moment the move is made. The only advice I can give is to try to identify these mannerisms and then work hard to eliminate them. Closely related to this problem is deceptive maneuvers carried out in a surreptitious or sneaky manner. Obviously, if you act in a suspicious manner, the members of your audience will suspect you. Deceptive actions should be done in a bold and matter-of-fact way. *Do them decisively.* Above all, don't sneak into them.

Physical misdirection, with its control of attention and its exploitation of nonattention, was undoubtedly the first and most basic form of misdirection that magicians understood and used.

In the past century, another, more subtle form has come to be recognized, and, while it has not replaced physical misdirection (and is, in fact, usually employed in conjunction with it), it has greatly influenced the thinking of magicians in recent years. *Mental misdirection* involves control of the logical thought processes that lead to the spectator's perception of a magic effect. In mental misdirection, the spectator's thinking is led down false paths which his mind, under the magician's suggestion, maps inaccurately. Dai Vernon (the Professor) has described it as a process in which "the mind is led ingeniously, step by step, to defeat its own logic."

As you are doubtless beginning to realize by now, mental misdirection is a far more abstract and subtle concept than physical misdirection. Its effectiveness depends not on direct control of the spectator, but on a surreptitious derailing of his logical train of thought. Perhaps the best way to understand mental misdirection is to think of each magic trick as a little self-contained drama. Like any drama, a magic trick has characters (coins, cards, silk handkerchiefs, even people and live animals), a story (the basic effect of levitation or vanish or whatever), and a plot (the way the story is played out) with a definite beginning, middle, and end. The beginning of the drama introduces the characters and sets up a situation, the middle adds complicating elements that build suspense and dramatic interest, and the ending resolves the plot. Sometimes the ending of a drama (like a joke or a mystery story) is a surprise. At other times, it ends on a note that fulfills the expectations of the audience.

There is a school of thought among some magicians that any trick, to be really effective, must have a surprise ending. It is true that many good tricks do have surprise endings, and are very effective for that reason. For example, most modern presentations of the classic Cups and Balls, in which the balls appear and vanish and transpose from cup to cup, have a surprise climax, in which something new is revealed under the cups—large balls, fruit or vegetables, or even live baby chicks. This unexpected surprise at the end adds immeasurably to the impact of the trick. There are other tricks that end, much to the satisfaction of the audience, in exactly the way they expect them to end. Take for example the classic stage illusion "Metamorphosis" or the "Trunk Substitution," in which the magician, who is on the outside of a locked trunk, changes places almost instantaneously with a girl tied up in a bag inside. When suddenly the girl appears outside the trunk, the audience knows the magician is inside the trunk. They are astonished at the lightning rapidity with which the exchange takes place. And when the trunk is unlocked, and a form is seen in the tied bag, they know it is the magician and are ready to applaud, enthusiastically, when the bag is untied to reveal him. The final revelation of the magician satisfies their expectations and is an effective dramatic climax. If the bag were to be untied and someone else found inside, they would be surprised, but also somehow disappointed. As many magicians who have experimented with this climax to the classic effect have discovered, the surprise ending is not always the best ending.

The plot of a magic trick must go beyond the basic story by supplying a certain internal logic to the sequence of events. The effect (story) of the famous "Chinese Rings" trick may be that rings link and unlink. The plot is the logical sequence in which they do this, starting with one ring linking into another, and ending with chains of rings linked in different ways and in different patterns. In many routines of this great trick, the rings all unlink again at the end. Again, here is a classic effect that packs no great surprises, and yet, when well presented, it is both beautiful and mystifying.

The dramatic impact of these tricks, which are really logically constructed magical playlets, lies in the fact that audiences perceive them as dramatic wholes, in which event A logically leads to event B, which logically leads to event C, and so on, until a satisfactory dramatic climax is reached. This is what the audience perceives, but is this *really* what happens? It should come as no great surprise when I tell you that it isn't. In reality, disguised by mental misdirection, the magician adds things of which the audience is not aware, and leaves out elements (which the audience, in their perception of the logical dramatic whole, thinks are there). As a result of this misperception of both *more* and *less* than is really there, the audience is fooled.

To illustrate how mental misdirection works, I will teach you a first-class card trick, the invention of the late Francis Carlyle, a fine magician. The effect is this: Two cards are selected, one by the spectator and one by the magician, and are replaced in the deck. The deck is then turned part face-up and part face-down. The deck mysteriously rights itself so that it is all facing the same way, except for the two selected cards. A very strong aspect of this effect is that the magic seems to take place while the deck is in the spectator's hands.

I will take you through the trick, step by step, pointing out as we proceed what is actually happening versus what the spectator *thinks* is happening, and how you as the magician do certain things of which the spectator is not aware, and do not do other things that the spectator thinks you do, in order to make the deception work.

1 The performer hands a deck of cards to the spectator, and asks him to look it over and then give it a thorough shuffle.

2 The spectator is asked to cut the deck into two piles and hand either one to the magician.

3 The magician invites the spectator to "do as I do," and explains that each will select a card from his respective packets and, so that "neither can see where the other's card came from," the packets will be held behind the back. This is done.

4 Both magician and spectator bring the cards out from behind their backs, holding the packet in one hand, the card in the other. They look at and remember their cards.

5 The magician then places his card (without showing it) face down into the spectator's packet, and the spectator places his card face down into the magician's packet.

6 The magician asks the spectator to cut the cards he holds into two face-up packets, and the magician sandwiches his face-down packet between them.

7 The cards are squared up and the magician asks the spectator to hold the complete deck between his hands.

8 *For the first time,* the magician and the spectator name their cards.

9 A magic pass is made over the spectator's hands, and when he spreads the cards out on the table, the face-up and face-down packets are found to have righted themselves, except for the two selected cards, which are reversed.

Now here are the same nine steps of the trick, but including the points where the deception is accomplished, and the mental misdirection that conceals these points from the spectator.

1 The spectator examines and shuffles the deck. The purpose of this is to convince the spectator that everything is open and aboveboard, and to lull him, from the very beginning, into a false sense of security about the fairness of what is about to take place.

2 The spectator is asked to cut the deck into two piles, and to hand either one to the magician. Again all is fair. No deception has yet taken place.

3 The magician invites the spectator to "do as I do," and each places his packet behind his back to select a card. This is where the first bit of trickery enters, both in what the magician says and in what he does. By inviting the spectator to "do as I do," the magician suggests that they will both be doing the same thing (nothing could be farther from the truth!), and, by suggesting that the packs be held behind the back "so that neither of us can see where the other's card comes from," he gives a completely bogus reason for putting the packet behind his back and out of sight. (Who really *cares* where the other's card comes from? It has nothing to do with the trick.) As the magician says this, he holds his packet in his left hand and casually looks at it. It is at this moment that he glimpses the bottom card of the packet and remembers it. The spectator takes no notice of this (why should he? He does not know what is coming anyway!). Once the magician and spectator put the packets behind their backs (ostensibly to select a card, unseen), the magician engages in two actions of which the spectator is unaware. First, he reverses the bottom card of the pack (the one he glimpsed earlier). Then he removes a face-down card from the packet and brings it around to the front in his right hand. Finally, he brings the packet forward in his left hand, but before he does this, he *turns it over.* Because of the reversed card on the bottom, it still looks face down. As this is done, the spectator is occupying himself with selecting a card and he brings to the front his card and the packet (really face down).

4 Both the magician and the spectator look at their cards. Here again, the magician *does not do* something the spectator thinks he does. He does not even pay any attention to the card he holds in his right hand! He does, however, emphasize strongly that the spectator must remember his own selected card and under no circumstances forget it. This is important for two reasons. From the standpoint of mental misdirection, it implies that the magician is doing the same (he is not) and, from a purely practical viewpoint, if the spectator forgets his card, you do not have much of a trick!

5 The magician places his card face down in the spectator's pile, and the spectator places his in the magician's pile. The magician should be very careful not to let his pile spread or open too much when the spectator inserts his card, for that would reveal that the cards (except for the top one) are really face down, not face up as the spectator believes them to be. As this is done, the magician should say something like, "I'll place my card in your pile and you place yours in mine." Under no conditions should he say, "I will place my face-down card in your face-down pile, and you place your face-down card in my face-down pile." That the piles and cards are face down is (to the spectator) self-evident. Why would you call attention to such an obvious condition unless such were not the case? To the spectator, the appearance of his pile and card and the magician's pile and card are *exactly the same*. It is visually implied, though *never* explicitly stated, that this is because they have done exactly the same actions.

6 The magician asks the spectator to take off half of his pile and give it to him. He turns it face up and places it *under* the apparently face-down pile in the left hand, overlapping it. The other half of the spectator's pile is also turned face up and placed above the face-down pile, overlapping it at the other end (see the figure). Again, the magician has *not done* something the spectator thinks he has done—that is, place his face-down pile between the two face-up ones. Actually, only the top card of the apparently face-down pile (the one the magician has glimpsed and remembered) is face down. The rest of the pile, unbeknownst to the spectator, is face up (except for the spectator's face-down card buried somewhere in the middle of it).

7 The deck is squared up and placed between the palms of the spectator's hands. At this point, all of the mechanical part of the trick is over, but the spectator does not know that it has started yet. Now is the time for the magician to use mental misdirection to convince the spectator that he is witnessing a miracle. From this point on, it's all done with words.

8 Explain that two cards have been selected, and that there is no possible way you could know the spectator's card, just as there is no way he could know yours (this is true).

THE SCIENCE OF ILLUSION

Point out that the deck is between his palms, so there is no way you could touch it, let alone manipulate the cards in any way (this is also true!). The magician says to the spectator, "Now, *for the first time,* please tell me your card and I will tell you mine." He names his card, and you tell him the name of the card you glimpsed and turned over behind your back. The implication is that, until the cards are named, the magic cannot begin to work. Actually, the naming of the cards has nothing to do with it, as they are already reversed in the deck.

9 The magician makes a pass over the spectator's hands and reiterates, "Remember, I have not touched the deck—except by magic." The spectator is asked to spread the cards on the table, and the face-up and face-down packets have righted themselves, except for the two selected cards.

Again, this quite simple but wonderful card trick is accomplished largely through mental misdirection; by what you say, and what you suggest, the spectator is led down a completely false path in terms of what he thinks has taken place.

There is also another important type of mental misdirection at work here, as there is in most good magic tricks. When the spectator thinks back on the effect he has seen, he is likely to remember something quite different from what really happened. Because of what you have verbally suggested, the spectator thinks the trick is just beginning when it is really over. He is led to believe by implication that you cannot make the cards in the deck turn over until you know their names and, by the time you know them, the deck is out of your hands. You constantly emphasize (after the physical trickery has been accomplished) that you do not touch the deck and, on thinking back, the spectator is likely to believe this. All of this has produced what mental-magician Bob Haines calls "the logical disconnect." Once this has taken place it is very difficult, if not impossible, for the spectator to reason his way back to the elements which, with false logic, led to the amazing climax of the trick.

All of these principles of psychology apply to any tricks you may perform, from close-up sleight-of-hand effects to big stage illusions to feats of mentalism and apparent mind reading. In the next section of this book we will see how to put these principles into practice.

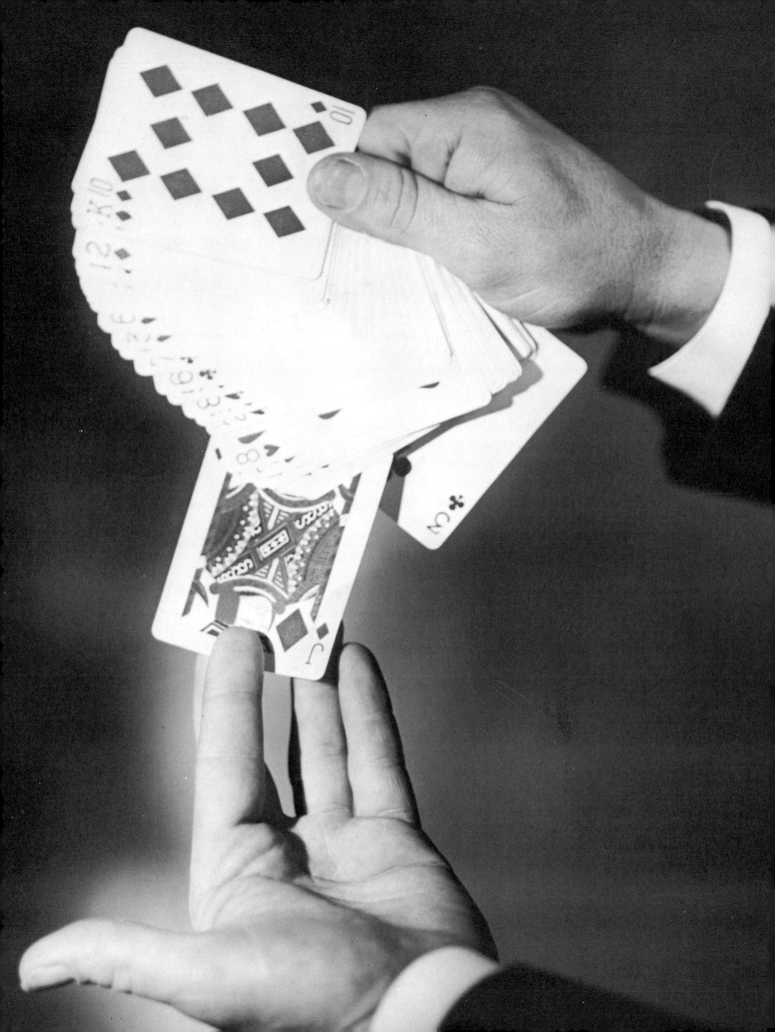

PERFORMING MAGIC

**B**efore we begin the trick section of this book I am going to pass along to you a piece of advice that my father gave to me when I was a young boy beginning in magic. It is the same advice that he always gave magicians who came to him for tips on how to learn the art. *"Don't waste your time on trying to learn every new trick you hear about. Instead spend that time in learning to do only a few really good tricks and learn to do them really well."*

There is a famous story about a young magician visiting the great British magician David Devant backstage after one of his performances. "I know how to do over two hundred tricks. How many do you know?" asked the young magician. "I know only eight," said Devant, "and I have devoted my entire life to learning how to entertain an audience with them."

Both of these stories illustrate the same truth about magic, and it is probably the single most important thing that you can learn from this or any other magic book. If you learn how to do only one trick really well, and learn how to entertain an audience with it, you are a magician. If you learn to perform many tricks in a clumsy and unentertaining way, you are not a magician. You are only a bore and a bungler.

Magic is a fascinating art that can elevate and entertain the audiences that witness it. If you are good to magic and approach it in the proper way, whether as a hobby or a profession, magic

(Opposite) **The hands of Harry Blackstone, Sr.**

will be very good to you. The greatest disservice you can do magic is to perform it badly.

Now, let's look at my father's advice more closely, and ask some important questions. How do you find some "really good tricks," and how do you learn to "do them really well"?

I would like to say that you will find some good tricks in the pages of this book, and, of course, I believe that is true. But there is more to it than that. The approach of this book is to follow the advice of my father and David Devant and to teach you a few good tricks in great detail so that, if you follow the explanation of how to perform the trick step by step, you will actually be able to do it. This is in contrast to many magic books, which explain a great many effects in a more abbreviated way and leave it to the readers to work out the details of performing them. In this book, I will try to give you all of those details, and for that reason the explanations may seem quite lengthy. All that I can ask is that you not be intimidated by their seeming complexity. If you follow along with the props in hand, you will find that many tricks that seem impossibly difficult and complicated in the reading are really quite easy in performance, if you start off on the right track and get each of the small details right as you go along.

Before you choose to spend the time and energy to learn a new trick, you should look at it carefully to evaluate, first, whether it is a good trick, and second, whether it is a trick for you. Sad to say, many of the hundreds of magic tricks that are created, published, and marketed each year are simply not worth doing. While they may be intriguing to magicians and magic hobbyists, they do not have the potential to entertain an audience of laymen. In the parlance of the professional magician, they are not "commercial effects."

I believe the first thing to look for in any magic is directness and clarity of effect. Is the action of the effect straightforward and easy to follow, or is it so devious and complicated that the audience simply will not want to make the effort to follow it and will consequently tune out?

If you cannot describe the effect of a trick in one simple sentence, it is probably not a good trick. All of the real classics of magic, many of which have lasted for hundreds or even thousands of years, will pass this test. A cage containing a bird disappears, steel rings link and unlink, an egg appears and disappears in a small cloth bag, three balls penetrate three cups and transpose beneath them, a woman is cut in half and then restored, a woman floats in the air. All of these are great tricks because each has a plot easy to understand.

Once you have decided on a good effect, the next step is to

find a good method of accomplishing it. Here again, directness and simplicity are the answer. The best method gets you through the action of the trick, where step A logically leads to step B, which logically leads to step C, and so on, in the easiest and most straightforward way possible. "Logically" is the operative word here, and it is essential in working out the action of a particular effect that this logic (or the *illusion* of logic) be maintained. Many effects appeal to magicians (not to audiences of laymen) because the method by which they are accomplished is so insidiously clever. But because the audience should not be aware of the method, *the way in which a trick is accomplished is of absolutely no importance to them.* It follows that the magician should use the method that is easiest for him and best fits his ability as a performer, and which allows for the most straightforward and logical action of the trick. This means that every necessary action used in accomplishing the effect should be motivated, so it does not arouse suspicion and break the magic spell the performer has cast. On the simplest level, if the performer puts his hand in his pocket for no apparent reason, the audience will immediately become suspicious. Why did the magician reach in his pocket? To get something? To get rid of something? If, on the other hand, the magician picks up something that has been utilized earlier in the trick, say a packet of matches, and puts it away in his pocket from which he earlier removed it, no suspicion will be aroused, and the magician can use this as an excuse to pick up or get rid of something else.

After you have decided on a "really good trick" (in terms of effect and method), the next part of my father's advice is to learn to do it "really well." There are two aspects to this: first, practicing the trick correctly, and second, learning to present it to an audience. Knowing a trick is not just knowing how to do it or even being able to perform it in the privacy of your home. Until you can perform a particular effect for an audience, and both fool and entertain them with it, you do not really know it.

No trick, even the most simple, apparently self-working ones, should be performed for an audience unless it has been practiced. It is through practice that you learn the mechanics of a trick, and also often discover if, at your present stage of development as a magician, a particular trick is right for you.

Most magicians first practice the moves of a trick in front of a mirror so they can see what the audience will see and perfect the action to the point (in terms of angles, movement, etc.) where it is most deceptive. There must come a time, however, when the mirror is finally abandoned, and the trick is performed with all the elements it would have in front of a real audience.

Here you no longer watch yourself perform, but perform for an imaginary audience. It will be interesting to see, in this rapidly advancing electronic age, how much the home video camera eventually replaces the mirror as a tool for magicians' practice. I can think of few better ways to correct your performing mistakes than being able to view, analyze, and criticize your work on the television screen.

The one place you should *not* practice the mechanics of your magic is in front of a real audience. By the time you are ready to do your magic in public, practice must become performance, and the action of performing the trick should be second nature to you. It is in front of a real audience that you will gain invaluable experience in how to *present* the trick and make it entertaining. In fact, it is only in front of a real audience that you can learn which lines, which bits of business and presentation, work and which do not. Trial and error in a real performing situation is something for which there is no substitute.

One final thing should be said about practice. Practice should not be a chore. It should be fun, and one of the most creative and stimulating times in learning a new effect. It is here that you take the moves you have been taught and make them work for *you.*

When you are finally performing in front of an audience, you will have practiced the effect so that you can do it automatically and can devote all of your attention to presentation—to selling the trick and making it entertaining. The most important thing to remember in doing this is that you know what's coming, but *the audience does not.* Because of this, you have a tremendous advantage in fooling and astonishing them. This is also why you *never* tell them in advance what you are going to do (they would then know what to look for), or repeat a trick in exactly the same way. On those rare occasions (I hope!) when a trick goes wrong (practice is the way to avoid this), you are able to correct the mistake and, if necessary, bring the trick to a different conclusion, because the audience does not know what is coming next.

Magic Up Close

In choosing the tricks for this book, I made one important basic assumption. It is that, in starting out in magic, you will not step directly onto a stage to entertain hundreds of people, or onto a television screen to entertain millions. I assume that you will start out performing magic for your friends, just as I did, and my father as well. The magic this book teaches is the kind that fits the performing situations you will encounter as you begin to get experience in this fascinating art.

Many magicians, myself included, make their livings by performing magic for large audiences in theatres or nightclubs, but even I must admit that there is nothing in magic as effective as a seeming miracle performed right under your nose. The first magic was unquestionably close-up magic, and there is little doubt that it supplied the foundation for all the larger magic that was to follow. In Scot's *Discoverie of Witchcraft* (1584), the first known book in English to explain magicians' tricks, we read: "The true act of juggling consisteth in legierdemaine: to wit, the nimble conveiance of the hand, which is especiallie performed three waies. The first and principall consisteth in hiding and conveing of balles, the second in the alteration of monie, the third in the shuffling of cards. He that is expert in these may show much pleasure and manie feats, and hath more cunning than all other witches or magicians."

How little magic has changed in four hundred years. The "oldest deception," the Cups and Balls, is still alive and well and in the repertoire of most close-up magicians, and magic with cards and coins is still a mainstay of close-up performers.

In this section of the book I will teach you some effective magic with all of these objects, as well as with other common props such as matches, salt shakers, and pocket handkerchiefs. What makes this magic effective is that it is done with common everyday objects and, of course, that it is done close up.

The Cups and Balls

The Cups and Balls is probably the oldest trick in magic, and for thousands of years it has survived as one of the best. While its plot is simple and easy to follow, it takes a considerable amount of practice to learn to do well, and its performance embodies many of the basic effects in magic productions, vanishes, transpositions, and penetrations. There are hundreds of different cup-and-ball routines of varying complexity and difficulty, as well as many related routines which, instead of the classic three cups and three balls, use other containers such as bowls, saucers, and even just the hands.

In this chapter, I will teach you a simple, effective ball routine that is related in basic principle to the Cups and Balls, and then, finally, a simple cup-and-ball routine on which you can build, if you wish, more complex routines as you become more proficient in sleight of hand.

One of the reasons the Cups and Balls (and its many spinoffs and variations) is such an effective trick is that much of the misdirection required is built into its physical action. For example, if a cup is lifted, revealing that a ball has appeared under it or that a ball previously placed under it has vanished, there is natural interest on the spectator's part and he will automatically direct his attention to this action. When this happens, the magician has a very powerful moment of misdirection in which to do something unobserved, like load an additional ball under the cup.

Let us look at a very good sleight-of-hand trick closely related to the Cups and Balls, but even simpler in its plot because it simply uses two objects without the complicating element of cups or other covers. This trick is called the "Chinese Count," and it has been popularized among magicians by the inimitable Dai Vernon. It will work with any two objects—balls of paper, matchsticks, coins, bottle caps—anything that can be easily palmed and with which you can do a false transfer. The basic "sleight" or "move" in this trick is to pick up an object in your right hand and apparently place it in the left hand (but actually you are not doing so). For the purpose of this discussion, let us say that we will use two small balls about one-half inch in diameter. These can be of rolled-up paper or they can be small rubber balls purchased at a toy store. Here is the action of the trick, which is performed as the magician counts aloud from one to ten.

Place the two balls on the table in front of you about ten inches apart.

1 Pick up the left-hand ball with the left hand, showing it, and count "one," placing it down again.

2 Pick up the right-hand ball with the right hand and place it down again, counting "two."

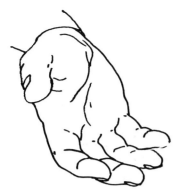

3 Place the palm-up right hand over the right ball (hiding it from view), counting "three."

4 Place the left hand, palm up, over the left ball, counting "four."

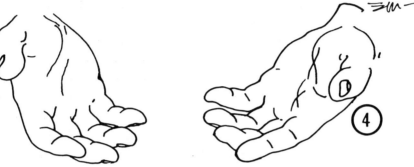

5 Turn your right hand palm down, curling all but the index finger into the palm. With the index finger, point at the ball that has been revealed on the table, and count "five."

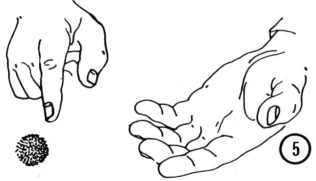

6 Pick up the ball between thumb and forefinger of the right hand, turning the right hand palm up as the ball is shown. Count "six."

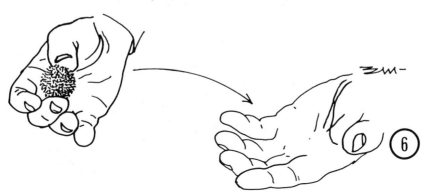

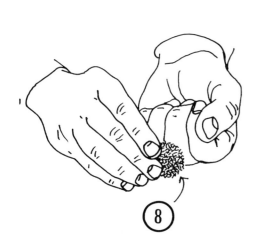

7 Now, here is the simple move upon which the deception is based. You are going to pretend to place the ball you have just shown in your right hand into the left hand, but you are not really going to do so. Instead, you will (unknown to the spectators) retain the ball in your right hand. This is a very simple move, but it must be done decisively and "acted" correctly in order for it to be deceptive.

Note that if the ball is displayed in the right hand, with thumb on top and fingers beneath, and the right hand is then turned at the wrist so that it is *palm down,* the ball is completely concealed. This is precisely what you will do when you apparently place the ball in the left hand. The right hand is simply turned at the wrist so that the ball goes out of sight, and the fingers are placed against the open palm of the left hand. The left-hand fingers close and *at the same time* the right hand (with the ball concealed behind its fingers) is withdrawn. It is very important to realize that no adjusting movement is made by the right-hand fingers (as if the ball were being palmed), as this would immediately give the game away. At this point, a crucial bit of misdirection takes place. As the left-hand fingers close to apparently take the ball placed by the right hand, the left-hand ball (previously concealed by the open left-hand fingers) is revealed. It is now, as the three fingers of the right hand are curling around the ball into the palm, that your right forefinger points to the revealed ball on the table. As you do this, count "seven."

8 On the count of "eight," the right thumb and forefinger pick up the ball, taking it into the closed right hand. At this point, the mechanics of the trick are over, but the dramatic climax will take place on the next two counts. This is the time to pause for a moment to give the audience a chance to digest what has happened. They think you have a ball in each hand. Actually, both balls are in the right hand.

9 On the count of "nine," open your left hand slowly and dramatically, showing it empty.

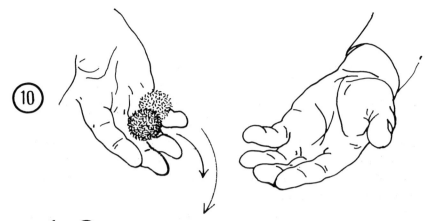

10 On the count of "ten," slowly open your right hand, allowing the two balls in it to roll out onto the table.

The trick is done, but now let's look at some of the fine points of misdirection that make it work. Once you have mastered the purely mechanical actions of your hands to do the "moves" of the effect, you should consider the equally important factor of what to do with your eyes.

As each ball is placed on the table, you must look at it, and as each palm-up hand is placed over the ball, you must look at that hand. On the counts of "six" and "seven," when the right hand picks up the right ball, you must look intently at that hand and at the ball it holds. Then on the count of "eight," when the ball is apparently placed in the left hand, you must look first at the left hand, and then at the ball that has been revealed on the table, as the left-hand fingers close. At this point, the right forefinger points at the ball and the eyes follow it as the right hand takes it. At the dramatic climax of the effect, you look intently at the left hand as it slowly opens and is seen to be empty. Then your attention shifts to the right hand, as it slowly opens, revealing the two balls.

In its misdirection, this very simple but very effective pure sleight-of-hand trick is closely related to the more complex effect of the Cups and Balls.

Now here is a good, basic cup-and-ball routine that, if practiced sufficiently to be performed smoothly, is guaranteed to amaze your audience.

Three cups are needed. These can be made of any material—paper coffee cups, plastic bathroom cups, or, if you prefer, special metal cups available at almost any magic store will do. The only requirements are that the cups must be opaque so that you cannot see through them, and they must be able to nest. They also must taper (or, in the case of some cups purchased in magic stores, have a ridge that keeps them separated), so that there is space between them, when nested, to conceal one or more balls.

If you are making the investment in a special set of cups at a magic store, be sure to check that *three* balls will fit on top of one cup, and will be completely concealed in the space between when another cup is nested on top. While this is not a necessity in the basic routine you will learn here, this advice about choosing the proper cups (given by Robert-Houdin more than a century ago) will prove useful in many of the more advanced routines you may want to learn later.

After you have chosen your three cups, the next thing you will need is *four* balls (the spectators know of only three of these). About three-quarter-inches in diameter is a good size, but they can be of any size that fits comfortably *between* the cups. Finally, in the right-hand pocket of your coat or pants, or your hip pocket, place a small lemon or lime.

To begin, have the three cups nested *mouth up* on the table. In the top mouth-up cup are three balls. Between the top cup and the second cup is the fourth ball, and nothing is concealed between the second and third cups (Figure 11).

1 Pick up the cups together and spill the three balls onto the table (Figure 12).

2 Now comes the major move of this basic cup-and-ball routine. It involves placing a cup, either mouth down and nested on another mouth-down cup, or mouth down by itself on the table, without letting the ball it contains fall out. This must be done in a continuous motion so that the ball stays inside due to the momentum of the movement (Figure 13). Experiment to see how slowly you can do this without the ball falling out. It requires a certain knack, but a few minutes of practice should

PERFORMING MAGIC

convince you how easy it is to learn. You will have occasion to do this move of placing a cup (which secretly contains a ball) mouth down on the table or on top of another mouth-down cup throughout the routine. You will also be handling other cups (which do *not* secretly contain balls) in the same way. It is very important that the empty cups and the loaded cup be placed down in exactly the same way and *at exactly the same speed.* If you place the "guilty" cups down faster and more suspiciously than the "innocent" ones, it will be a dead giveaway that you are trying to get away with something.

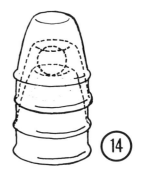

After the balls are spilled on the table, the cups (held mouth up and nested in the left hand) are shown in the following manner: The first cup is taken mouth up in the right hand, inverted, and placed mouth down on the table. The next cup (remember that, unknown to the audience, this cup contains the fourth ball!) is inverted and placed mouth down on on top of the first cup. This should be done at exactly the same speed that you placed the first cup down. Finally, the last cup is inverted and placed on top of the other two (Figure 14). As this is done, say, "Three balls, one, two, three cups, and [showing your hands] two empty hands."

3   Pick up the cups again in the left hand, turning them mouth up. Removing each cup singly, place them mouth down on the table from left to right. Remember, the second cup contains a ball that must not drop out as the cup is placed mouth down. We will call the cups, from left to right, cup 1, cup 2 (the one with the fourth ball secretly under it), and cup 3 (Figure 15).

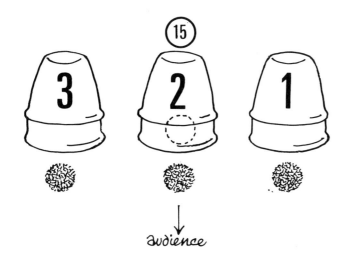

4 Explain that the balls can magically penetrate the cups and, picking up one of the balls, place it on cup 2 and cover it with cup 3. Lift *both* cups with the left hand, and show that the ball has penetrated. When this penetration takes place, it's a good idea to do something to indicate that something amazing is about to happen. The traditional cup-and-ball manipulators have, for thousands of years, used a wand or magic stick to tap the cups and apparently make the magic take place. You can do the same, or you can merely make a pass with your hands over the cups. Whatever you decide to do, be sure you "point up" the penetration so the audience will properly appreciate it (Figures 16–18).

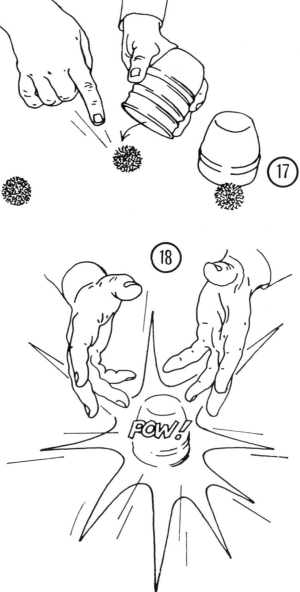

When the audience sees that the ball has penetrated, they will look at it in amazement. Under cover of this misdirection, separate the cups, taking the top mouth-up cup into your right hand. Place the cup in your left hand (remember it contains a ball), mouth down, over the ball already on the table. Place another ball on top of the cup, cover it with the other cup, and (after making the appropriate magical gesture) lift them both to show that another ball has penetrated and that there are now *two* balls underneath (Figures 19–20).

5 "I'll make it *twice* as hard," you say. "I'll make a ball penetrate *two* cups." Again place the bottom cup (with its hidden ball) over the two balls on the table, and nest a second cup on top of it. Place the third ball on top of it, and the third cup nested mouth down on top of that (Figure 21). Make an even bigger magical gesture (remember this double penetration is *much* more difficult!).

You are now going to do something that is pure bluff, but if done boldly it will convince the spectators that there is no ball between the cups and that it has, indeed, achieved a double penetration. With your left hand, lift the top *two* cups off the bottom cup. No ball will be on the bottom cup (remember, it's one cup above), and as this registers on the spectators, separate the two cups, taking the bottom one (with the concealed ball) in your left hand. Hold the cups tilted with their bottoms toward the audience and their mouths toward you so the ball doesn't fall out (Figure 22). Immediately place the right-hand cup on top of the face-down cup on the table, and the left-hand cup on top of that. Lift all three cups, showing the three balls underneath. Note that in replacing the top two cups, you have put them back in *reverse* order so that the concealed ball is between the top cup and the one beneath it.

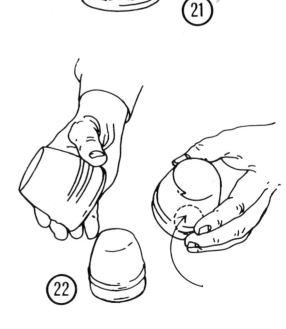

6 Again, place the cups on the table from left to right (the ball is under the left-hand cup). Say, "I'll do it again for those of you who weren't watching." Place one ball on top of the right-hand cup and place the middle cup on top. Make a gesture and lift both cups. Act surprised that nothing is underneath. Put the cups down and make the gesture again. Lift them and register surprise that there is still nothing beneath them. Say, "It must have gone over here," and lift the left-hand cup, showing the missing ball beneath it (Figure 23).

While the spectators are reacting to this unexpected development, place the two nested cups on top of the cup you have just lifted to reveal the ball.

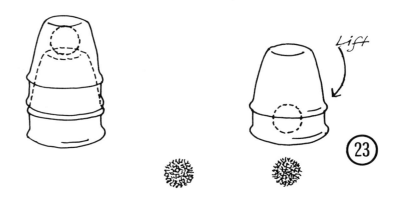

7 At this point in the routine, there are three balls on the table and three nested mouth-down cups, with the concealed ball between the top and middle cups. Now tell the audience you will show them something "really amazing." Line up the three balls. You will now cover them with the cups, but in a special way. Pick up the cups and hold them nested, mouth up, in the left hand. Remove the top mouth-up cup with the *right* hand. Show it empty by pointing its mouth toward the audience, and place it over the ball on the left. Take the next cup, mouth up, in the *left* hand and show it empty. As you do this, the final cup in the right hand is tilted mouth down, and the ball is allowed to roll into the right-hand fingers, where it is retained with the hand in a natural position (Figure 24). The misdirection for this steal of the ball is that the spectators are looking at the cup being shown empty by the left hand. The last cup is removed from the right hand by the left hand, shown empty, and placed over the right-hand ball. As this is done, the right hand (holding the concealed ball) drops naturally to the side.

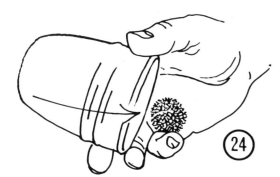

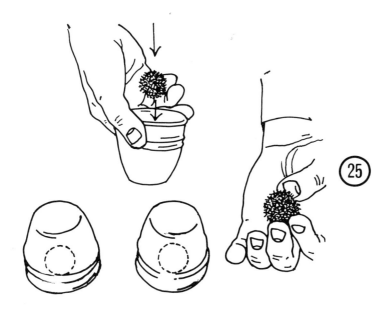

8 In this final phase of the trick, the three balls are apparently removed from under each cup and placed into a right-hand pocket. This is the pocket containing the small lemon or lime and, while it can be any right-hand pocket (choose the one that, with the outfit you are wearing, shows the least bulge), let us for the purposes of this explanation say that it is the right pants pocket.

Lift the left-hand cup with your left hand, showing the ball underneath. Transfer the cup, mouth up, into the right hand (which has the concealed ball), and pick up the ball on the table with the left hand, *looking at it.* Under cover of this misdirection, allow the ball in the right hand to drop into the mouth-up cup it holds (Figure 25). With the right hand, place the cup face down on the table, with the ball under it. Put the ball that you're holding in your left hand into your right hand, and apparently place it in your right pants pocket. Your attention now returns to the second (middle) cup, lifting it with the left hand to reveal the ball underneath. *At exactly the same time as this is happening,* the right hand comes out of the right pants pocket to take the cup that is put into it by the left hand. What the spectators do not know is that this right hand retains (curled in the fingers in a natural position) the ball that they think you just put away in your right pocket. *Exactly the same sequence of moves is repeated as with the first cup,* as the left hand picks up the ball, and the right hand loads its ball into the mouth-up cup (Figure 26). This is repeated once again with the third cup, as the third ball is apparently put into the right pocket. This time, however, the ball is dropped in the pocket, and the right hand grasps the lemon in its curled fingers, but for the moment remains in the pocket. You will remember that because each time a ball was removed from under a cup another ball was loaded in, there is

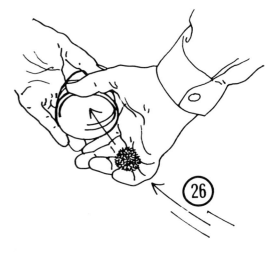

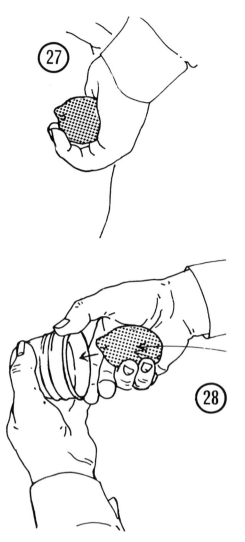

still, unknown to the spectators, a ball under each cup. You are now going to surprise them by revealing this, and under cover of the strong misdirection created by this surprise, you will load the lemon under one of the cups. Here's how to do it.

With the left hand, lift the center cup, revealing a ball. *As the cup is being lifted,* the right hand is coming out of the pocket with the lemon. The back of the hand is toward the audience and the lemon is held in the natural-looking curled fingers. The cup is placed mouth up from the left hand into the right hand, and the lemon is allowed to drop in (Figure 28). The ball is picked up by the left hand as you and the spectators look at it, and the right hand places its cup (with the lemon now inside) back on the table. Now the other two cups are lifted, revealing the balls underneath. These are nested, mouth down, on top of the cup concealing the lemon. Finally, all three nested cups are lifted for the surprise climax, revealing the lemon underneath (Figure 29).

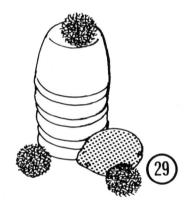

This very effective cup-and-ball routine may seem complicated in the reading, and it may sound impossible to load such a large object as a lemon under a cup right under the noses of the audience. I assure you that this is not true. If you continue in your study of the Cups and Balls, you will discover that some more advanced routines accomplish such large loads not once, but as many as six times. And all with the audience none the wiser. If you follow this routine step by step, with props in hand, you will discover that it flows along very simply, with the misdirection built in so that each time an object is revealed it covers the load of another. This is why the Cups and Balls remains, after thousands of years, the undisputed masterpiece of sleight-of-hand magic.

Card Magic

If one were to poll magicians, particularly amateur magicians, about their favorite tricks, I suspect that card tricks would prove to be the most popular. More is published each year on card tricks than on any other field of magic. In magic magazines, in pamphlets, and in books literally hundreds of new moves and methods, many of them extremely clever and deceptive, are offered to the card magician. Unfortunately for the general public, there are relatively few fundamental card *effects*, and there is a great danger that after several card tricks are done, they all begin to look alike. The most basic, and perhaps the best, card effect is that in which a spectator chooses a card and the magician finds it. The problem with this effect, as in all magic, is that it must be presented entertainingly—a fact that many magicians lose sight of.

There are literally hundreds of ways to find a selected card, and hundreds of ways to reveal that card. Since these methods are hidden from the audience (or should be), to the spectators they all appear identical. If a magician knows fifty ways to find a card and only one way to reveal it entertainingly, as far as an audience of non-magicians is concerned, he knows only one card trick. If, however, he knows only one way to find a card and fifty ways to reveal it, he knows fifty card tricks. I would not be so foolhardy as to suggest that you show any audience (even an audience of magicians, many of whom, sadly, will applaud a good method before they will applaud a good effect) fifty card tricks, each involving the selection of a card. Nevertheless, it's good to remember that in the "take a card"-type card tricks, it's the revelation of the card that supplies the entertainment, and the mechanics of how you find the card should be something of which the audience is both unaware and unconcerned.

There are, of course, many kinds of card tricks other than finding selected cards. Cards can be made to change, to move from place to place, to penetrate and levitate, and to do most of the basic magic effects that we discussed earlier in this book. One of the very best of all non-"take a card" card tricks is called "Out of This World," and was invented by Paul Curry, an amateur magician who also happens to be a magic genius. It involved a spectator separating a face-down deck into red and black cards without knowing how he did it. Because the trick takes place in the spectator's hands, and he apparently does it all himself, it is a very strong "commercial" effect. I cannot reveal how the trick is done because Mr. Curry sells it (at a very reasonable price) through magic dealers, but it was a great favorite of my father's, as it is of mine, and it is an excellent example of how a card effect other than the classic location can be top-notch entertainment.

There is so much material available to the beginning card magician that it is understandably confusing to know where to start. There are, however, some basic techniques that you can master that will allow you to perform most of the card magic you could ever wish to perform.

A Control. This technique will allow you to have a card selected and replaced in the deck and still keep track of it, bringing it to the bottom or the top of the pack as you wish.

A False Shuffle. This is closely related to a control because it allows you to apparently shuffle a card into the deck so that you seemingly do not know where it is while, in reality, this is not the case at all. Other false shuffles allow you to keep all or part of the cards in the deck in a particular order, rather that just keeping one selected card where you want it.

A Palm. It is a widely held conception among the general public that magicians "palm" cards and other objects. This is one of the few magic clichés that happens to be true, which makes it even more difficult for magicians to palm things and not get caught. Fortunately, with proper technique and strong misdirection, palming remains one of the most powerful techniques at a magician's disposal. In card magic, a card is usually palmed from the top of the deck, although in some tricks it can come from the bottom or even the center.

A Force. This is a technique by which a spectator is made to take a particular card that the magician wants him to select. The lay public is not entirely unaware of the ability of magicians to "force" cards, so it is important that the particular technique used be as direct and apparently fair as possible. If the spectator even suspects that he has not had an absolutely free choice of a card, the trick is over before it begins.

A Change. The effect of one card magically changing into another is one of the most startling and entertaining in card magic. In some tricks, the change of a card, sometimes visibly, is the entire effect. In others, the magician apparently fails to find the spectator's card and then, for a surprise climax, changes the wrong card into the right one.

There are dozens of other techniques in card magic, but if you master these basic five, you will have an excellent foundation upon which to build your repertoire. There is, however, another complicating factor. There are hundreds of ways to accomplish each of these basic techniques, some quite easy and others quite difficult. It often takes considerable experimentation to decide which particular method is the best for you and your particular style and ability.

In the card tricks I will teach you in this chapter, you will learn an effective and relatively easy version of each of the five basic techniques of card magic. It may well be that, as you advance as a card magician, you will want to learn more difficult ways to accomplish the same thing, because *to a lay audience* they appear more direct. For example, the cleanest and most direct way to control a card and bring it to the top of the pack remains, in many tricks, the classic "pass." This sleight, in which the two halves of the pack are rapidly transposed, was considered to be the foundation of all card magic a century ago. It remains a very useful sleight, but a difficult one to master. Consequently, many substitutes have evolved that are easier to do. It is questionable, however, whether many of them are as straightforward as the pass skillfully performed with the proper misdirection.

Exactly the same is true of the force. The best and most direct way to force a card is the classic technique, in which the spreading of the cards in front of the spectator is skillfully timed so that he will withdraw the correct one. Again, this is not an easy sleight to learn and requires plenty of practice to do properly.

In the card tricks explained here, I have in some cases given you easier, but nevertheless effective, ways of accomplishing moves than the classic and still preferable methods. This is done to get you immediately started doing effective card magic, rather than getting bogged down right at the beginning learning difficult sleights. In some cases, such as the palm of a card from the top of the deck, I am teaching you what I consider to be the very best way to do it, as there is simply no "easy" substitute for this basic sleight. As you go on in card magic, I hope you will pursue the more difficult but often more direct ways to achieve the five fundamental techniques. The excellent books on card magic listed in the Bibliography will help you in this.

THE LIE DETECTOR

This is a basic card trick in which you simply find a chosen card, but the presentation makes the revelation of the card very dramatic. The effect is this: A card is selected and returned to the deck. The magician explains that, through diligent practice, he has developed the ability to tell from the tone of someone's voice whether that person is lying or telling the truth. He tells the spectator to deal the cards face up on the table, one by one, from a face-down deck, and to call out the name of each card. When the spectator comes to his chosen card, he is to "lie" about its name, and call out the name of another card. When he does so, the magician stops him and tells him he has lied, and that he is holding the chosen card in his hand.

Let's look at two versions of this trick. In the first, you reveal that the person is lying, and is holding the card in his hand. In the second, you also reveal the name of the card.

In the first version, we make use of one of the most effective controls in card magic, the "key card." In its simplest form, a key card is a card that is secretly known to the magician and that is brought, unbeknownst to the spectator, to a position in the deck either above or below the spectator's card. Once the key card is located, the spectator's chosen card can be found next to it. In the basic Lie Detector effect, the performer secretly glimpses the bottom card of the deck (this can be easily done as he shuffles it), and then has a spectator select and remember the card.

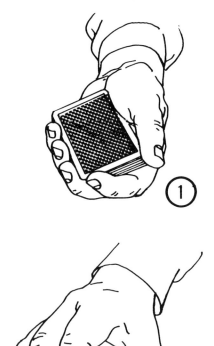

Throughout all of these tricks, there are two basic grips of the deck. The Left-Hand Basic Grip is to hold the deck in the palm of the left hand, thumb high along the left long side of the deck, forefinger of the left hand on the narrow end of the deck (toward the spectators), and the remaining three fingers along the right-hand side of the deck (Figure 1). The Right-Hand Basic Grip is holding the deck face down in your right hand, thumb over the narrow near end of the deck (toward yourself), forefinger of the right hand curled on top of the deck, and the remaining three fingers on the far end (toward the spectators) of the deck (Figure 2).

1 Spread the deck, asking the spectator to choose a card. Tell him to look at and remember the card. (A word of caution here about spectators remembering their cards. Sometimes they don't! Needless to say, this ruins the trick, so it is a good idea to emphasize the importance of not forgetting the card they looked at and, if possible, to have the card shown to several other people, just in case the original spectator does forget it.)

During this time, you have secretly taken the opportunity to look at and remember the bottom card.

2 After the card is selected, ask the spectator to replace it in the deck. Extend the deck to him, holding it in the Left-Hand Basic Grip, and, as you do, pull the bottom half from the deck's narrow end toward you with your right hand

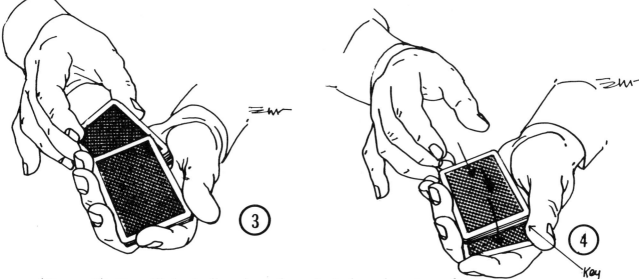

(Figure 3). He will, logically, place the selected card on top of the cards held in your left hand. Continuing your movement, place the portion of the deck held in your right hand on top of his card (Figure 4). *His card is now under your key card* (magicians call this undercutting).

Now, offering the deck, ask the spectator to cut it twice, completing the cut each time he does. (Cutting, incidentally, will never disturb the order of the deck, and cannot possibly separate the chosen card from the key card above it.) By specifying that the deck be cut *twice,* this ensures that the chosen card will end up somewhere in the body of the deck and not on the top or bottom. In fact, by watching where the card is replaced and where the cards are cut, you should know approximately in which part of the deck the card is located. Now, you have only to ask the spectator to read off the cards, one by one, from the top of the deck. When you hear the key card called out, you know that the *next* card is the chosen card, and therefore the spectator will lie about its name.

Normally, a trick in which a major portion of the deck is dealt and called out could be rather tedious, but this one is an exception because of the dramatic plot of catching the spectator in a lie. The audience will be listening intently to the tone of his voice to see if they can detect a difference. Be sure to "sell" this plot strongly, calling out, with all the showmanship you can muster, "Stop! You are telling a lie! The card you are holding in your hand is the one you selected."

Now here is another version of the same effect in which you also reveal the *name* of the card. In this version, you again use a key card to tell you when tbe spectator reaches the selected card, but you also know the name of his card because you have forced it on him. This force is so simple and bold that at first you will find it hard to believe that you can get away with it, but let me assure you, magicians *have* been getting away with it for many years. It is the trick's very simplicity and apparent direct-ness that make it so effective.

In this effect, you will have to remember *two* cards instead of one—the top card of the deck (the one you will force), and the bottom card (which is the key card). You can glimpse these cards easily as you display the deck at the beginning of the trick.

It is useful at this point to learn a simple false shuffle, the purpose of which is simply to keep the top and bottom cards of the deck (which you have secretly glimpsed) in place while the deck is riffle shuffled. Cut the deck into two piles so that one pile can be riffle shuffled into the other. Let the first few cards from the bottom half be released first, and the last few cards from the top half be released last, so that after the riffle shuffle, the same top and bottom cards remain in position (Figure 5). You probably do this automatically much of the time when you riffle shuffle a deck of cards. A few minutes of experimentation with deck in hand should make this clear.

Now for the trick.

1 Place the deck on the table and ask that it be cut about in the center into two piles (by specifying "into two piles" you assure that the cut is not completed). The spectator will place the top portion either to the right or left of the bottom portion. Note where he puts it (or else you may end up fooling yourself with this force). Now look the spectator in the eyes and ask him a question such as, "Do you know anything about lie detectors?" As he ponders an answer, his attention will be momentarily off the deck.

2 At this moment, casually reach down and pick up the bottom portion of the deck and place it crosswise on the top half, as if simply to mark the cut (Figure 6). Now, completely ignore the cut deck as you further explain to the spectator that you have developed the remarkable ability to detect whether a person is lying or telling the truth, simply by the tone of his voice.

Your attention now returns to the deck.

3 Picking up what is now the top portion of the deck, and indicating the top card of what is now the bottom pile, explain that you will turn away, and as you do so, the spectator is to look at the card he cut to, replace it, and put the rest of the cards on top.

When the deck is reassembled, your key card (the bottom card of the deck, which you have remembered) will be right on top of his chosen card.

From here on, you proceed exactly as in the previous version, but with the baffling addition of being able to tell him the *real* name of the card he just lied about.

WRONG INTO RIGHT

In this trick, you will learn a very effective card change (there are dozens of good ways to change a card, including the classic "top change" and "bottom change," both of which you may want to learn as you advance in card magic). I will also teach you a more sophisticated way to use the key card control in conjunction with what magicians call the Hindu Shuffle.

The plot of this effect is very simple, which, of course, is why it's good. A card is selected and the magician tries to find it. He fails. Finally, the wrong card is magically changed into the right one.

First, let's look at our new way to use the key card.

The Hindu Shuffle is a very useful way of mixing a pack of cards, and can be employed in many card tricks. Hold the deck face down in the Left-Hand Basic Grip. With the right hand, placing the thumb on the left long side of the packet and the middle two fingers on the right long side, undercut about three-quarters of the deck. Now, with the left fingers, strip successive small packets off of the top of the right-hand packet onto the top of the left-hand pile, until the right-hand packet is exhausted (Figure 1).

This shuffle can also be done *face up* into the left hand, in which case the card on the face of the right-hand packet continually changes as the cards are stripped off into the left hand. Whichever way this is done, the cards on the *top* of the pile held in the right hand continually change as they are stripped onto the top of the left-hand pile, while the bottom card of the right-hand pile remains the same. This allows you to use that card as a key card.

1 Have a card selected from the middle of the face-down deck (you have already glimpsed the bottom key card).

2 Now, Hindu Shuffle the cards from the right hand into the left, asking that the selected card be replaced "anywhere at all."

3 Once the card has been put on top of the left-hand pile, drop the right-hand pile casually on top and square up the deck (Figure 2).

The key card is, once again, directly above the selected one.

Practice the Hindu Shuffle until you can do it smoothly and casually, and you will see that having a card replaced in the middle of it looks entirely offhand and it seems impossible that the card could be controlled in any way.

Key Card

Selected Card

②

4 Now, spread the cards, faces toward you, and pretend to be having trouble finding the card. Finally, cut the cards (completing the cut) so that the selected card is *second* from the bottom of the deck.

5 Turn the deck face up, and with your right-hand fingers at the front, and your thumb at the back, lift off the top two face-up cards in perfect alignment. This is done by lifting the top face-up card *and then* the second card with the right thumb. As soon as these two cards are separated from the deck *at the end of the deck toward you,* allow the little finger of the left hand to slightly enter the break at the back right-hand corner of the deck, in order to keep the two cards separated from the remainder of the deck.

6 Now, with the two middle fingers of the right hand at the outer end and the right thumb at the inner end, move the two cards *in perfect alignment* to the right for about half their width, and hold them there (still perfectly aligned) with the left thumb (Figure 3).

③

7 Now comes the deceptive move. Turn your right hand palm up and with the first two fingers (first finger on bottom and second finger on top), grasp the two cards in a scissors grip (Figure 4). Turn both hands palm down simultaneously, retaining the scissors grip on the cards, and at the same time, with the thumb of the left hand, pull back the first face-up card of the two aligned cards so that it is even with the deck (Figure 5). The grip of the right-hand first two fingers remains on the other (the selected) card, which is immediately pulled away and placed face down on the table (Figure 6). As all of this is done, the spectator is asked if that is his card. He will, of course, say no. Make a magic pass over the card and dramatically turn it over to reveal that it has changed to the correct one.

◆

Here is an effective "quickie" that can be used as an interlude in a card routine when you want to get away from "take-a-card" effects. It uses the same scissors change that is employed in the previous effect (so, of course, it should not be used in the same performance). To do this trick, simply bring a six of any suit to the bottom of the deck with a nine of the same suit directly above it. Move the two cards, in alignment, to the right and, turning the hands, remove them face down, scissored between the right-hand first and second fingers, exactly as in the previous trick. Before you turn the card over and change it, call attention to the fact that it is a six and ask the spectator if he knows anything about "visualization." As he is thinking this over, the card is placed face down on the table and, of course, it has been changed to the nine. Tell the spectator to visualize a large six written on the back of the card. When he says he has done this, slowly turn the face-down card end for end, keeping it, of course, face down on the table. "Now, what does the six look like?" you ask him. If he is awake and intelligent, he will probably say, "A nine." Slowly turn the card over and watch his reaction!

A DOUBLE REVERSE

Now, let's look at a trick using the moves you have already learned, plus a new sleight that must be covered by strong misdirection to produce the effect of two selected cards magically reversing themselves in the deck, one at a time. We will also use a new kind of key card, which can be identified from the edge instead of the face. It is called a "crimp key," "crimp" being the magicians' term for putting a bend in a card so you can easily identify it out of all the others in the pack.

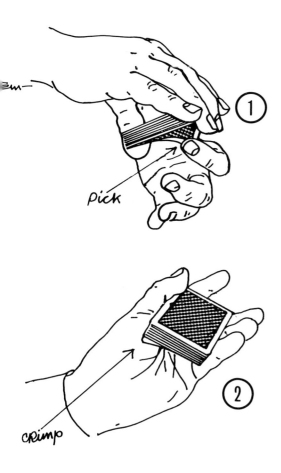

pick

crimp

Hold the face-down pack in the left hand with the thumb over the back of the top card and the four fingers along the right long side. With the right hand square the deck, and as you do this, under cover of the right-hand fingers, the first finger of the right hand crimps (bends slightly, but not so much as to crease or break it) the upper right corner of the bottom card (Figure 1). After this is done, the face-down deck is immediately turned, end for end, and put back in the left hand. This should all be done casually and without undue attention to the deck. After all, the trick has not yet started! From the front of the deck (facing the spectators) everything looks fair. From your angle, at the end of the deck facing you, you can easily see the crimped lower left-hand corner of the bottom card (Figure 2). Even if the deck is cut, putting the key card somewhere in the middle, this crimp is clearly visible. With a little practice, you will see that it is easy to casually cut this crimped card back to the bottom of the deck, as the crimped corner forms a natural break in the apparently squared-up deck. With the crimped card on the bottom, a chosen card can be replaced by means of the Hindu Shuffle, and the key card immediately above it can then be cut back to the bottom of the deck, placing the selected card on top. With a little practice, this handling of the crimp key will become second nature.

1 To begin the trick, have a card selected, shown to several spectators, replaced via the Hindu Shuffle, and, by means of the crimp key, casually cut to the top of the deck.

2 Now a second card is selected, and while all attention (including yours) is focused on its being shown around, a very simple sleight takes place. The first selected card, face down on top of the deck, is reversed onto the bottom of the deck. This is done by the four fingers of the left hand, which pull the card to the right and over the right edge of the deck (under cover of the right hand), reversing it as they do (Figure 3). Remember as this is done that you should be looking at the

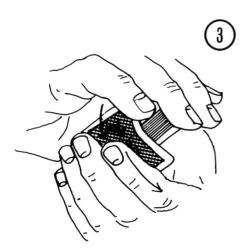

PERFORMING MAGIC

spectator, who is showing his card to the other spectators. *You are not looking at your hands.* This sleight is easily covered, but some practice will be necessary so you can do it *silently.*

3 After the second card is selected, it too is replaced in the pack, again by means of the Hindu Shuffle. The first selected card, now reversed on the bottom of the deck, acts as a key card and goes directly on top of the second selected card. A magic pass is made over the deck and it is spread to show that the first card has miraculously turned face up. This face-up card is cut to the top of the deck and shown.

4 The right-hand fingers now lift off this card *and the face-down card under it* in perfect alignment, just as you learned to lift two cards together in the scissors change.

5 The deck in the left hand is turned over by the left-hand fingers and the cards (apparently only one card) are placed face up on the face-up deck.

6 The deck is now cut, turned face down, and put on the table. The second spectator names his card, and when the deck is spread, it too has magically turned face up.

THE DETECTIVE CARD

Here is an effective, quick card trick that also makes use of the Hindu Shuffle and a key card—but in this case the key card does not end up next to the card, but a known number of cards away. This principle of the "remote key card" is used in many card tricks, and you will no doubt come across it again as your study of card magic continues.

This trick requires a small bit of advance preparation, but it can be done very quickly as you are toying with the deck after another card trick. Look for a seven of any suit and reverse it on to the bottom of the deck. Then count off *six* face-down cards and put them under the seven so that it is now located *face up* and seven cards up from the bottom of the deck. If this is the first of several card tricks you are going to do, this preparation can be done before you pick up the deck.

1 Fan the deck, and have a card selected, being careful not to expose the reversed seven near the bottom of the deck.

2 Now have the card replaced, using the Hindu Shuffle. When the card is replaced, drop all the cards remaining in the right hand on top, exactly as in the standard handling of a bottom key card that you have already learned. *This places the reversed seven just seven cards above the selected one.*

3 Square up the deck after the card has been replaced, and make a magical gesture over it. Spread the deck, either in your hands or on the table, to show the reversed seven.

4 Cut the reversed seven to the top of the deck. That is, place all the cards *above* the reversed seven onto the bottom of the deck.

5 Remove the seven as you explain that it is a very special card. In fact, it is a detective card and has been trained to find other cards. Say that since it is a seven, that means that the selected card is exactly seven cards down in the pack. Allow the spectator to count down in the pack and he will, much to everyone's amazement, find his card to be the seventh down from the top.

COMPUTER ACES

Here is a trick that is effective because the spectator seems to do it all himself, and the patter story ties in with the eternal interest in gambling as well as the contemporary interest in computers. When you have entertained people with a few card tricks, one of the most common remarks will be, "I wouldn't want to play cards with you!", or the question "Do you know how the gamblers control the cards in a game?" Explain that crooked gamblers have a new technique in which they treat the deck as a computer. Under your direction, the spectator programs the deck and carries out the computer program. Without your even touching the cards, he locates the four aces!

This trick takes a small amount of advance preparation. Put the four aces on top of the deck, with any other single card above them. The trick is more effective if you seem to casually shuffle the deck before you begin. You can do this with a riffle shuffle, simply allowing the last five cards of the top pile to fall last on the other pile without interweaving, or you can hold the deck, face up, in your left hand, pull a packet of cards from the *center* with your right hand, and overhand shuffle them onto the left-hand cards. This will show the faces of many different cards as you shuffle, and strongly suggests that the cards are thoroughly mixed. The setup of five cards remains on top of the deck (against your left fingers) and is not disturbed in any way.

1 Explain that to program the computer, the deck must be cut into four fairly even piles. Have the spectator do this, placing the first pile (off the top of the deck) to the right, the next pile to the left of it, and so on. The far right-hand pile will, of course, contain your setup of five cards on the top.

2 Point to the far left-hand pile and explain, "This is pile number one. To program it, we take *one* card from the top, place it on the bottom, and deal a card on each of the other three piles." Make sure the spectator does this. Indicate the next pile to the right and say, "This is pile number two. To program it we take *two* cards from the top, place them on the bottom, and deal a card on each of the other three piles." Now, indicate pile number three (the next one to the right), and have *three* cards transferred from the top to the bottom, and, as before, a card dealt on each of the other piles. At this point, you will have reached the right-hand pile (number four) and it will have (unknown to the spectator) four cards on top of it *followed by the four aces.* Have four cards transferred from the top to the bottom and one card dealt on each of the other three piles. There is now (unknown to the spectator) an ace on top of each pile.

Now is the time to stop and talk a little so that the spectator will not remember *exactly* what he did. "You will remember, we shuffled a deck of cards and *you* cut it into four piles. Just exactly where you cut was *your* choice. You could have cut anywhere. We then turned the deck into a computer and *you* programmed the computer by transferring and dealing cards. Remember, *I* never touched the cards. Here's how a gambler would use the deck as a computer to win the game."

3 Pause dramatically at this point, and turn the aces over on the top of each pile (Figure 1).

CARD THROUGH THE HANDKERCHIEF

For the final effect in this section of the book, I am going to teach you a classic sleight-of-hand card trick. It was a favorite of my father's and of mine, and it is so strong in effect that the great nightclub magician Paul Rosini performed it as one of the features of his act. While the mechanics of the trick are not complicated, it requires plenty of practice and assurance to do well. All I ask is that you give it the time and work that it deserves, before you perform it for an audience.

It requires that you learn to palm a card, and the technique that I will teach you here will prove useful to you in many other tricks as you advance in card magic.

1 Begin the trick by having a card selected and replaced in the deck. Control it to the top by means of the crimped key card and Hindu Shuffle that you learned in previous effects. It will make the trick more effective to give the deck a casual overhand or false riffle shuffle at this point, simply leaving the selected card on top of the deck.

The next step is to palm the card off the top of the deck into the right hand. I will explain to you in great detail how to do this correctly, but, as with any other sleight, you do not want the spectators looking directly at your hands when you do it. It must therefore be covered by proper misdirection, in this case the borrowing of a handkerchief from one of the spectators, or the displaying of your own handkerchief (I prefer to use my own handkerchief for the trick so I can be sure it is completely opaque, and also because it is sometimes difficult to find a clean, unused handkerchief which, for obvious reasons of taste, is what you are looking for). I have my handkerchief folded in my *left* pants pocket.

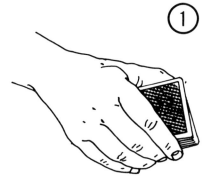

2 After the card has been replaced, and the deck false shuffled, hold it face down with your *right* hand, with all four fingers at the outer end and the right thumb at the end near you (Figure 1). At this point, the right hand almost completely covers the deck. With your left hand, reach into your pants pocket and remove the folded handkerchief (or, if you wish, ask for a borrowed one). Instruct the spectator to unfold the handkerchief and examine it carefully. As this is going on, and with your eyes on the spectator as he looks at the handkerchief, your right hand, *without letting go of the deck,*

places it momentarily into the left hand. The deck is taken in the left hand, with the left thumb at the outer left corner, the left forefinger on the narrow edge away from you, and the other three fingers of the left hand along the right long side of the deck. You are now going to lift the top card into the right palm, and this is done with *only two fingers*—the *left* thumb and the *right* little finger. Here is how it's done: The right little finger presses on the right upper corner of the top card (remember, the right hand is still over the deck), and presses slightly forward and down. This should cause the card to pivot up between the fulcrums of the left thumb and right little finger, and literally pop into the right palm (Figures 2 and 3). There is a definite knack to this that will require considerable practice, but once you learn it, it happens practically instantaneously. My only advice is, stick with it and don't be intimidated by the thought that your hands might be too small. Many magicians with small hands have been successfully palming cards for years. It's not the size of your hand that is important, but the correct technique and misdirection.

Once the card is in the right palm, the right fingers slide to the right along the deck (which is still in the left hand) until they can hold it by the right first finger at the upper right corner and the thumb at the back right corner. At this point, the left hand is removed and the deck is held by its right edge in the right hand (which also has the card palmed). All of this should take less than two seconds and is well covered by the misdirection of the spectator unfolding the handkerchief.

3   Now, say to the spectator, "I'll take the handkerchief, you shuffle the cards." Under the misdirection of the spectator coping with this new request, the following action takes place. The deck, which until now has been held in the right hand and parallel to the floor, is now tilted up into a vertical position so that the thumb is on top and roughly parallel to your body, and the fingers are on the bottom. Check to see that the back of the deck is facing away from you, and the face of the deck is toward you. If you look directly down at the deck, you should be able to see the card palmed in the right hand, but because of the angles, the spectator cannot (Figures 4 and 5).

4   Now, the left hand comes in from the back and takes the deck with the thumb on its right side and the fingers on its left (Figure 6). This is important (a subtlety of the brilliant British magician Pat Page), as the spectators can look through the space formed by the right fingers holding the deck, and this suggests that the right hand (even though it contains a

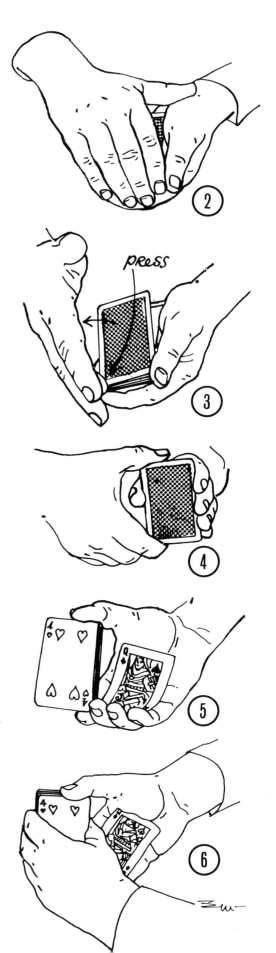

palmed card) is empty. The deck, now taken in the left hand, is handed to the spectator while the right hand (with its palmed card) takes away the handkerchief. Angles must be carefully watched here so that none of the spectators can see the card in your right hand, but there is so much misdirection created in handing the spectator the deck and taking back the handkerchief that strong attention is not likely to be on the hand with the palmed card.

5 As the spectator is shuffling the deck (and remember, you are watching him do this), you casually drape the open handkerchief over your palm-up right hand, which, of course, conceals the palmed card. When the shuffled deck is handed back to you, it is taken in your left hand and placed face up into the handkerchief-covered right hand, directly over the face-up card that is in the right palm. Once the deck is in place, the thumb and fingers of the right hand can grip the deck through the handkerchief with the palmed card in alignment (Figures 7 and 8).

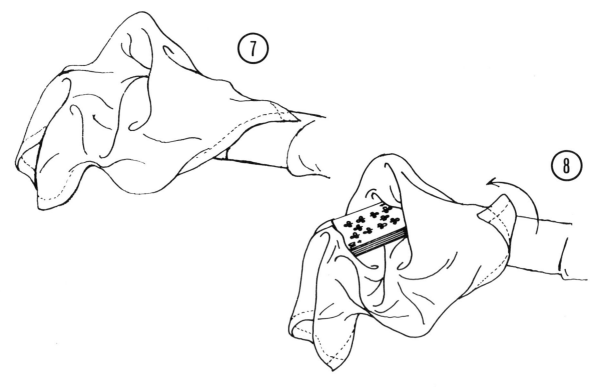

6 Now, with the left hand, take the corner of the handkerchief closest to you and drape it over the deck, covering it completely. The face-up card in your right palm should be fully covered by the draped deck. Make sure that none of the edges of the concealed card show.

7 Now, hold the deck (and the concealed card under it) in place with the right hand, thumb on the top edge of the deck, fingers on the lower edge (Figure 9). With the left thumb and forefinger, grasp the deck at its upper left-hand corner, holding the selected card in place. The right hand now grasps the handkerchief from the front, at the bottom. This automatically folds the handkerchief over the concealed card sufficiently to hold it in place at the back of the wrapped deck (see Figures 10 and 11 for the front and back views of this).

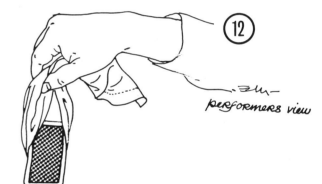

8 Being careful to keep the wrapped card toward you and away from the audience, turn the deck end for end (Figure 12). Gently shake the handkerchief; the card will slide out. When the card is almost entirely exposed, and before it drops to the floor, pull it free with the left hand and display it triumphantly as the right hand displays the still-wrapped deck.

Again, let me emphasize that the palming of the card (as with any "move" in a magic trick) must be done boldly and decisively (with what they used to call in old magic books "address"). If you make it look like a surreptitious and guilt-ridden act, you will almost surely be caught at it.

The Card Through the Handkerchief is one of the classics of card magic. Performed correctly, it is as strong an effect as you could wish for.

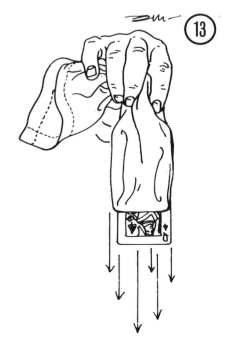

Tricks with Coins

Magicians probably started doing tricks with coins from the time that coins first came into use, between the eighth and the sixth centuries B.C. Almost surely the first coin tricks were vanishes, productions, and transformations adapted from the sleights of the Cups and Balls, that most ancient of magic tricks. We can assume that coin magic predates card magic by almost two thousand years, and that by the time the first coin tricks were introduced, magicians had been manipulating the Cups and Balls for many centuries.

There are both advantages and disadvantages to the practice of coin magic. One important advantage is that coins are almost always available and are familiar objects that audiences understand. As nearly everyone is interested in money, tricks with coins have a built-in fascination. However, coins are not the easiest objects to manipulate, which may be a disadvantage. To become a first-rate coin magician requires a considerable amount of practice. The number of really good coin effects as compared to, say, card tricks is relatively small, and compared to other major branches of magic there has been little written on coin magic (although many books, beginning with Scot's *Discoverie* way back in 1584, have some coin tricks in them). The modern classic work on coin magic is undoubtedly J. B. Bobo's *Modern Coin Magic* (see the Bibliography), and it will tell you nearly all you will ever need to know about the subject.

The great archetypal coin trick, with its roots deep in myth and dreams and wish-fulfillment, is catching coins out of the air. By the mid-nineteenth century, "The Shower of Money" had become a standard feat in the repertoires of Robert-Houdin and others. At the turn of the century, the great coin magician T. Nelson Downs (the King of Koins) created a sensation in vaudeville performing the effect, now billed as "The Miser's Dream," and it remains to this day probably the most popular effect in coin magic.

The basis of all sleight of hand with coins is palming. There are dozens of different ways to palm coins and hundreds of other coin sleights. If you are going to learn a repertoire of coin tricks, it is important that you learn some of the techniques that are right for you. That will require research in books on coin magic and experimentation to see which tricks fit your particular performing style and ability (the Bibliography at the end of this book will describe what I believe to be the best text on the subject).

The first thing to learn is how to palm a coin, and the best palm to learn first is the classic one in which a coin is placed in the palm of the hand and held there by the contraction of the muscles between the base of the thumb and the opposite side of the palm. This palm can, with practice, be executed with either hand. For the purpose of this explanation, we will assume that you will be palming the coin in the right hand.

To begin, hold the coin in the right hand between the two middle fingers and thumb. Turn the hand so that the coin is parallel to the floor, then remove the thumb so the coin remains balanced on the middle two fingers. Now, using these two fingers only, press the coin into the palm where it is gripped between the base of the thumb and the other side of the palm. By contracting the muscles of the palm, the coin should be held firmly in place by its edges. This will take some practice to do smoothly and to place the coin in exactly the right position where it can be gripped firmly and will not fall out of the palm. By relaxing the muscles of the palm, you should be able to drop the coin out of the firm grip at any time.

Once you have mastered getting the coin into the classic palm position, you must now learn to hold the hand in a *natural position* so that it does not appear that a coin is concealed there. You should be able to use that hand normally, picking up objects with the fingers while the coin remains palmed. While all of this takes practice, it is not as difficult as it sounds. A good way to practice holding the coin naturally is to look in the mirror at the way your hand appears when you do not have a coin palmed, then imitate that look when the coin is palmed. Try keeping a coin palmed in your hand as you go through your day's activities, using the hand as you normally would. After a while, concealing a coin will begin to feel natural to you. When the coin is palmed the fingers should not be unnaturally splayed out, but should be naturally curled as they are when the hand is at rest. The hand is supposed to be empty so you cannot stare at it as if you are concealing some guilty secret. If you learn to hold your hand with the palmed coin naturally, and pay no attention to it, the chances are that your audience will also pay no attention to it.

This classic palm is the basic sleight used in the coin routine I will teach you here, but there are a few other simple sleights that you will need to know. I'll take you through them as we go through the routine.

This is a routine embodying several different effects. The moves involved are relatively simple, but once they are practiced and thoroughly mastered they will pave the way for many other coin tricks you may want to learn. The props are very simple: a

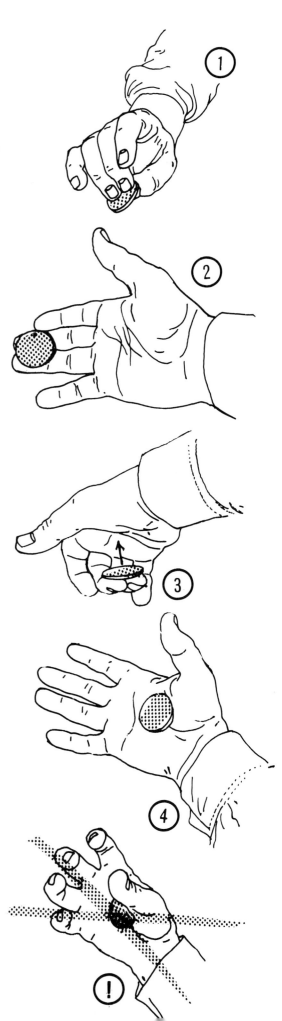

coin (a half dollar is preferable, but a silver dollar can be very effective if your hands are large enough to handle a coin of this size; a quarter can be used, though it is a bit small and not as effective as the larger coins); a handkerchief, any one that is opaque; a patterned man's silk dress handkerchief, of the type that can be purchased in the men's department of any large department store; and finally, a pen or pencil that will be used as a magic wand.

Each effect in this routine flows into the next one and secretly sets up the effect to follow, an excellent example of what magicians call routining. Although this sequence depends as most coin tricks do on palming, the sequence of the routine is cleverly designed to suggest that the magician does not have anything concealed in his palm. As important as understanding the moves themselves is understanding the psychology behind them, which I will explain as we go along. The thinking behind this routine, once it is understood, can be used to create other coin routines that are equally effective.

Here is what the audience sees, or *thinks* they see. The magician shows a handkerchief and a pencil or pen that he explains is really a magic wand, the thing that makes the magic work. To begin, the magic pencil penetrates the handkerchief without leaving a hole—not a coin trick itself, but a surprising effect that sets up a trick to follow. After the pen has penetrated the handkerchief, it is waved over the handkerchief and a coin magically appears. Now the coin penetrates the handkerchief in much the same way that the pen did. The magician explains that, in order for a pen or coin to penetrate a handkerchief, it must be *dematerialized* into invisible molecules and then *rematerialized* on the other side of the handkerchief. He offers to show how a coin can be dematerialized. He places the coin in the left hand and waves the magic pencil over it. When he opens his hand, the coin is still there, but it has become "soft," a condition the magician demonstrates by bending it back and forth. He explains that this softness indicates that the dematerialization has begun. He places the coin back in his left hand and again waves the pencil over it. This time the coin has disappeared completely. The magician now pantomimes the collecting of the "invisible molecules" of the coin out of thin air. The magician gives a spectator the magic pencil and asks him to wave it over his empty left hand. When it is opened, the coin has magically reappeared.

Here is the "preset" for the routine: In your right pocket (pants or jacket, whichever is more convenient), have the handkerchief and the coin. In the inner left pocket of a jacket, or left pocket of a shirt (covered by a jacket), have the pencil or pen which will serve as the magic wand. Explain that you will present "an experiment in materialization and dematerialization." With your right hand reach into your right pocket, classic-palm the coin, and remove the handkerchief, being careful not to "flash" the coin palmed in the right hand. Hand the handkerchief to a spectator to examine and, with the right hand (containing the palmed coin), reach for the pencil in your inner jacket or shirt pocket. As you do this, drop the coin down your left sleeve at the armpit. Keep your left arm bent so that the coin does not fall out. You will, in fact, keep your left arm in this position, with the coin concealed in the sleeve, for the first phase of this routine in which the pencil penetrates the handkerchief. Throughout this first phase it is constantly seen that both of your hands are empty, thus setting up the audience for later phases when your right hand is *not* empty, but conceals the classic-palmed coin. Notice also that at this point in the routine, you do not even mention a coin, and the audience, which does not know what is coming, thinks that you are going to do a trick with a pencil and a handkerchief, which in fact you do. This amazing penetration of a pencil apparently through the center of a handkerchief was marketed many years ago by the late Duke Stern, one of magic's most beloved personalities. It is very simple to do, but looks astounding.

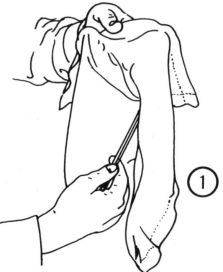

1   Hold the pencil at the bottom with the thumb and first two fingers of the right hand. Have the spectator drape the handkerchief over the pencil. After this is done, the left hand apparently grasps the top of the pencil through the cloth of the handkerchief, *but actually holds only the cloth* as the right fingers tilt the pencil back toward you to a horizontal

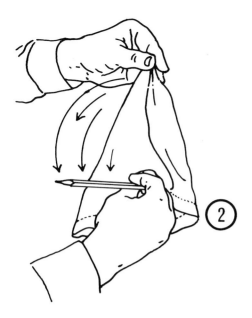

(2)

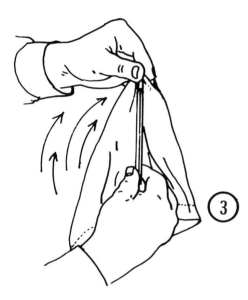

(3)

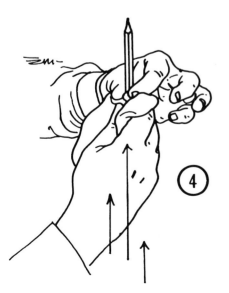

(4)

position and immediately up behind the handkerchief. This move is masked by the handkerchief (which should have its straight edge toward you, *not a corner*), and happens very quickly. As soon as the pencil is behind the handkerchief, the left thumb grips the top of the pencil, holding the entire pencil out of sight behind and within the folds of the handkerchief (Figures 1 through 3). The left fist now closes around the pencil and handkerchief and the right hand reaches underneath, grabbing the pencil through the cloth and pushing straight up. It looks as if the pencil is penetrating straight up through the center of the handkerchief (Figure 4). All of these actions should be done quickly and smoothly and the result will be a visual surprise.

2 After the pencil has "penetrated," immediately hand it to the spectator and open out the handkerchief, showing it spread out between your two hands with the palms of the hands toward the audience. This gives the spectators another chance to see (without your calling specific attention to it) that your hands are empty. A good principle of magic to remember, in this and any other effect, is that it is much more convincing for the spectators to see and deduce for themselves that your hands are empty than for you to *tell* them that they are. Remember also that throughout this pencil-through-handkerchief effect, your left arm has remained in a bent position and the coin has been reposing in the left sleeve.

After you have shown the handkerchief with both hands, let go of the left-hand corner of the handkerchief and look at it as it dangles from the right hand. *As this is done,* drop your left hand naturally to your side and allow the coin to slide out of the sleeve into your hand. Bring your cupped left hand up and immediately drape the handkerchief over it. Remember, at this point, that for all the audience knows the trick is over and they are not looking for anything. Take advantage of this moment of relaxation to cover the left hand simply. Under the handkerchief, work the coin to your left fingertips, wave the magic pencil over it, and replace the pencil in your right pocket with your right hand. Bring your right hand out of your right pocket, clearly empty after having deposited the pencil, and whip the handkerchief away, revealing the coin.

3 Hand the handkerchief to a spectator. Take the coin in your right hand and spin it into the air as you talk about materialization and dematerialization. Offer to repeat the penetration (where an object dematerializes under the handkerchief and rematerializes outside it). Hold the coin in your right

fingertips and have the spectator drape the handkerchief over it. Have him feel the coin through the handkerchief. As you are doing this, arrange the draped handkerchief so that one corner is toward the audience and the opposite corner is along your right arm (Figures 5 and 6). Adjust the coin with your left hand and, as you do so, move your right thumb back and allow your left thumb to move down, making a little well in the handkerchief behind the coin. Move your right thumb forward, grasping the coin, and remove your left thumb so that a small fold of the handkerchief is trapped behind the coin (Figure 7). Offer to show the spectator that the coin is really under the handkerchief. Lift the front corner of the handkerchief, revealing the coin, and, with the left hand, carry the corner of the handkerchief back until it lies directly on top of the corner lying on the right arm (Figure 8). Now comes the secret move, as the left hand lifts *both* corners of the handkerchief and carries them forward to apparently cover the coin again. As this is done, the coin is really transferred outside the handkerchief, but is hidden underneath the folds held by the right finger and thumb (Figure 9).

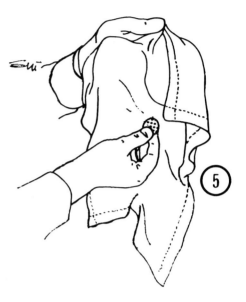

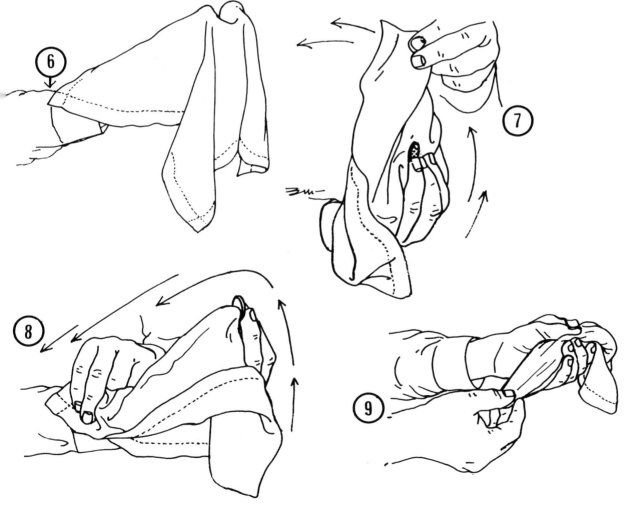

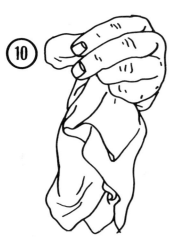

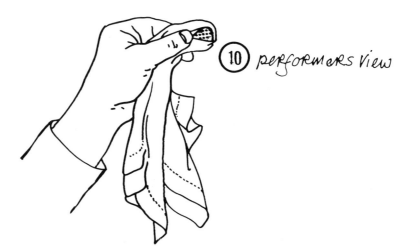

⑩ *performers view*

4 The handkerchief (with the coin hidden behind the fold) is now transferred to the left hand, which grasps it below the coin, being careful not to reveal the coin (Figure 10, front and back views). The right hand reaches into the right pocket and removes the pen, waving it over the handkerchief as the left thumb pushes up on the coin and the coin apparently penetrates right through the center of the handkerchief (Figure 11).

Again show that the handkerchief has no hole in it and place it aside. Replace the pen in your right pocket. This act of taking the pen in and out of the right pocket becomes commonplace to the audience, and the fact that your hands are casually seen to be empty each time conditions them for the deception to follow.

5 Offer to demonstrate how the magic pen makes the coin dematerialize and rematerialize. Show the coin in your right hand, holding it by its edges, with the thumb on top and the coin's bottom edge resting along the first finger (Figure 12). Allow the coin to fall onto the fingers of the right hand and from there into the partially cupped left hand, which is held palm up to receive it. When the coin is in the left fingers, close the left hand. Reach into the right pocket for the magic pen (casually letting your right hand be seen empty as you do so), and wave the pen over the closed left hand.

6 At this point, the spectators will expect that the coin has vanished or changed in some way. Replace the pen in your right pocket and open your left hand, revealing the coin unchanged. Say, "It seems to be getting soft." Now you present an optical illusion that makes it look as if the coin is bending. Hold the coin flat side to the audience in both hands, with fingers in front and thumbs in back (Figure 13). Now, move the hands

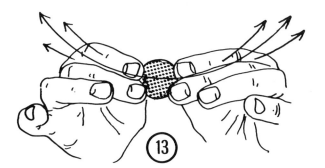

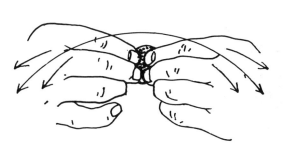

forward and backward in unison, still holding on to the coin.
The coin actually moves slightly (always flat on to the audience),
as the hands holding it bend forward in unison and then bend
back. The illusion (try it in front of a mirror) is that the coin is
bending. Do this about three times. Now you are going to
apparently place the coin back in the left hand. You will do this
in what appears to be exactly the way you did it before, but
actually you will retain the coin in the right hand. Here's how to
do it.

7 Hold the coin, flat side toward the audience, in the right
hand, the thumb on top and the bottom edge resting along
the first finger (all just as you did before). Hold the left
hand palm up (fingers toward the audience) and slightly cupped.
Bring the right hand down so that its fingers lie across (at right
angles to) the fingers of the left hand (Figure 14). At the exact
moment the fingers touch, raise the right thumb and tip the right
hand slightly inward (away from the left fingertips and the
audience). The coin will fall on the right fingers but will be out
of sight of the audience. The right hand continues its movement
as the left fingers close as if retaining the coin (Figure 15). The
right hand (with the coin lying on the fingers) is dropped naturally to the side.

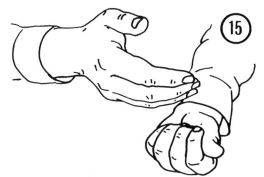

Now the right hand, holding the coin in its naturally curled
fingers, reaches into the right pocket, drops the coin and brings
out the pen. As the pen is waved over the left hand, the right
hand is casually seen to be empty. The pen is replaced in the
pocket and the coin is classic-palmed in the right hand. As the
right hand (with the palmed coin) is removed from the pocket,
the left hand is slowly and dramatically opened and seen to be
empty.

8 Explain that you must gather the dematerialized "invisible molecules" of the coin out of the air. Close the left hand loosely, and with the right hand (classic-palmed coin and back of hand toward the audience), reach into the air for a molecule. Pretend to put it into the left hand and allow the coin to drop into the loosely held left fist (Figure 18). Now, reach for more molecules (this time, of course, the right hand can be casually seen to be empty), and repeat this several times, making sure that the empty right palm is seen. For the first time, reach in your right pocket for the magic pencil, but this time hand it to the spectator to wave over your hand. Dramatically open your left hand (remember this is the big climax of the trick), and show that the "invisible molecules" have "rematerialized" into the coin.

Tricks with Small Objects

THE PENETRATING MATCHES

Some of the most startling effects in magic are ones in which one object seems to visibly penetrate another. A classic effect in this vein is the "Chinese Linking Rings," in which solid metal rings seem to visibly link and unlink, a trick that is hundreds of years old yet remains an impressive part of many magicians' repertoires today. It takes a considerable amount of practice to do the Chinese Rings properly, and also a considerable amount of research among the dozens of different ring routines available, and if you want to perform this trick you will have to find the version that best suits you and your style of working. The Chinese Rings requires special apparatus that must be purchased in a magic store, so it is outside the scope of this book, but I will teach you an impromptu effect using two ordinary matches, either wooden or paper, that, in its own way, is just as amazing as the most effective Chinese Ring routine.

The effect, as in all good tricks, is a simple one. A match held in full view between the fingers of one hand visibly penetrates another match held between the fingers of the other hand. What makes this feat so amazing is that the penetration seems to happen visibly and one match seems to melt through the other. While the effect and the method are very simple, it will require some practice for you to get the knack and the proper timing to make the illusion deceptive.

First we'll learn the easiest way to do the trick. This is very baffling on its own, and by learning to do it that way first, you will develop the proper feel for how the moves must be timed. Then I will show you an even better way to do it that requires considerably more practice, but looks even more impossible to an audience.

1 To begin, get two ordinary wooden matches and hold one horizontally between the thumb and first finger of the left hand, and the other vertically between the thumb and first finger of the right hand (Figure 1). Display the matches freely and tap the vertical match in the right hand against the center of the horizontal match in the left hand a couple of times. Look intently at the horizontal match in the left hand and, as you do this, you subtly adjust the grip on the vertical match in the right hand. Until this point, the matches have been held between thumb and forefinger of each hand. As you begin to move the right-hand match toward the left-hand match for the penetration to take place, the second finger of the right hand moves up so it is parallel to the first finger, and the end of the match is gripped *between* these two fingers. It is now possible to allow the thumb to move away a fraction of an inch, allowing a small gap between the bottom of the match and the ·ball of the thumb while the match remains firmly gripped at the top by the first and second finger (Figure 2). It is through this gap (which should be ¼" or less) that the horizontal match in the left hand passes. This adjustment of the fingers of the right hand and the opening of the gap take place while the right hand moves down and forward, apparently penetrating the horizontal match in the left hand. It is important that the left hand not move, and that all your attention be on the horizontal match it holds. By utilizing the basic principle of physical misdirection—that a large motion will always serve to conceal a smaller motion—the movement of the match in the right hand should not be seen.

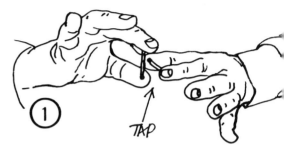

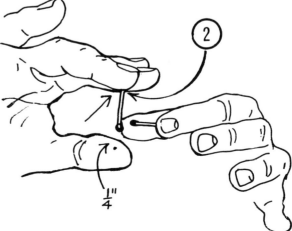

2 As soon as the matches have apparently penetrated, and under the very strong misdirection of the surprise at the visual miracle that has just taken place, the right second finger drops down a fraction of an inch and presses *inward* on the side of the match so that it is pushed into a grip where its top can be held only by the pad of the first finger, with the right thumb, of course, still holding the match at the bottom (Figure 3). At this point, the other three right fingers are moved away and held opened out so the match can be seen to be held only by the thumb and first finger. The hands can now be moved about in different positions showing that the matches are clearly linked, one through the other.

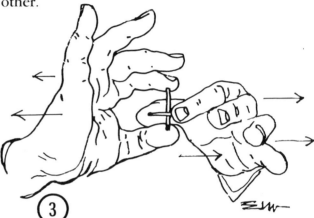

3 To unlink the matches, the left hand returns to its position of holding its match horizontally, and, as the hands are moved apart, the right first and second fingers again momentarily grip the top of the vertical match so that the gap at the thumb end can be opened as the horizontal match passes through. Again, the adjustment is made so that the match is held only between the first finger and thumb, and the matches can then be displayed vertically in each hand, clearly held between thumbs and first fingers (Figure 4), with the other fingers spread wide. Practice these moves well so that the moving right hand with its match swoops down and forward and the left-hand horizontal match passes through the smallest possible gap. By practicing diligently in front of a mirror, you will soon develop the proper timing so that you will fool even yourself.

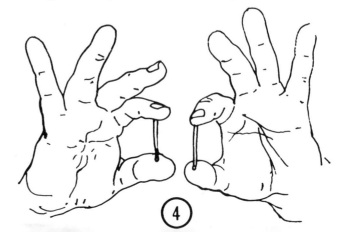

Now let's look at a more difficult but even more effective method for doing the trick. This often works better with paper matches because they are not as heavy as wooden matches, but it can be done with some lightweight wooden matches as well. In this method the horizontal match passes through the gap between the right thumb and the bottom of the vertically held right-hand match, just as in the previous method you learned. The timing is exactly the same. The only difference is that the top end of the right-hand match is not clipped between the right first and second fingers, but instead *sticks* to the pad of the right forefinger so that when that finger is lifted slightly, the match comes with it, and the gap at the bottom thumb-end occurs (Figure 5). For this to work, the *head* end of the right-hand match must be up and the forefinger must be slightly moist. It will also be found that some matches work better than others. For some reason that I do not completely understand, matches with white heads seem to work better for me than ones with colored heads. Only experimentation will tell you whether particular matches work or not. If they do not work well, don't take a risk. Simply use the first method you have learned, which is much surer and less likely to foul up. In fact, the reason I have emphasized learning the other method first is that it will teach you the knack of moving the gap between vertical match and thumb in the right hand over the horizontal match in the left with sureness and accuracy. In the second method, if you do not do this absolutely accurately, the match which is only lightly stuck to the pad of the right forefinger will hit the left-hand match and be knocked off.

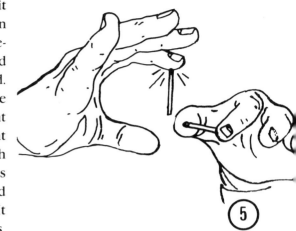

Here are a couple of final tips. A good way to wet the right forefinger is to do it with your tongue as you pretend to cough, and raise your right fist to cover your mouth. No one will pay any attention to this natural action. When the match is first held in the right hand with the head end against the moistened forefinger, it is a good idea to talk for a little to give the match time to stick to the finger as it dries slightly. If you have a chance to rub the head of the match against a hard surface so that it is flattened slightly, it will also stick better. And, the most important tip, practice in front of a mirror until you can do the penetration surely and deceptively. Then, just to be on the safe side, practice some more!

RING ON RIBBON

There are many effects in magic in which an examined ring is put on or taken off a string, ribbon, or stick without apparently passing over the ends. Many methods have been created for doing this, including various sleight-of-hand moves as well as gimmicked rings and, occasionally, gimmicked strings, ribbons, and sticks. This effect is my handling of an ingenious principle, created by that magical genius Stewart James, who gave it the strange name "Sefalaljia." It has the advantage of using borrowed objects, being easy to do, and seeming completely impossible. The effect is simply that a borrowed ring is put on an examined ribbon while the ring and the center of the ribbon are covered with a handkerchief, and while the ends of the ribbon seem to remain in full view. There is a strong psychological reason why the "Sefalaljia" principle is so baffling. It would seem it could only be done by slipping the ring over one end of the ribbon. This does not happen because of the ingenious way in which the ring is fastened to the ribbon. One end of the ribbon is secretly pulled *out* of the ring instead of the ring being slipped over it. Nevertheless, the ring ends up on the ribbon. This pulling of the ribbon out of the ring is cleverly covered by strong misdirection so the audience is never aware that it happens.

To begin, show a length of ribbon (silk if possible) about ½″ wide and approximately four feet long. You also need a handkerchief, either your own or a borrowed one. You can carry these simple props with you and they can be thoroughly examined. It is very important, however, that you borrow the finger ring, because the effect is much stronger if a spectator's obviously ungimmicked ring appears on the ribbon.

It is best to do this effect either seated or standing at a table. Spread the ribbon out horizontally in front of you and place the ring *on top of* the ribbon in about the center (Figure 1), calling attention to the fact that the ring is not on the ribbon and could only be put on by threading it over one of the ends. Cover the ring and the center of the ribbon with the handkerchief, pointing out that the ends of the ribbon protruding beyond either side of the handkerchief remain at all times in full view. Place both of your hands under the handkerchief, where some simple actions take place. You can easily learn to do these entirely by feel and, with a little practice, they can be done quite quickly. Here, step by step, is what happens under the handkerchief.

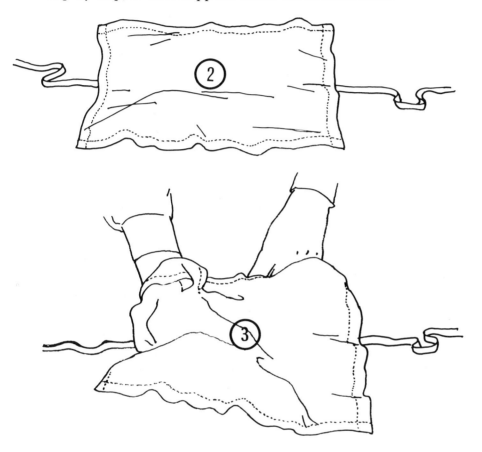

1 With the thumb and first finger of the left hand, hold the ring while the fingers of the right hand pull a loop of the ribbon up through the ring (Figure 4).

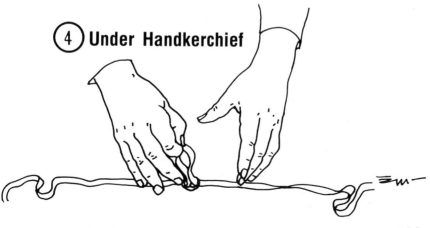

2 Hang the loop of ribbon pulled up through the ring over your right little finger. It is important that this loop remain in position over the little finger during the action that follows, and that it not fall off (Figure 5). If bending the little finger over into the palm helps you to anchor the ribbon securely, do this.

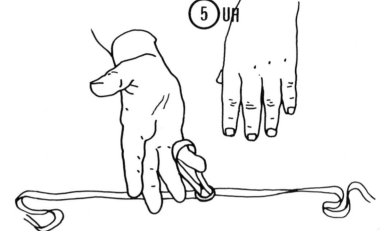

3 Now, using the remaining fingers of the right hand and the fingers of the left hand, grasp one of the lengths of ribbon running through the ring at either side of it so that the ring hangs on the length of ribbon held between your fingers (Figure 6). Tie this ribbon in a simple slip knot *around* the ring (Figure 7). Make sure this knot is pulled tight so it will not come undone prematurely.

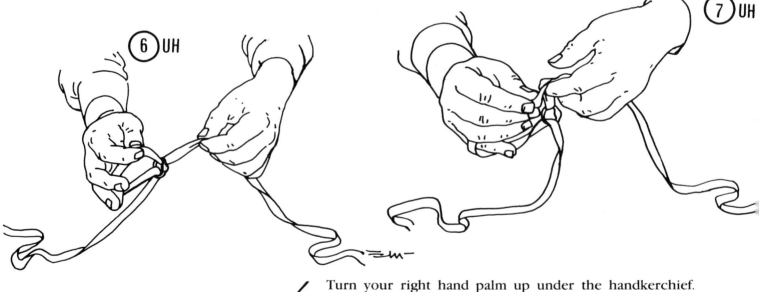

4 Turn your right hand palm up under the handkerchief. Remember that the ribbon remains looped over your right little finger.

5 With the fingers of the right hand, grasp the approximate center of the handkerchief from underneath. Remove your left hand from beneath the handkerchief. Remember that throughout this brief action of tying the ring onto the ribbon, the ends of the ribbon remain in full view at either side of the handkerchief (Figure 8).

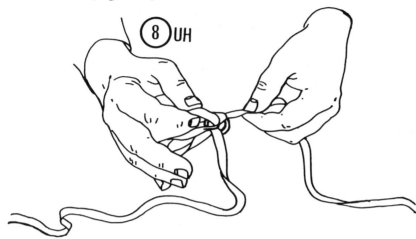

6 Pause for a moment and announce to the audience that "believe it or not, the ring is now *on* the ribbon." With your left hand, pick up the end of the ribbon, which comes out of the left side of the handkerchief, and pull it to the left. Your right hand, with the ribbon around the little finger, and which is also holding on to the handkerchief, remains in position. As the ribbon is pulled out from under the handkerchief, the right end of the ribbon will be pulled through the ring. This happens under the handkerchief, which conceals the fact that your right little finger is looped in the ribbon and causes this to happen. By the time the tied-on ring comes into sight at the left of the handkerchief, the right end of the ribbon should be pulled completely through it (Figure 9). Check to make sure that this has happened. This must all be done quite quickly, and your attention should be on the ring as it appears. As soon as the ring appears, move the right hand, holding on to the handkerchief, to the right, and place the handkerchief aside.

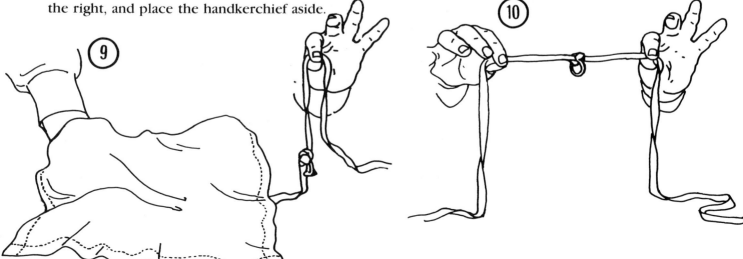

What has actually happened is that, for a brief instant, one end of the ribbon has gone out of sight under the handkerchief, but the misdirection is such that the spectators never notice this. Remember that at the point when the deception takes place, and the end of the looped ribbon is pulled out of the ring, the audience thinks the trick is already over. Why? Because you have told them so! Therefore, their attention is relaxed, and they are looking at the ring (*not* at the other end of the ribbon, which momentarily goes out of sight) because *you* are looking at the ring. The deed is done, and the deception is accomplished before anyone has a chance to notice it.

7 As you display the ribbon in your left hand, with the ring tied to it, many people will not believe that the ring is actually on the ribbon, and their reaction may be one of skepticism. At this point, you perform the climax of the trick and it happens visibly, not under the handkerchief. Hand one end of the ribbon to a spectator as you hold the other end, and both of you pull. The slip knot holding the ring will pop out, and there will be the ring, actually threaded on the ribbon, while both ends are held. Pause for the miracle to sink in, and acknowledge your well-earned applause.

MAGIC AT THE TABLE

Here is a baffling routine containing many surprises, one that is best performed at the table when the conditions are right. It involves a coin, a paper napkin, and a salt (or pepper) shaker. We will assume that you are seated at the table with people across from you, and, possibly, at your sides (in which case, you must be more careful to maintain the proper "angles," as we shall see).

In this routine, a coin vanishes from the magician's hand after it is covered with a paper napkin. The coin reappears under a salt shaker. Then the magician attempts to make the coin disappear from under the napkin-covered salt shaker and fails, but the salt shaker disappears instead! The salt shaker is reproduced from under the performer's jacket, and a little salt is shaken on the coin, finally making it disappear completely.

This routine is an excellent example of how a very old magic technique can be brought up to date and adapted to modern-day performing conditions. In many of the magic books of almost a century ago, various tricks worked by means of what was known as a "servante." This was a bag or tray, usually concealed behind a draped table (most magicians used draped tables in those Victorian times, and oddly enough some even do today), or on the back of a solid-backed or draped chair. Objects were, unknown to the audience, dropped into and picked up from the servante under cover of appropriate misdirection. For a considerable period of time, the loads in such tricks as the Cups and Balls were picked up from a servante; most of today's performers use their pockets. In the Middle Ages and after, many conjurors wore a special apron with pockets called a *gibecière*, a sort of portable servante, and for over half a century, some magicians produced near-miracles by means of a special servante worn secretly under the coat (known to magicians as a "topit"), a device that is currently experiencing a renaissance among close-up workers. It remained for a charming Sicilian-born magician named Slydini (real name: Quintino Marucci), who is now in his mid-eighties but continues to entertain and astound audiences with his amazing skill, to invent (or, probably, re-invent) a technique in which the performer is seated and uses his lap as a natural servante. This technique of secretly dropping things in the lap and, often, picking them up again later is known to magicians as "lapping." When the magician's performing circumstance involves his being seated at a table, it is a powerful tool of deception.

This table routine involves lapping in several places, but as you will see, each time an object is dropped into or retrieved from the lap, it is covered by strong misdirection.

This trick, like many others, requires a "preset," but in this case, it is a very simple one. It merely requires that you place a coin, of which you have a duplicate, under a salt shaker. This can be done sometime before the trick begins, and since the audience does not know what is coming, or even that a salt shaker is involved in the trick, this should be easy to do. It is best to do this trick with as large a coin as will conveniently fit under the shaker. A nickel will do, but if the bottom of the shaker is large enough a quarter is even better.

1 To begin, show a coin and a paper napkin, explaining that you will perform an amazing trick with them. Unfold the napkin and lay it on the table so that one corner overlaps the edge of the table just above your lap. Drop the coin, to display it, in the middle of the napkin. Pick it up in your right hand and pretend to place it in your left hand. Use the false transfer that you previously learned in the stand-up coin routine (page 193). Look intently at your left hand (which is supposed to contain the coin), and with the right hand (which really contains the coin) reach for the corner of the napkin that overlaps the edge of the table toward you. As you do this, relax your fingers

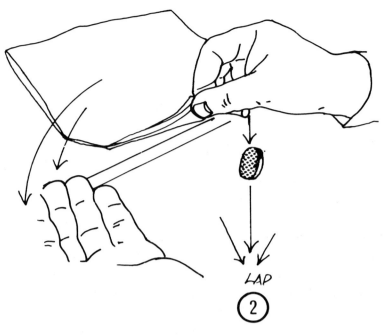

LAP

②

and allow the coin to drop into your lap (Figure 2). Be sure to have your knees tightly together so that the coin does not drop *through* your lap and onto the floor.

2 Place the paper napkin over your left hand and make a few passes over it with the right hand, which is, incidentally, seen to be empty. Ask a spectator to remove the paper napkin and slowly open your left hand, showing it empty. As this happens, look intently at your left hand and casually allow your right hand to drop into your lap. Pick up the coin in your lap and place it on the chair under your right leg (Figure 3). This is to avoid having other objects that will later be dropped into your lap hit the coin and make a noise. This moving of the coin is easily accomplished if it is just done casually. There is plenty of action on the table to attract the spectators' attention. When the fact that the coin has vanished has sunk in, remove your right hand from your lap (you have, by now, ditched the coin), and lift the salt shaker, revealing the duplicate coin that you planted there earlier.

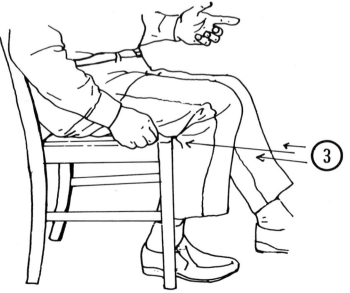

③

3 Explain that you will make the coin disappear while it is under the covered salt shaker. Shape the paper napkin over the shaker and place it over the coin. Make some passes over the shaker, and lift it off the coin with the right hand, holding the shaker under the covering napkin. As you remove the shaker, move it back toward you, almost but not quite to the edge of the table, just over your lap. Act amazed that the coin did not vanish, and replace the covered shaker over it. Again make the passes, and lift off the covered shaker. The coin is still there. Pick it up with the left hand and look at it quizzically, saying something like, "That's funny, it's supposed to disappear" (say something even more clever, if you can think of it). At *exactly the same moment* you pick up the coin, let the covered shaker in the right hand move just beyond the edge of the table. By relaxing your grip just slightly, the shaker will drop noiselessly into your lap, but the napkin covering it will retain the shape of the shaker (Figure 4). Cover the coin with the napkin (remember, the audience sees the shape of the shaker and thinks it is under the napkin). Make a pass over the coin again and slam your left hand down on the shape of the shaker, smashing the napkin flat on the table (Figure 5). Say, "If the coin won't vanish, we'll make the shaker disappear." Under cover of the surprise, let your right hand drop to your lap, and pick up the shaker with its end held in your curled fingers, and its length concealed by the palm.

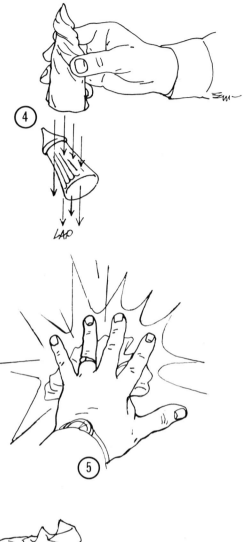

4 Rest this hand lightly on the edge of the table, keeping the shaker concealed (Figure 6). At the same time, with the left hand, lift the napkin, revealing the coin which *still* has not vanished. Pick up the coin with the left hand and toss it a couple of inches into the air, catching it in the left hand, which closes around it. Turn the left hand over so it is back-up and as you do so, work the coin down so it is held (unseen by the audience) between the finger and the heel of the hand. Rest the hand lightly on the table, about a foot from the edge. With your right hand (holding the concealed shaker), quickly reach under the left side of your jacket, apparently removing the shaker. Move the right hand to place the shaker down at approximately the same place as occupied by the left hand. As this happens, the left hand moves out of the way to the table edge, where the coin clipped between the fingers and heel of the hand is dropped into the lap. As soon as this happens, the left hand immediately moves forward and rests on the table. The right hand then picks up the shaker and shakes a little salt on the left hand, which then dramatically opens to show that the coin has finally vanished.

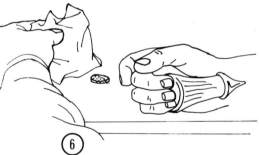

The Double Ropes: An Exploration of a Classic Magic Principle

In the art of magic the basic effects are few (a vanish is a vanish whether a coin or an elephant disappears), but the principles by which the effects are accomplished are many. In a given magic performance, we may see many variations of the basic effect. Many different things may appear and disappear and be transformed. As long as the objects used, the principles, and the presentation of the mystery are varied, they will appear to the audience as different tricks. The really important principles of magic are, as we have seen, psychological. The rest are mechanical and, of these, the best are the simplest and most foolproof in their working.

In this final section, I will show you how one basic effect (that of a magical penetration of solid through solid) can be presented in many different guises, and appear to an audience as entirely different tricks. In each of these variations, different props and presentations are used, but the basic effect remains the same, and so does the simple but very clever mechanical principle by which it is accomplished. It would not be a good idea in the course of one performance to do several tricks all depending on exactly the same principle, but, as you will discover as you progress in the study of magic, there are many methods by which an effect can be performed.

The basic principle we will examine can be adapted to many different tricks, from close-up mysteries to stage illusions.

No one knows what early magic genius invented the trick that has become popularly known as "My Grandmother's Necklace," but we do know that it was probably a standard part of the conjuror's repertoire, perhaps for centuries, by the time it was explained in Scot's *Discoverie of Witchcraft* (1584). The book explains, "a notable feate of fast or loose; namelie, to pull three beadstones from off a cord, while you hold fast the ends thereof, without removing of your hand." Both this description of the trick and the illustration that accompanies it leave out one important fact, and it is this that makes the trick work. The beads are not removed "from off a cord," but, in fact, off *two* cords. Not only that, but they are tied on by a single knot in one of the cords. These factors, which would seem to make the trick more difficult, are really the basis for the deception. The explanation of the secret in the *Discoverie* makes it very clear that two cords are used. By 1722, Henry Dean's *The Whole Art of Legerdemain, or Hocus Pocus in Perfection* titles the trick "How to take Three Button Moulds off Two Strings," but the illustration (obviously patterned after the one in Scot) shows the button on *one* string.

By 1876, when Professor Hoffmann wrote his classic *Modern Magic*, we see clearly not only the two strings, but additionally how the beads are tied on by making a knot with two ends of the cords run through them. The trick has been explained in literally hundreds of magic books and included in magic sets over the centuries under such varied names as "The Pater Noster Beads," "Grandmother's Rosary," "The String and Corals," "The Ropes and Rings," "The Cords of Phantasia," and many others. In all cases, the basic effect is the same. Objects such as beads and rings threaded on cords, or silk handkerchiefs tied to the cords, magically penetrate them and come free. Sometimes, by means of the same extremely clever principle, the cords penetrate a coat, the back of a chair, or even a human body. Some magic historians believe that the origin of this trick was probably with ancient Hindu magicians, who performed it with tapes and a wooden ball, and that it eventually passed in only slightly altered form into the hands of medieval European magicians, from whom it has come down to magicians of the present day.

The secret of the trick is this: the two tapes, ropes, or strings used are doubled in the middle and held together in some way, often by a loop or knot, or tied together by thread, middle to middle (Figure 1). This fact is concealed from the audience, which believes that the tapes or ropes run side by side. The place

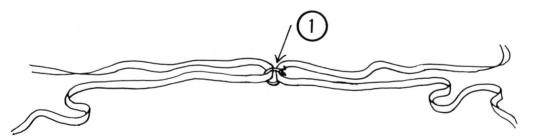

where the middles of the two looped-over ropes are joined is concealed in some way, such as having a handkerchief tied around it (Figure 2) or, as in the original version, having it be inside a bead or wooden ball that has a hole run through it. When a *single* (not a *double*) knot is tied using one side of each rope

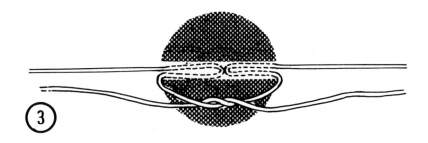

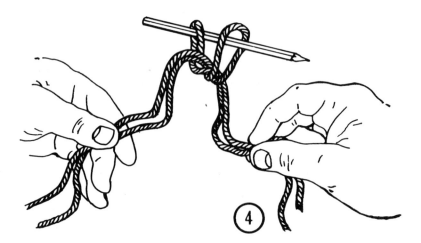

(Figure 3) the looped ropes will naturally straighten when the thread or other device holding them middle to middle is released. The object threaded or tied on seems to penetrate the double cords. After the object or objects have seemingly penetrated the knotted cords, the magician is left with two cords running parallel to one another with no knots or breaks in them. In most versions of the effect, they can be thoroughly examined by the audience (as can the objects that have penetrated the cords) without the audience being any the wiser.

There are two basic ways of handling the two cords so that they are really looped middle to middle while the audience mistakenly believes them to be running parallel to one another. The simplest way is to tie the two ropes to a stick, wand, or pencil. Here is a simple close-up effect that depends on that method: Show two strings, ribbons, or shoelaces, and tie them around a pencil that you have borrowed from a member of your audience. To tie the knot around the pencil, you must take care to do it in the correct way. Drape both cords over the stick and, holding both strands of one cord in one hand, and both strands of the other cord in the other hand, tie a single knot (Figure 4). Do not make the mistake of holding one strand from each rope in each hand and tying the knot, as then the trick will not work.

After the pencil is tied on, hand the two ends coming from one side of the knot to one spectator to hold, and the other two ends to another spectator (Figure 5). Note that if, at this point, you were to pull the pencil out of the knot, each spectator would be left holding one complete cord doubled over at the center. Fortunately, the spectators will not have analyzed the tying of the knot (which should be done casually and without calling undue attention to it). Now, borrow several finger rings and bracelets from various members of the audience and thread them onto the cord at each side of the pencil (Figure 6). Draw these along the

cord until they are right up against the pencil. Now ask each spectator to give you *one* of the cords he is holding, and, with these two ends, tie a *single* knot (Figure 7). To the spectator, this tying of an additional knot seems to secure the rings and bracelets even more tightly onto the cords. What it actually does is exchange the ends of the doubled-over cords so that, when the knot that holds them center to center is pulled out, they will run parallel to one another. Slowly pull out the pencil and hold your other hand under the seemingly knotted-on rings and bracelets. Have the spectators pull on their ends and the jewelry will

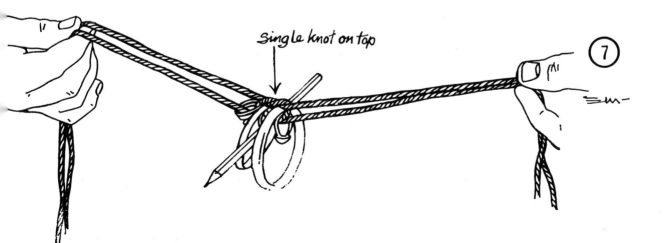

Single knot on top

apparently penetrate the knotted cord, leaving the two cords running parallel to one another between the two spectators (Figure 8).

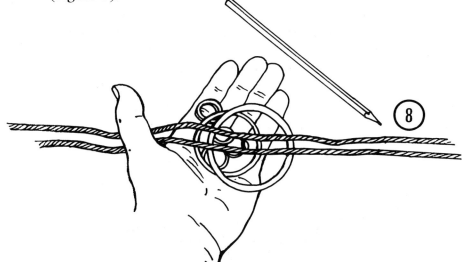

This effective close-up trick utilizes the double-rope principle in its simplest form. Now let's see how it can be "dressed up" as a more elaborate effect for stage or platform presentation.

One of the most obvious ways to make the trick more flashy is to increase the size of the objects used. Instead of strings and rings and a pencil, you can use a wand or a Chinese fan and tie ropes or colorful ribbons around them. Be sure, if you are using ribbons, that both are of the same color or else it will become obvious that they are center to center as they are tied around the wand or fan. Wooden embroidery hoops, painted different colors, can be threaded on the ropes, and different-colored silk handkerchiefs can be tied on at intervals. Note that even though these handkerchiefs are tied securely around the double ropes, at the climax of the trick, when the ropes are straightened out, they will pull through the knots and the handkerchiefs will come free. This additional factor of things being *tied*, and not just threaded, on the ropes adds to the mystery. At the end of the effect, after the single knot is tied, remove the wand and wave it over the knotted-on objects as they come free or open the Oriental fan and fan the objects as the magic happens.

The great Dante (1882–1955) turned this simple but effective trick into a charming feature of his big show, which contained scores of large stage illusions. Dante called his presentation "The Lazy Magician." In it he sat center stage in a chair, his legs crossed, puffing on a cigar, his top hat tilted rakishly on his head. The two long ropes stretched all the way across the stage and were held at the ends by two glamorous women assistants. At the center the ropes were tied by Dante around his black cane with a silver head. One by one, other women assistants brought the magician large silk scarves matching the color of their evening dresses. Rather than move to different areas of the stage to tie the scarves on the rope, Dante, who was obviously too lazy to move from his comfortable chair, indicated with an imperious gesture that the girls holding the ends should move the rope to the proper position. Each girl handed Dante a scarf as he flirtatiously ogled her and puffed his cigar as the orchestra played *Smoke Gets in Your Eyes.* At the end of the effect, when the silks penetrated the ropes, they were caught in his opera hat and the cane around which the ropes were tied also vanished. The Vanishing Cane is a standard trick available at magic dealers, but here a master magician integrated it into a charming and original presentation of a classic effect. The trick was simply the ancient "Grandmother's Necklace," but Dante, through his showmanship, made it into one of the highlights of his big show.

The presentational variations of this trick are limited only by your imagination, but, without going into great detail, let me suggest two others that may get you thinking in different directions. Suppose you find (or you can make it yourself if you are handy with tools) a fancy jewel chest of such a size that a wand can fit through holes in the narrow ends, and ropes can be strung through two holes in the other sides. You can borrow women's bracelets or perhaps wristwatches (those with closed bands, like expansion bands, would be best), and string them on the cords. Then place the wand, with the ropes tied to it, into the chest so it protrudes from either end. Run the ropes through the holes in the sides, close and latch the chest, and tie the single knot over the top of the chest (Figure 9). As a climax, the chest and its contents penetrate the ropes and then the chest is opened and taken to each spectator as they remove their jewelry from it.

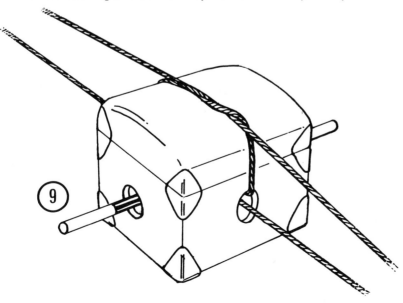

Another idea is to use a wooden coathanger instead of a wand and tie the ropes around one end of it. Then hang a coat borrowed from a spectator on the hanger, running the ropes down the sleeves. Tie the single knot over the coat. Remove the hanger and the coat miraculously penetrates the ropes (Figure 10).

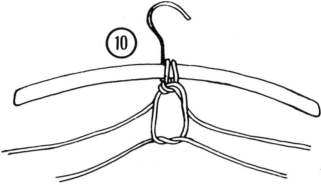

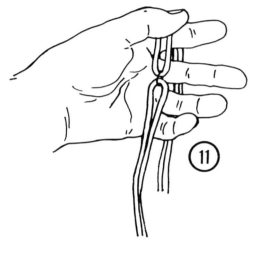

Now that you are thinking about different presentations of this effect, let's look at ways in which we could alter the method slightly to eliminate having to tie the ropes around a stick or other object.

The simplest way to avoid the necessity of tying the ropes around something is to tie them to each other. For example, the ropes can be tied at their midpoint with some lightweight, easily-broken thread the same color as the ropes or ribbons. The ropes can be displayed (though, of course, they cannot be separated as in the previous method), and, under cover of gathering them up, can be arranged so that they are doubled back but tied together at their midpoint. The point where they are tied together can be hidden in the hand (Figure 11). The ropes can be displayed and a silk handkerchief can be tied around just to the side where the tied-together midpoints are concealed in the hand (Figure 12).

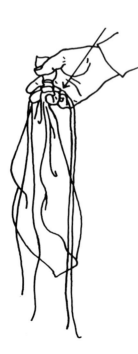

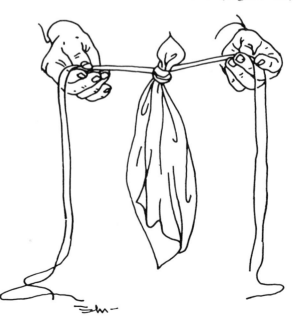

After this is done, the silk handkerchief can be moved over to cover the junction, which is now *inside* the knot of the handkerchief. Now, as many other handkerchiefs as desired can be tied onto the double ropes at either side of the center one that conceals where they are tied together. If you wish, a borrowed jacket can be threaded on with the double ropes running through the sleeves, and the single knot, with one rope from each side, tied on top of everything. At this point, you can reach inside the jacket, and (breaking the thread) magically remove the tied-on handkerchiefs. Then, for a grand climax, show that the jacket itself has magically penetrated the ropes.

A very pretty presentational idea is to get a tube about ten inches long and big enough in diameter to allow the two ropes to be easily threaded through it. Tie on the silk handkerchief, hiding the place where the doubled-back ropes are tied together, as in the previous version. Then lower the ropes into the tube until the silk handkerchief is inside. Have the two ends of the rope held by two spectators, and the single knot tied on top (Figure 13).

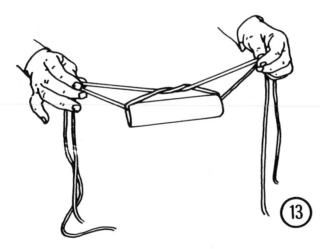

Now, the tube, with the handkerchief inside, penetrates the ropes. Place one end of the tube to your lips and blow the handkerchief high into the air, catching it in the other hand as it descends (Figure 14). You are thus in a position for a perfect applause

cue—the silk handkerchief in one hand, the tube in the other, and the two ropes, which they have mysteriously penetrated, stretched out in front of you. When you are performing tricks for a larger audience, and not just for a few friends, it's a good idea to plan for moments at the climax of your tricks that will suggest, in a reasonably subtle way, that it's time to applaud. This trick supplies an excellent example of such a moment.

◆

As you can see, an imaginative performer can create many different effects using the double rope principle. It can even be used to create some effective stage illusions that can almost be carried in one's pocket (instead of requiring the hundreds of pounds of equipment that stage illusions usually need). An effective patter theme is stating that you are going to perform the world-famous feat of cutting a woman in two. Explain that most magicians use a saw for this effect, but you prefer a less bloody version and will use two ropes. Invite a woman up on the stage, and two men to hold the ropes. Show the ropes (they are secretly tied together with thread at the center) and gather them up so that they are doubled over, center to center, where the thread ties them together, but conceal this in your hand. Now, stretch the ropes out *behind* the woman, giving two ends to each of the men. Have the men standing slightly forward ("downstage" in theatre terminology) of the woman so that they cannot see the tied-together centers of the ropes that are behind her and hidden by her body. To the audience it simply appears that the woman is standing center stage with two ropes, the ends of which are held by two men, stretched out behind her (Figure 15). Now, taking

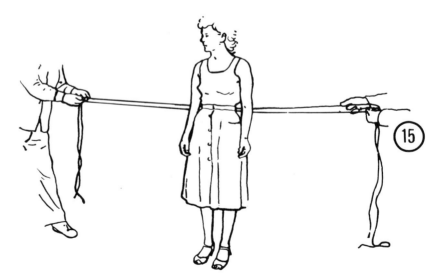

PERFORMING MAGIC

one end from each man, tie a knot in front of her and return the ends of the rope to the two men (Figure 16). Now is the time for a big buildup. Ask the woman if she has ever been cut in half before. The chances are that she has not. Caution the men to hold their ropes tightly and explain that, if anything goes wrong, they will be held responsible. Ask the woman if she is ready. Ask the men if they are ready. Tell them that on the count of three, they should pull hard on their ropes. Count slowly and impressively, one, two, three, and when they pull, the ropes should appear to pass right through the woman and end up stretched parallel in front of her. As in most magic tricks, the effectiveness is largely dependent on the showmanship with which it is done. Presented effectively, any of these tricks using the venerable double rope principle can be a high point of a magic act. Hundreds of years after its invention, grandmother's ancient necklace lives on in countless modern forms and remains one of magic's most clever and baffling principles.

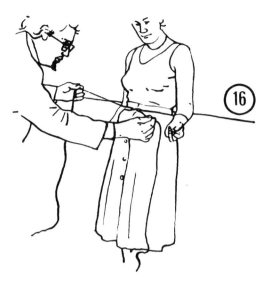

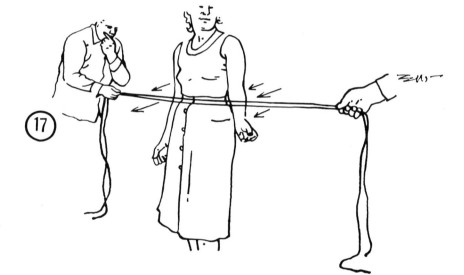

Final Thoughts and Secrets

As you progress in magic as a hobby, or even as a means of entertaining the paying public, you will probably discover that you want to specialize. You may find that the kind of magic that fits your particular personality is a silent manipulative act, or an act of stage magic, or even illusions. You may find that comedy magic or mentalism (in which you apparently read the minds of your audience) or children's entertainment are the particular approaches that work best for you. The only way you will determine this is by starting on a modest level, learning to do a few tricks well, and trying different approaches until you find the ones that fit your personality. The final section of this book, with the Appendix and Bibliography, will tell you where to learn more from books and magazines and from magic organizations. As you learn more about the specialized areas of magic, and perhaps decide to concentrate on one or more of them, you will discover that the basic principles taught you in this book apply to all of them, and that, as you move on, your biggest concern will be to find the tricks and presentations that suit you best.

As you read about new magic effects in magazines and catalogues, and ponder whether they are worth an investment of your time and money, you will occasionally come across seductive phrases like "self-working" and "no skill required." Do not be seduced by these. To present any effect well requires a considerable amount of work, and that work should be part of the joy of mastering the trick. Depending upon the trick, this work may be expended in different areas. In close-up magic or manipulative sleight of hand, the work may have to be put in on mastering the moves required, whereas in an illusion show the same time and effort must be expended on learning the stagecraft that makes the deception work. In mentalism, which at its best depends on neither elaborate stagecraft nor difficult sleight of hand, just as much work must be put in on mastering the psychological subtleties and the exact spoken words that will convince the spectators that you are reading their innermost thoughts. In the art of deception, as in any other endeavor, the old adage holds that "there is no free lunch." Somewhere along the line, the time and effort must be put in to make the magical presentation effective—so never believe anyone who tells you that this work is not necessary or that it takes less practice and skill to perform a stage illusion or mental effect than it does a sleight-of-hand trick. It just isn't so! Just as there is no trick whose weak points need not be concealed by proper misdirection, so there is no "self-working" trick. To present any trick with the proper deception and entertainment value, work is the key ingredient.

Once you have put in the requisite work to learn to present a trick correctly, there are some other things you should do (and not do) to make sure that your magic will be presented with its maximum effectiveness.

Do protect the secrets of how the tricks work. Much of the power of magic as an entertainment form lies in the fact that it fools people. Your audience does not know what is going to happen next in your performance, and by *never* telling them in advance what you are going to do (so that they know what to look for), and by *never* repeating a trick in the same way (so that the second time around the audience can analyze the action and perhaps discover the method), you have a considerable advantage over them. By resisting (in a pleasant and non-superior way) their pleas to tell them "how it's done" you will protect your prestige as a performer and not spoil the audience's sense of wonder. You will discover that when spectators learn how a trick is done, they are invariably disappointed and give you far less credit for skill than you should receive.

Don't bore people with your magic. Only perform tricks when you are asked (and preferably asked more than once). Never force people to watch a trick when, perhaps, they are not in the mood to see one.

Do try to cultivate an amusing line of patter to go with your tricks. This does not mean that you must learn the words by rote, but you should have a general idea of what you are going to say. What you do say should advance the plot of the trick without being redundant. Nothing is more ridiculous than a performer holding up a silk handkerchief (which everyone can plainly see) and saying, "Here I have a silk handkerchief." Avoid telling the audience things they are intelligent enough to see for themselves.

Don't try to be funny and tell jokes along with your magic if you are not naturally funny. If you are naturally funny, and your purpose is to make audiences laugh by telling them jokes, then forget the magic and become a comedian. (As a profession, you may even find that it pays better.) You will discover, however, that magic well performed will almost always elicit laughter. The audience is not laughing *at* the magician, but rather because they are surprised and amazed. An old magic book had a wonderful term for this, "laughter born of bewilderment," and even if you are not a natural comedian, you can expect a lot of this wonderful laughter in the course of your performance.

Do try, when performing magic, to quit while you are ahead. A few tricks done well and leaving the audience wanting more are far more effective than doing so many tricks that your audience becomes bored. In magic, as in many other artistic endeavors, less is more.

Don't become so fascinated by the clever working of a trick that you lose track of its entertainment value. Some tricks that magicians love to perform (because they are so ingenious) are very boring to audiences.

Do study the work of other good magicians in live performances and on television and try to analyze why they are effective. This does not mean that you should copy the other performer's patter or tricks, but that you should try to find out *why* he or she is good and how you can apply that to your own personal approach to performing.

Don't try to be something that you are not. The teenage magician who introduces an effect with patter like, "While traveling through the Orient, I chanced upon a most amazing legend," is cultivating laughter from his audience, but for all the wrong reasons. They will surely be laughing *at* him and not *with* him.

Do treat magic with the respect that it deserves. The greatest disservice you can do to magic is to perform it badly, to bore people with it and to present it with a superior attitude that is sure to be more infuriating then entertaining. If you are good to magic, it will be good to you. For me and my father before me, it has not only provided a rewarding livelihood and a fascinating lifetime study, but also opened doors to many wonderful friendships with people all over the world. Entertaining people and making them happy is a heady experience. It is a form of giving that in return gives back even more to you. I can think of no better way of doing that than through magic.

Xmas 1947

To My Son Harry
I hope he grows up to be a better man than I
Harry Blackstone

(Opposite page) **Harry Blackstone, Sr., 1961.**

THE GREAT MAGIC BOOKS: AN ANNOTATED BIBLIOGRAPHY

In a field in which there are literally thousands of books in print and dozens of books and pamphlets published each month, it is obviously a difficult task to choose a list of the greatest books on magic. Naturally, such a choice must be a very personal and subjective one. In order to keep the list to manageable size, I have set certain limitations on the kinds of books chosen. First, the list is limited to books in the English language, and second, they are all books of general interest. There are hundreds of books on specific magicians, their histories, and their tricks. Many of them are excellent and offer valuable insights into how these particular performers worked and achieved their success. To dip into this fascinating fund of information on magic would result in a list many times longer than this.

While most bibliographies are listed alphabetically by author, this very informal one is divided into specific areas of interest. Within each of these areas, the books are listed chronologically so that, if they are studied in order, they will give an indication of the development of each facet of the conjuror's art. Most of the books listed are readily available in new editions and can be found through the magic dealers listed in this book. A few are very rare but sometimes can be found in public libraries or in the libraries of magic organizations such as the Academy of Magical Arts (at The Magic Castle in Hollywood) or The Magic Circle in London.

I THE CLASSICS

The first section of the bibliography is certainly the least subjective one, for these books, spanning a period of nearly three centuries, are the ones that shaped the art of magic. Most magicians and magic historians would, I believe, be in agreement about most of them, though some would probably have some particular favorite that they would like to see on the list, perhaps in the place of some book that is included.

The Discoverie of Witchcraft, Reginald Scot, 1584.

This is the first book in the English language to describe the tricks of the conjurors, many of which are still being performed today. All the early books on magic that followed were based, to a large degree, on Scot. The real purpose of the book was to prove that witches did not exist. In an age when the execution of people accused of witchcraft was a popular pastime, this was a highly controversial thesis and, in fact, King James found the view so heretical that he ordered all copies of the book burned. A few copies survived and formed the basis of the many editions that have been passed down to the present day. Though only a small part of the book is devoted to the art of the magician, and it may be slow reading because it is written in early English, it is still important because it contains the roots of the magician's art. It is available in an inexpensive paperback edition, published by Dover Publications, that is an unabridged republication of the 1930 edition with an introduction by Montague Summers.

The Secrets of Conjuring and Magic (Les Secrets de la Prestidigitation et de la Magie), Jean-Eugène Robert-Houdin, 1868; English translation by Professor Hoffman (Angelo John Lewis), 1878.

Considered by many to be the greatest general text on the principles of conjuring ever written, this brilliant book is as vital today as it was when it was first published over a century ago. This book has recently been reprinted in a facsimile edition by Magico, New York.

Modern Magic, Professor Hoffman, 1876.

The great classic of Victorian magic that, along with Robert-Houdin's *Secrets of Conjuring and Magic,* remains one of the two most influential magic books of all time. It has been through at least eighteen editions, the latest in paperback by Dover Books with a new introduction by Charles Reynolds. Along with its two sequels, *More Magic* (1890) and *Later Magic* (1904), it exhaustively documents the magic of the day.

Sleight of Hand, Edwin T. Sachs, 1877.

A classic manual of general magic that, despite its somewhat misleading title, does not concentrate only on sleight of hand but also on stage magic with apparatus. This is another work that can be considered a foundation of contemporary magic; the Fleming edition (1953) is still available through magic dealers.

The Modern Conjuror, G. Lang Neil, 1903.

This book, which concentrates on small magic and is, in fact, subtitled "The Drawing Room Entertainer," exerted a strong influence on many young magicians at the beginning of the century, among them Blackstone and Dunninger. It is the first magic book to make extensive use of photographs (over five hundred of them), and contains contributions by such leading conjurors as John Nevil Maskelyne, Felicien Trewey, Charles Bertram, Paul Valedon, and T. Nelson Downs (all of whom posed for the photographic illustrations). In addition to magic tricks, the book contains sections on plate spinning by Maskelyne, chapeaugraphy and shadowgraphy by Trewey, and paper folding by Ellis Stanyon. The last American edition was published in 1947 by Wehman Bros., New York. Check used book dealers or your library.

The Art of Magic, T. Nelson Downs, edited by J. N. Hilliard, 1909.

One of the first books to deal primarily with the art of the close-up magician, this classic text remains one of the most sophisticated books ever written on intimate magic. It contains detailed explanations of the featured effects of such masters as Nate Leipsig and Max Malini, who were at the height of their fame when the book appeared. Although the great vaudeville coin manipulator Tommy Downs is credited with its authorship, it was almost certainly written by John Northern Hilliard, a journalist and theatrical advance man for the Thurston show who was later to write another conjuring classic, *Greater Magic* (1938). It is available in a Dover paperback edition (1980) with a new introduction by Charles Reynolds.

Magicians' Tricks: How They Are Done, Henry Hatton and Adrian Plate, 1910.

A standard work on general magic with more than one-third of its pages devoted to card tricks (a field of magic that was to undergo tremendous advances in the ensuing seventy-five years) and the rest on general magic. The book is particularly interesting because it contains contributions by such master magicians of the day as Felicien Trewey, Karl Germain, Okito, Frank Ducrot, Dr. Elliott, and Clement De Lion. It supplies a comprehensive view of magic as it was being performed just after the turn of the century. Not available in a modern reprint edition; check your library.

Our Magic, Nevil Maskelyne and David Devant (David Wighton), 1911.

This was probably the first book to treat magic as one of the fine arts. The first section of the book (which was published separately by Dover Publications as *Maskelyne on the Performance of Magic* in 1976) details the elements of magic performance that the author feels can turn a performing magician into a true artist, including Maskelyne's twenty-three principles of artistic presentation. The second part deals with the theory of magic, and is probably the first attempt to analyze in detail the types of magic. The third and final section, by David Devant, England's greatest magician of the time, is devoted to the practical application of the principles from the previous sections, with twelve tricks from his own program comprehensively taught. The beautiful Fleming edition (1946) is still available through magic dealers.

The Tarbell Course, Harlan Tarbell, 1927.

This is a complete and very comprehensive course in all aspects of the art of magic, truly one of the monumental works of magic literature. Originally it was issued in sixty parts, which were periodically mailed to the students who subscribed. Fortunately for all serious students of magic, the course was republished in revised form in a series of seven volumes (issued from 1941 through 1972) by the Tannen Magic Co. They are all in print and contain some ninety-one lessons in all. They constitute a complete magic library in themselves.

Greater Magic, J. N. Hilliard, 1938.

This is one of the greatest, and certainly the biggest, works on magic ever produced. Over one thousand pages in length, over half of which are devoted to card tricks, it was written by John Northern Hilliard, the advance man for Thurston who did the actual writing for T. Nelson Downs's *The Art of Magic*. All other branches of magic—Cups and Balls, Coins, Ropes, Chinese Rings, and dozens of others—are included. In 1956, this wonderful book was reprinted in five volumes as *The Greater Magic Library* (A. S. Brown, New York). Today, unfortunately, *Greater Magic* in its single and multi-volume forms is rather hard to find and definitely costly to purchase. Perhaps it will someday be reprinted. Again, check your library.

II HISTORY AND THEORY

Almost all of the classics listed in the previous section are, in a sense, history, for they document the particular tricks that were popular at the time of their publication and tell you something about the magicians who performed them. Many of the classics also touch on the theory of magic and one of them (*Our Magic*) is one of the major theoretical works.

The Annals of Conjuring, Sidney W. Clarke, 1929.

This comprehensive history of magic, from prehistoric times to the late 1920s, was originally published as a serial in the British magazine *The Magic Wand*. Only four copies were actually bound as a book (excluding the many that were bound from the magazine pages), making it among the rarest of all magic publications. Fortunately, in 1984 a new limited edition of the book (a bound facsimile of the magazine pages with an excellent index by Robert Lund, curator of the American Museum of Magic) was published by Magico in New York. This history, though strongly oriented toward the history of magic in Great Britain and particularly strong in its account of the Maskelyne and Devant years, is probably the best general history of magic ever written.

Neo-Magic, S. H. Sharpe, 1932.

A classic of magic theory by magic's greatest philosopher. Sam Sharpe, though now in his eighties, is one of magic's most prolific writers and is still producing valuable text on the history and theory of magic. Anything by Sam Sharpe is well worth reading. Out of print but sometimes available through used-booksellers.

Programs of Famous Magicians, Max Holden, 1937.

This small paperbound book lists the effects in the acts of the magic greats of the time. In some cases, descriptions of the effects are given. It is particularly valuable as a source of information on the tricks the great magicians did and how they routined their acts. This fascinating book is available in a new edition from Magic, Inc., in Chicago.

The Fitzkee Trilogy, Dariel Fitzkee (Dariel Fitzroy), 1943, 1944, 1945.

These three books were written by an acoustical engineer with an analytical mind and an enthusiasm for magic. The first of these, *Showmanship for Magicians* (1943), is an analysis of what makes magic entertaining. You may not agree with everything that Fitzkee says but you will almost surely find it thought-provoking reading. The second Fitzkee book, *The Trick Brain,* is a stimulating discussion of basic effects and the various means by which they can be accomplished. Also included is a method to help you invent your own tricks.

The final book of the trilogy is *Magic by Misdirection,* an in-depth analysis of the misdirectional principles that underlie all magic. Fitzkee had very personal likes and dislikes but he was always stimulating. In addition to his famous trilogy, he wrote books on rope tricks, contact mind reading, card tricks, and linking rings. Any product of his searching mind is worth reading. Available in magic shops.

Panorama of Magic, Milbourne Christopher (New York: Dover Publications, 1962).

A fascinating picture book containing items from the author's extensive collection. Available in paperback, it is an excellent companion volume to Christopher's *Illustrated History of Magic.*

Illustrated History of Magic, Milbourne Christopher (New York: T. Y. Crowell, 1973).

The most important general history of magic since *The Annals of Conjuring.* It is extensively illustrated and full of fascinating information from one of magic's major historians.

The Great Illusionists, Edwin A. Dawes (Secaucus, New Jersey: Chartwell Books, 1979).

A fascinating book of essays about specialized areas of magic history by a distinguished British historian, this is not really about "The Great Illusionists" (a title the British publishers insisted on) but rather about "The Pursuit of Illusion" (the title the author preferred).

The books listed in this section have been limited to *general* histories and books on theory. There have been many wonderful books on specific magicians, including biographies and autobiographies (the greatest of which is the immortal *Memoires of Robert-Houdin,* which has been published in many editions including a recent one in paperback by Dover). As your general interest in magic increases, you will probably want to read many of these.

III GENERAL MAGIC

In addition to the ten great classics listed in the first section of this bibliography, there have been many fine books, most of later vintage, that have made significant contributions to teaching the magician's art.

Lessons in Conjuring, David Devant (David Wighton), 1922.

A wonderful introduction for beginners teaching in detail many of the popular effects of its day and full of

good performing advice along the way. Out of print, but check used-book dealers and libraries.

Secrets of Magic, Harry Blackstone (Harry Bouton), 1929.

A good general introduction, with instructions to many basic effects and some unusual ones. It was "ghosted" by Walter B. Gibson. Available in bookstores.

Illustrated Magic, Ottokar Fischer, 1931.

An English translation of a 1929 German text, which explains a great many magic secrets without really teaching how to do them. Nevertheless, it is fascinating in its scope and the English edition boasts an excellent introduction by Fulton Oursler, giving a capsule view of the magic scene in 1931, and a previously unpublished chapter by the great Harry Kellar that should be read by all magicians. Available in many libraries.

Marvels of Mystery, John N. Booth, 1941.

A successful working professional details his approach to many of the classics of magic as he actually performed them in his nightclub act in the 1930s. With fully detailed information on staging, patter, and even music, it gives a valuable insight into how to effectively present magic. This book is part of a volume called *The Booth Classics,* published in 1975 and available at magic shops.

The Fine Art of Magic, George G. Kaplan, 1948.

An excellent book of subtle principles and practical routines greatly influenced by the thinking of such masters as Vernon and Horowitz. Available in magic shops.

Classic Secrets of Magic, Bruce Elliot, 1952.

The sophisticated editor of one of magic's best small magazines of the 1940s and 1950s, *The Phoenix,* offers his analysis of the classic effects, including presentations of them by many top professionals. The routines are modernized by some of the best magic thinkers and performers of the day. Available in bookstores, libraries, and magic shops.

Stars of Magic, edited by George Starke, 1961.

A one-volume edition of a high-quality series of photographic pamphlets issued during the 1950s, containing effects by magic greats Vernon, Slydini, Bertram, Horowitz, and others. Strictly sleight of hand, meticulously taught. Published by Tannen's and available in magic shops.

The Mark Wilson Course in Magic, Mark Wilson with Walter B. Gibson and U. F. Grant, 1975.

This meticulously detailed course in magic covers everything from close-up to simple stage illusions. Originally sold with some of the basic props needed, it is now available separately in bound form. The course text has 472 pages with over two thousand illustrations taking you step by step through the performance of each trick. Available in magic shops.

The Big Book of Magic, Patrick Page (New York: Dial Press, 1976).

One of Great Britain's best and most knowledgeable magicians has written this book for beginners—but, because of his unique approach to classics like the Cups and Balls, the Linking Rings, and the Miser's Dream, there is much that all magicians can learn from it. Available from magic shops and bookstores.

The Magic Book, Harry Lorayne (New York: G. P. Putnam's, 1977).

Harry Lorayne has written over a dozen books on advanced sleight of hand (mostly with cards) and publishes his own monthly magazine, *Apocalypse.* This is his first attempt to produce a book for the general public. The explanation of basic magic effects is excellent and, as in all his writings, Lorayne skillfully communicates his own unbounded enthusiasm for the subject. Available in bookstores and magic shops.

Encyclopedia of Impromptu Magic, Martin Gardner, 1978.

This big book by Martin Gardner, renowned author on mathematical recreations, pseudo science, and philosophy, has assembled an exhaustive collection of impromptu effects with every conceivable object from apples to zippers. Gardner has been collecting these tricks with ordinary objects requiring no special apparatus or advance preparation for well over a quarter of a century. The result is an invaluable reference work. Published by Magic Inc., Chicago, and available in magic shops.

The Complete Illustrated Book of Close-up Magic, Walter B. Gibson (New York: Doubleday & Co., 1980).

The title of this book is a misnomer, for much of it is devoted to manipulation of coins, thimbles, and, most extensively, billiard balls. This latter section is over one hundred pages long and is the most exhaustive treatment of the subject in more than half a century. Available in bookstores and libraries.

Impromptu Magic, Bill Severn (New York: Charles Scribner's Sons, 1982).

With the single exception of Walter Gibson, Bill Severn is America's most prolific writer of magic books for the general public. This latest book of magic with ordinary objects is up to his usual standards. It is listed here as representative of his highly original approach to teaching magic by creating new effects and very clever twists on old ones. Any of Bill Severn's books on magic is well worth your study. Available in bookstores, magic shops, and libraries.

IV CARD MAGIC

Unquestionably, more books have been written on card tricks than on any other subject in the literature of magic. After the early classic by Erdnase and the excellent card sections in the books listed in the first section of this bibliography, one must choose from hundreds of books explaining thousands of sleights and card tricks, with many more being published each year. To keep our list from being impossibly long, we have reluctantly omitted the books devoted to the originations of particular card magicians, however brilliant. These include the excellent books written by or devoted to the work of Hofzinser, Leipzig, Vernon, Marlo, Enfield, Lorayne, Hamman, and many others. Any of the books by or about the acknowledged masters are important reading if you are to become truly knowledgeable in card magic.

The Expert at the Card Table, S. W. Erdnase, 1902.

This book, the single most influential work on card sleight of hand, has been through many editions and has been continuously in print since its publication just after the turn of the century. Although card magic was a part of most of the classic books, Erdnase supplied a great step forward in his accurate and detailed explanation of the fine points of card sleights. It remains, even today, the masterwork on which most modern card magic is based. A bit more than half the book is devoted to "card table artifice," or the sleights used by the gambler, but many of these are also useful to the card magician. The second part is devoted to "legerdemaine," the sleights useful to the card magician (but often *not* to the gambler), and to the explanation of some fourteen card tricks. Several editions of this seminal work remain in print today, the most fascinating new one being part of a book entitled *Revelations,* which contains the comments and annotations of Dai Vernon (a lifetime student of Erdnase) on the text. For the serious student of card magic, this is obviously the edition to find. Available in magic shops.

Modern Card Tricks, Harry Blackstone (Harry Bouton), 1932.

This book, often combined with Blackstone's *Secrets of Magic,* was written by Walter B. Gibson in collaboration with Blackstone, who contributed many of his pet ideas. It contains clear explanations of many sleights, card locations, and card discoveries, as well as excellent card tricks. It is a good introduction for the beginner in card magic and also contains effects for the more advanced performer. Available in bookstores.

Expert Card Technique, Jean Hugard (John Boyce) and Frederick Braue, 1944.

A standard reference work on advanced card magic, this excellent book is best approached after you have learned the basics. It is available in a paperback edition (Dover), but without the extra chapters by Dai Vernon and Dr. Jacob Daily, which serious students of card magic will want. Available in magic shops.

The Royal Road to Card Magic, Jean Hugard (John Boyce) and Frederick Braue, 1949.

We believe this to be the best basic text for the beginner in card magic. Meticulously written and beautifully illustrated, each chapter explains a basic technique or sleight and then teaches excellent tricks utilizing it. This is the book to read before you tackle the same authors' more advanced *Expert Card Technique*. Available in bookstores, magic shops, and libraries.

The Complete Illustrated Book of Card Magic, Walter B. Gibson (New York: Doubleday & Co., 1969).

Magic's most prolific author has included a lifetime of knowledge of card magic in this gigantic book, illustrated with hundreds of photographs. It's a bit overwhelming to read straight through but if you want to look up a sleight or a trick, the chances are it's in there. Available in bookstores and libraries.

V COINS

Coins were among the earliest objects to be manipulated by magicians and almost all general magic books from *The Discoverie of Witchcraft* onward have contained coin tricks. However, there have been very few really great books exclusively devoted to coin magic. The first of these was undoubtedly *Modern Coin Manipulation* by T. Nelson Downs, published in 1900. It is very hard to find and does not exist in a modern edition. There is only one modern book exclusively devoted to coins that we can unqualifiedly recommend to beginner and advanced magician alike.

The New Modern Coin Magic, J. B. Bobo, edited by John Braun (Chicago: Magic, Inc., 1966).

This second and greatly enlarged edition of Bobo's *Modern Coin Magic* (1952) is *the* classic in the field and one of the great magic books. You need go no further, but after you have digested Bobo (which should take a long time), you may want to study the work of such outstanding modern coin magicians as David Roth, Ross Bertram and Derek Dingle. The original edition is available in a Dover paperback but it is better to invest the extra money and get the revised and expanded edition, published by Magic, Inc., which contains much new and important material.

VI MENTALISM

The field of pseudo mind reading is a separate branch of magic with an entirely different approach to its presentation, though many of the basic principles of magic are used to achieve the end result. Mentalism is, generally speaking, less visual than magic and depends more on psychological subtleties than upon sleight of hand, elaborate props, or clever stagecraft. Mentalism does not usually mix well with magic tricks on the same program, and many of its practitioners have specialized in mental magic to the exclusion of conjuring. The literature of mentalism is vast and many general books on magic contain a section on mental effects. We will confine ourselves to recommending what we consider, because of their scope, to be the two great books on mentalism. From these you can go on almost end-

lessly exploring the subtleties of the mind reader's art. If you do decide to go further in the study of mentalism, some of the authors you should seek out are George Anderson, Larry Becker, Bruce Bernstein, C. L. Boarde, Robert Cassidy, Burling Hull, Robert Nelson, Al Mann, and Tom Waters. Their books are available through major magic dealers. In mentalism, equally as important as understanding the secrets is understanding the psychology of the pseudo psychic. Three books that will give you a good background are Milbourne Christopher's *ESP, Seers and Psychics* (1971), James Randi's *Flim Flam* (1980), and John Booth's *Psychic Paradoxes* (1984). There are, of course, dozens of books available in almost any bookstore that will tell you that mind reading is genuine—but that is another story.

Practical Mental Effects, Theodore Annemann, 1943.
Ted Annemann was one of the undisputed geniuses of mental magic and all of his books are essential reading for anyone seriously interested in the field. This book, however, is his masterwork, compiled from effects published in his great magazine *The Jinx*. Understanding not only the effects but the thinking behind them will tell you virtually all you need to know about mentalism. Available in magic shops.

Thirteen Steps to Mentalism, Tony Corinda (Thomas W. Simpson), 1960.

Originally published (between 1958 and 1960) as thirteen small booklets, this invaluable work is now available in a single bound volume. It is a virtual encyclopedia of mentalism, its methods and its presentation. Essential reading for anyone aspiring to do a mental act. Available in magic shops.

VII ILLUSIONS

Sad to say, there has never been a really good general book on the creation of, the building of, or the presentation of stage illusions. This has been a matter of considerable frustration to those in magic who want to learn about them, and considerable solace, I suspect, to those who make their living either performing illusions or building them. Both groups have learned about illusions the hard way, through long and often costly experience. Suffice it to say that the number of people *in the world* who are really good builders of illusion equipment are probably less than a dozen, and those who can *present* them well are not many more. Many books on general magic contain a section on stage illusions. This information is usually sketchy and sometimes entirely wrong (for example, the classic magic text *Greater Magic* has an explanation of Amac's legendary "Find the Lady" illusion that is totally incorrect).

As good a place to start as any is in some of the books published around the turn of the century. The illusion sections of Professor Hoffmann's books (see the first section of the bibliography) will give you an idea of some of the standard illusions of the day, and Hopkin's *Magic Stage Illusions and Scientific Diversions* (1897), which has been available in many editions through the years and can often be found in libraries, is quite useful. This book has a good explanation of a few illusions and an excellent introduction by the eminent magic historian Henry Ridgley Evans, but much of it is concerned with stage effects, early motion pictures, and trick photography.

After studying these early effects, the next best advice I can give you is to look at books of illusion plans, available through magic dealers. Most of these books are not nearly as good as they could or should be, but they will give you a general idea of how illusions are built. Most of these are very expensive and it is a matter of personal judgment and motivation whether they are worth your time and money.

APPENDIX A: MAGIC SOCIETIES

There are hundreds of magic societies, large and small, that you can join, and by attending meetings, have contact with other magicians and what they are doing. Many of these have annual conventions, publish their own newsletters or magazines, and sponsor periodic lectures by luminaries of the magic world. The following are some of the major national and international organizations; it is likely that there are chapters and local clubs in or near the particular area in which you live.

International Brotherhood of Magicians

This is the largest magic organization, with chapters (or "rings," as they are called) all over the world. For information: I.B.M., P.O. Box 227, Kenton, Ohio 43326, U.S.A.

Society of American Magicians

The major magic society exclusively oriented toward the United States. For information: S.A.M. Membership Chariman, Frank F. Buslovich, 4 Stanley Terrace, Lynn, Massachusetts 01905, U.S.A.

Academy of Magical Arts

This society is made up of members of Hollywood's famous Magic Castle, the major meeting place for magi-

cians and magic enthusiasts. For information: The Magic Castle, 7001 Franklin Ave., Hollywood, California 90028, U.S.A.

The Magic Circle

This is England's major magic society and probably the most prestigious magic organization in the world. The Magic Circle has its own clubroom, museum, and small theatre at 84 Chenies Mews, London, and its members meet there every Monday. For information: John Salisse, Honorable Secretary, 12 Hampsted Way, London N.W.11, England.

The Magic Collectors Association

This organization counts as its members those magic enthusiasts who collect books, posters, film, tapes, magic ephemera, and information on all areas of the magic art. For information: Walter J. Gydesen, Executive Secretary, 179 Greenwood St., New Britain, Connecticut 06051, U.S.A.

The Psychic Entertainers Association

This organization is made up of mentalists, hypnotists, and other performers whose entertainment has a "psychic" theme. For information: Psychic Entertainers Association, 3733 Eliot St., Denver, Colorado 80211, U.S.A.

APPENDIX B: MAGIC CONVENTIONS

The largest United States conventions are those of the I.B.M. and S.A.M., usually held mid-summer (see Appendix A for information on those organizations). The very large British I.B.M. organization also holds a convention in the fall, usually at an English seaside resort. There are dozens of small conventions held by various magic clubs in the United States and abroad. Others of interest are:

F.I.S.M. (Federation International de Societies Magique)

This is a world congress of magic held every three years in some European city (although it may someday be held in the United States), and encompassing all of the world's magic societies. It is usually the biggest and most diversified in content of all the magic conventions. The 1985 congress will be held in Madrid, and the following one (1988) will be in Amsterdam. Check magic magazines for details.

The Abbott Get-Together

A very homey magic convention, held in the small town of Colon, Michigan (hometown of the Blackstones and many other magicians). It is the favorite of many magicians because it is small and friendly, without the impersonal quality of many of the very big conventions. It is hosted annually (usually in August) by the Abbott Magic Company. Write to them in Colon, Michigan 49040, U.S.A.

Meeting of the Minds

The annual meeting of the Psychic Entertainers Association, usually held in the spring in different cities (see Appendix A).

Collectors Weekend

The annual meeting of the Magic Collectors Association, usually held in Chicago in the early spring (see Appendix A).

APPENDIX C: MAGIC MAGAZINES

There are many publications put out by the various societies listed above. The largest of these is *The Linking Ring* (I.B.M.) followed in size and scope by *MUM* (S.A.M.). Others of interest are *The Magic Circular* (The Magic Circle), *Magicol* (the Magic Collectors Association), and *Vibrations* (Psychic Entertainers Association). Best among the general magazines are:

The Genii (P. O. Box 36068, Los Angeles, California 90036, U.S.A.). Probably the slickest of all the magic magazines, it is published and edited by Bill and Irene Larsen of Hollywood's Magic Castle, and is an excellent source of what is happening in the world of magic with particular emphasis on the West Coast. Periodic theme issues on specific magicians and their effects are particularly interesting.

Magic Manuscript (Tannen's, 6 West 32 St., New York, New York 10001, U.S.A.). Published by the Louis Tannen magic shop, this slick magazine with lots of color is the East Coast attempt to do what *Genii* does for the West Coast. It is well worth reading, both for news and for the tricks it publishes.

Tops (Abbotts, Colon, Michigan 49040, U.S.A.). This monthly, published by Abbotts, is not nearly as slick a production as the previous two publications, but in content it is just as valuable (particularly for the columns by such magic experts as Sid Lorraine, George Johnstone, and Bruce Posgate).

Apocalypse (Harry Lorayne, 62 Jane St., New York, New York 10014, U.S.A.). The most sophisticated monthly dealing with close-up magic.

Magick (Bascom Jones, 1065 La Mirada St., Laguna Beach, California 92651, U.S.A.). This bimonthly is the best periodical on mentalism and related deceptions since Theodore Annemann's fabled *Jinx* of the 1930s and 1940s. It is must reading for anyone interested in this type of mystery entertainment.

Abracadabra (Davenports, 7 Charing Cross Underground Concourse, The Strand, London WC2 4HZ, England). *Abracadabra* is the world's *only* magic weekly and has to date published over two thousand issues without missing a deadline. It is full of tricks, news, and articles of historical interest, and is essential reading to anyone interested in what is happening in magic in Great Britain.

Pentagram (Supreme Magic Co., 64 High St., Bideford, Devon, England). This small British monthly is edited by Peter Warlock, a man of vast knowledge both as a performer and a historian. The quality of the material is excellent, as would be expected.

The New Invocation (Tony Adruzzi, 2727 N. Pine Grove #303, Chicago, Illinois 60614, U.S.A.). This is a bizarre publication about bizarre magic (much of it with the theme of witchcraft, demonology, and all that strange stuff). Its editor is "Maskelyne le Mage."

Ollapodrida (Alton Sharpe, 8306 Wilshire Blvd., #37, Beverly Hills, California 90211, U.S.A.). This bimonthly is aimed at collectors but also prints some very good effects, many from the past, that have somehow been overlooked by modern performers. Its editor, Alton Sharpe, has been a working professional for many years and has a wide knowledge of the field.

Magigram (Supreme Magic Co., 64 High St., Bideford, Devon, England). This is the house organ of Supreme Magic, Britain's largest magic dealer, and has many interesting columns and tricks.

APPENDIX D: MAGIC DEALERS, MANUFACTURERS, & PUBLISHERS

Here is a selected list of magic dealers, manufacturers and publishers. A letter to any of them should get you information on available catalogues and mailings.

Abbotts Magic Manufacturing Co. (Colon, Michigan 49040, U.S.A.) Dealer, manufacturer, and publisher.

Academie de Magie (47 Rue Notre Dame de Lorette, 75009, Paris, France). Dealer.

Al's Magic Shop (1012 Vermont Ave., N.W., Washington, D. C. 20005 U.S.A.). Dealer and manufacturer.

Sam Berland (5175 Jefferson, Chicago, Illinois 60607, U.S.A.). Manufacturer of original effects.

Jeff Busby Magic, Inc. (10329 MacArthur Blvd., Oakland, California 94605, U.S.A.). Dealer, manufacturer, and publisher.

Mario Carrandi (122 Monroe Ave., Belle Mead, New Jersey, 08502, U.S.A.). Used equipment, books, posters, etc.

Ted Carrothers Magic Studio (1951 Sylvania Ave., Toledo, Ohio 43613, U.S.A.). Dealer.

Chu's Magic Studio (P. O. Box 95221, T.S.T., Kowloon, Hong Kong). Dealer, manufacturer.

Davenports (7 Charing Cross Underground Concourse, The Strand, London WC24HZ, England). Dealer, manufacturer, and publisher.

Paul Diamond Magic & Fun Shop (903 N. Federal Highway, Searstown, Ft. Lauderdale, Florida 33304, U.S.A.). Dealer, manufacturer, and publisher.

Steve Dusheck (1000 Seybert St., Hazelton, Pennsylvania 18201, U.S.A.). Dealer and manufacturer.

Flosso-Hornmann Magic (45 W. 34 St., New York, New York, 10001, U.S.A.). Dealer. America's oldest magic shop, specializing in antique magic.

John Gaughan (5223 San Fernando Rd., Los Angeles, California, 90039, U.S.A.). Custom builder of illusions and special props.

Micky Hades International (Suite 500, 110 Union St., P. O. Box 2242, Seattle, Washington, 98111-2242, U.S.A., and 2407 Burrend St., P. O. Box 4786, Vancouver, British Columbia, Canada V61 3J3). Publisher and manufacturer.

Haines House of Cards (2514 Leslie Ave., Norwood,

Ohio 45212, U.S.A.). Dealer specializing in trick playing cards.

Hollywood Magic (6614 Hollywood Blvd., Hollywood, California 90028, U.S.A.). Dealer.

Lee Jacobs Productions (P. O. Box 362, Pomeroy, Ohio 45769, U.S.A.). Publisher.

La Galeria (Apartido Post 34009, Mexico DF 11619). Manufacturer and dealer.

Hank Lee Magic Factory (24 Lincoln St., Boston, Massachusetts, 02111, U.S.A.). Dealer and manufacturer.

Magic Hands (Postfach G, D-7033, Herrenberg, West Germany). Dealer and manufacturer.

Magic Inc. (5082 N. Lincoln Ave., Chicago, Illinois 60625, U.S.A.). Dealer, manufacturer, and publisher.

Magic Methods (P. O. Box 4105L, Greenville, South Carolina 29608, U.S.A.). Dealer and publisher.

Magical Publications (572 Prospect Blvd., Pasadena, California 91103, U.S.A.). Publisher.

Magico Magazine (P. O. Box 156, New York, New York 10002, U.S.A.). Dealer and publisher of original magic books and facsimile editions of classic magic books.

Mayette Magie Moderne (8 Rue de Carines, 75005 Paris, France). Dealer.

O'Dowd Conjuring Books (7313 Kohler Dr., Barnhardt, Missouri, 60312, U.S.A.). Rare books and magazines.

Osborne Illusion Systems (P. O. Box 36155, Dallas, Texas 75235 U.S.A.). Stage illusions and illusion plans.

Owen Magic Supreme (934 N. McKeever Ave., Azuza, California 91702 U.S.A.). Custom illusion builders.

Repro Magic (46 Queenstown Rd., London S.W.8, England). Dealers and manufacturers.

Show Business Services (1735 E. 26 St., Brooklyn, New York 11229, U.S.A.). Dealer of books and audio and video tapes.

Silk King Studios (640 Evening Star Lane West, Cincinnati, Ohio 45220 U.S.A.). Dealers, manufacturers, and publishers specializing in silk handkerchief tricks.

Bill Smith Magic Ventures (7842 Northlake Dr. Huntington Beach, California 93467, U.S.A.). Custom builders of stage illusions and props.

Stevens Magic Emporium (3238 E. Douglas, Wichita, Kansas 67208, U.S.A.). Dealer, manufacturer, and publisher.

Supreme Magic Co., (64 High St., Bideford, Devon, England). Dealer, manufacturer, and publisher.

Louis Tannen, Inc. (6 W. 32 St., New York, New York 10001, U.S.A.). Dealer, manufacturer, and publisher.

Tayade's Magic (64–65 Bhatia Bhuvan, Ash La, Dadar, Bombay, India). Dealer and manufacturer.

Venture III (6016 Montgomery Rd., Cincinnati, Ohio 45213, U.S.A.). Dealer in antique magic and manufacturer.

Wellington Enterprises (55 Railroad Ave., Box 315, Garnerville, New York 10923, U.S.A.). Custom builders of illusions and props.

PHOTO CREDITS

x, photo by Ken Howard; p. 6, photo by Ken Howard; p. 9, Blackstone collection; p. 10, Blackstone collection; p. 12, courtesy Dover Publications, Inc.; p. 13, courtesy Dover Publications, Inc.; p. 14, George Johnstone collection; p. 16, Reynolds collection; p. 20, courtesy Edwin Dawes, *Isaac Fawkes*; p. 21, Ricky Jay collection; p. 22, *top left:* courtesy Dover Publications, Inc.; *top right:* courtesy Robert Olson; *bottom:* courtesy Dover Publications, Inc.; p. 24, Reynolds collection; p. 25, Reynolds collection; p. 27, *top:* collection of Posters Please, Inc., New York City; *bottom:* Reynolds collection; p. 28, Reynolds collection; p. 29, *top:* collection of Posters Please, Inc., New York City; *bottom:* Reynolds collection; p. 31, collection of Posters Please, Inc., New York City; p. 32, collection of Posters Please, Inc., New York City; p. 34, collection of Posters Please, Inc., New York City; p. 35, collection of Posters Please, Inc., New York City; p. 36, collection of Posters Please, Inc., New York City; p. 37, collection of Posters Please, Inc., New York City; p. 39, Reynolds collection; p. 40, Stanley Palm collection; p. 41, collection of Posters Please, Inc., New York City; p. 43, Daniel Waldron collection; p. 44, Daniel Waldron collection; p. 45, courtesy Robert Lund, American Museum of Magic; p. 46, Dr. Joseph Inzima collection; p. 47, collection of Posters Please, Inc., New York City; p. 48, Blackstone collection; p. 50, collection of Posters Please, Inc., New York City; p. 51, collection of Posters Please, Inc., New York City; p. 52, Stanley Palm collection; p. 53, Stanley Palm collection; p. 54, *left:* Stanley Palm collection; *right:* courtesy Robert Lund, American Museum of Magic; p. 55, courtesy Robert Lund, American Museum of Magic; p. 56, Stanley Palm collection; p. 57, courtesy Robert Lund, American Museum of Magic; p. 58, Blackstone collection; p. 59, Blackstone collection; p. 61, Blackstone collection, photo by George Karger; p. 62, Blackstone collection; p. 63, Blackstone collection; p. 64, George Johnstone collection; p. 65, courtesy Robert Lund, American Museum of Magic; p. 66, Blackstone collection; p. 67, Blackstone collection; p. 68, Blackstone collection; p. 69, Blackstone collection; p. 70, photo by Ken Murray; p. 72, Blackstone collection; p. 73, *top left:* Blackstone collection; *top right:* George Johnstone collection; *bottom:* courtesy Robert Lund, American Museum of Magic; p. 74, *top left:* Blackstone collection; *top right:* George Johnstone collection; *top middle:* George Johnstone collection; *bottom:* courtesy Merrillyn Merrill; p. 75, *top left:* Blackstone collection; *top middle:* Blackstone collection; *top right:* courtesy Floyd Brown; *middle left:* George Johnstone collection; *middle right:* photo by Ken Murray; *bottom left:* courtesy Caroline Merrill; *bottom right:* George Johnstone collection; p. 76, *top left:* courtesy Robert Lund, American Museum of Magic; *top right:* Blackstone collection; *middle left:* courtesy Robert Lund, American Museum of Magic; *middle right:* Blackstone collection; *bottom right:* Blackstone collection; p. 77, *top left:* courtesy Merrillyn Merrill; *top right:* George Johnstone collection; *middle* left: Stanley Palm collection; middle right: Blackstone collection; bottom: Blackstone collection; p. 78, top left: photo by Irving Desfor; top right: Blackstone collection; bottom: Blackstone collection; p. 79, top left: photo by Regina Reynolds; top right: photo by Pete Biro; bottom: photo by Jim Feldman; p. 80, Blackstone collection; p. 82, left: courtesy Robert Lund, American Museum of Magic; right: Blackstone collection; p. 83, Stanley Palm collection; p. 84, Stanley Palm collection, reproduced by permission of Street & Smith; p. 85, Stanley Palm collection, reproduced by permission of Eliott Caplan; p. 87, collection of Posters Please, Inc., New York City; p. 88, Blackstone collection; p. 90, top: Reynolds collection; bottom: courtesy Jay and Frances Marshall; p. 91, courtesy Robert Lund, American Museum of Magic; p. 92, collection of Posters Please, Inc., New York City; p. 93, courtesy Jay and Frances Marshall; p. 95, courtesy Robert Lund, American Museum of Magic; p. 97, Stanley Palm collection; pp. 98 & 99, Blackstone collection; p. 100, Blackstone collection,

photo by George Karger; p. 101, photo by Ken Howard; p. 102, Blackstone collection, photo by George Karger; p. 103, left: George Johnstone collection; right: Blackstone collection; p. 104, Blackstone collection; pp. 106 & 107, Blackstone collection; pp. 108 & 109, Blackstone collection; p. 110, George Johnstone collection, photo by George Karger; p. 111, photo by Ken Howard; drawing from Blackstone collection, reproduced by permission of Al Hirschfeld; p. 112, courtesy Doug Henning; p. 113, courtesy Siegfried and Roy; p. 115, courtesy William Larsen, Jr.; p. 116, Blackstone collection; p. 119, Blackstone collection; p. 122, Blackstone collection; p. 123, Blackstone collection; p. 124, photo by Ken Howard; p. 125, Blackstone collection; p. 126, photo by Ken Howard; p. 128, Blackstone collection; p. 129, courtesy Robert Lund, American Museum of Magic; p. 131, Blackstone collection; p. 132, George Johnstone collection; p. 139, Reynolds collection; p. 152, Blackstone collection; p. 218, Blackstone collection; p. 219, photo by Charles Reynolds

INDEX

12 PEACHTREE

793.8
Blacks- Blackstone, Harry.
tone   The Blackstone book of magic & illu-
          sion / Harry Blackstone, Jr., with
          Charles and Regina Reynolds. New York
Copy ①   : Newmarket Press, 1985.
            230 p. : ill. (some col.)

          Bibliography: p. 220-224.
          Includes index.

          1.Conjuring--History. 2.Conjuring.
          I.Reynolds, Charles R. II.Reynolds,
          Regina. III.Title.

GV1543.B57 1985   793.8
ISBN 0-937858-45-5   84-29486

          001 415   © 1960 BRODART   LC-MARC8